Three Plus One Equals Billions

The Bendix-Martin Marietta War

Three Plus One Equals Billions

The Bendix-
Martin Marietta
War

BY ALLAN SLOAN

ARBOR HOUSE *NEW YORK*

For Nancy. Doing this book has made me love and appreciate her more than ever.

Library of Congress Catalogue Card Number: 83-70468

ISBN: 0-87795-504-2

Manufactured in the United States of America
10 9 8 7 6 5 4 3 2 1

Photograph of Mary Cunningham Agee by Richard Lee provided courtesy of the Detroit *Free Press*.

This book is printed on acid free paper. The paper in this book meets the guidelines for permanence and durability of the Committee on Production Guidelines for Book Longevity of the Council on Library Resources.

ACKNOWLEDGMENTS

I would like to thank Nancy Stesin and Marie D'Amico, friends and colleagues of mine at Money magazine, for the excellent reporting assistance they provided me; Marshall Loeb, managing editor of Money, for his graciousness in granting and then extending my leave of absence, and for having said "I-told-you-so" only one time during the leave; and Stanley Brown, my friend and teacher, without whom this book would not have been possible. Many people risked their jobs and reputations to provide information to me to help with the book. They have asked not to be named. To them, my thanks. I would especially like to thank my wife, Nancy J. Sloan, and our children, Sharon, Susan and Dena, for their tolerance and understanding above and beyond the call of duty.

Information about the early days of the Bendix Corporation and the life of Vincent T. Bendix was obtained from the Discovery Hall Museum, South Bend, Indiana, which graciously made its files available. Other sources included "Where Ideas Unlock the Future: The Story of the Bendix Corporation," by A. P. Fontaine, an address given in 1966 to the Newcomen Society and printed in 1967; "Bendix: Brainy and Bothered," by William B. Harris, in the June 1956 issue of Fortune magazine; *My Life at General Motors,* by Alfred P. Sloan, Jr.; and *Ernie Breech: The Story of His Remarkable Career at General Motors, Ford and TWA,* by J. Mel Hickerson (Meredith Press, 1968).

Information about the history of the Martin Marietta Corporation was obtained from Marietta, which provided the author with the text of a slide show illustrating the company's history.

The author also wishes to thank Forbes magazine and staff writer Thomas Jaffe for providing access to an interview that Mr. Jaffe conducted in 1981 with Edward L. Hennessy, Jr., chairman of the Allied Corporation.

A BRIEF CHRONOLOGY OF THE BENDIX–MARTIN MARIETTA WAR

APRIL 1982– JULY 29, 1982	Bendix uses Salomon Brothers investment banking firm to secretly buy 4.5 percent of Martin Marietta's stock, prepares its attack.
AUGUST 25	Bendix launches the war by announcing it will offer to buy Marietta for $43 a share.
AUGUST 30	Marietta rejects the Bendix offer, retaliates by offering to buy Bendix for an average of about $65 a share; Marietta gives its executives "golden parachute" employment contracts.
AUGUST 31	Bendix tries to defend against Marietta bid by changing corporate charter to make takeover by Marietta harder.
SEPTEMBER 1–2	Bendix auditions investment bankers because William Agee doesn't like Salomon Brothers anymore.

8

SEPTEMBER 7	Marietta unveils its secret weapon, as United Technologies enters the war by offering to buy Bendix for an average of about $62.50 a share; Bendix launches second strike by raising its Marietta bid to $48; Bendix gives its executives golden parachutes.
SEPTEMBER 9	Bendix switches generals by hiring First Boston investment banking firm.
SEPTEMBER 13	Its defenses failing, Marietta sets up "doomsday" machine, so that if Bendix buys a majority of Marietta shares, Marietta will be legally forced to buy Bendix shares.
SEPTEMBER 15	United Technologies raises Bendix offer to about $67.50.
SEPTEMBER 16	Bendix rejects offer.
SEPTEMBER 17	Spurning peace terms offered by Marietta and United Technologies, Bendix buys a majority of Marietta's stock. But Marietta fights on, because Bendix, though its majority holder, has no way to control the Marietta board of directors without holding a special shareholders meeting to elect a new board. The possibility of Bendix and Marietta owning majorities of each other grows.
SEPTEMBER 20	Bendix holds "Unity Day" rally to show it wants to stay independent. But belatedly realizing Marietta's doomsday threat is serious, Bendix tries to sell 20 percent of itself to Allied Corporation, hoping the Allied purchase will delay

Marietta's purchase of Bendix stock for ten days because of securities laws. But Allied turns down Bendix deal, leaving Bendix powerless to stop Marietta.

SEPTEMBER 20–21 Agee holds last-ditch talks with Thomas Pownall of Marietta; talks fail.

SEPTEMBER 22 Majority of Bendix board votes to sell out to Allied to avoid annihilation by Marietta doomsday machine, four Bendix directors quit. Allied and Marietta arrange a separate peace, giving Bendix to Allied faster and cheaper than the Allied-Bendix deal. At midnight, Marietta buys tendered Bendix stock, gives Allied the right to buy it.

SEPTEMBER 23 Allied renegotiates terms with Bendix.

SEPTEMBER 24 Full armistice reached; Allied to own all of Bendix, 39 percent of Marietta.

DECEMBER 21 Allied buys Marietta's Bendix stock.

DECEMBER 22 Marietta buys some of Bendix's Marietta stock.

JANUARY 31, 1983 Allied completes victory, buys the rest of Bendix.

FEBRUARY 2 Alonzo McDonald, Bendix president, is fired by Allied chairman Edward Hennessy, Jr.

FEBRUARY 8 Hennessy accepts Agee's "resignation," effective June 1.

Contents

down for low entrance exam scores * Accepted on
second application with help from Rollins * Graduates
with honors from Harvard * Rollins recruits for Boise
Cascade Corporation * Boise Cascade Chairman
Robert Hansberger, a Rollins protege, promotes Agee
rapidly * Agee becomes chief financial officer at age
thirty-one * Agee learns to handle securities analysts,
press * Agee's role in Boise Cascade's problems *
Agee recruited by W. Michael Blumenthal of Bendix,
joins Bendix before Boise's troubles peak

Profile of W. Michael Blumenthal, Agee sponsor at
Bendix * History of Bendix Corporation, including
Vincent T. Bendix—inventor, promoter * General
Motors assumes control of Bendix in 1937 * Bendix
prospers during World War II * General Motors sells
Bendix stock in 1948 * Blumenthal chairman in 1972
* Agee, Blumenthal and unsuccessful acquisition *
Agee becomes candidate to succeed Blumenthal *
Agee named Bendix president * Blumenthal becomes
United States Treasury Secretary * Agee becomes
chairman * Agee looks afield * Enter Mary
Cunningham Gray as Agee's executivè assistant

Harvard Business School dean recruits her for Bendix
* Analysis of her "strategic planning" role at Bendix *
Her early life—New Hampshire, Wellesley, Notre
Dame Law School * Marries Howard (Bo) Gray, Jr. *
Trainee at Chase Manhattan Bank * Harvard Business
School * Harvard classmates' recollections of her *
Early days as Agee's assistant at Bendix *
Agee–Blumenthal estrangement, Mary's ascent *
Promoted to Bendix vice-president * Rumors about
Agee-Cunningham relationship * Agee seeks national

political appointment * Agee divorce * Cunningham
promotion of Agee for vice-president of United States

14

Profile of Allied Chairman Edward Hennessy, Jr.,
seminarian turned businessman * Hennessy negotiates
with Agee, who seeks Allied offer to save Bendix from
Marietta-United * United raises offer for Bendix *
Bendix turns down United * Agee nears go, no-go
decision on Marietta * Bendix board authorizes Agee
to buy * Judge freezes Bendix, Marietta * Bendix gets
freeze overturned * Pownall nixes white knights for
Marietta * Peace negotiations break down * Bendix
banker Bruce Wasserstein vs. Marietta's Marty Siegel
* Agee bets a billion, buys tendered Marietta shares

Bendix buys 70 percent of Marietta * Pownall refuses
to resign the game, Marietta plays on * Allied hires
investment banker, lawyer * Agee seeks "Great
Extenders" to delay Marietta * Agee meets Pownall
face-to-face, talks fail * Bendix stages "Unity Day" *
All Agee Extenders except Allied fall through *
Bendix board approves Allied Extender deal * Allied's
board does not approve deal, Extender falls through *
Shark repellants fail to pass * Agee spends afternoon
talking to Pownall in Bethesda, talks fail * Agee
returns for more talks, talks fail

Judges refuse to halt Marietta bid for Bendix * Agee
agrees to sell Bendix, 70 percent of Marietta to Allied
* Four Bendix directors resign, board approves sale *
Allied board approves purchase * Papers not filed in
time to halt Marietta * Allied's Hennessy negotiates
separate peace with Marietta's Pownall * Allied buys
Bendix, frees Marietta * The "magic minute" and

16

Any information in this book that is not otherwise attributed comes from at least two sources the author believes to be independent of each other, or from such as public records, newspaper or magazine stories, transcripts, Bendix internal documents he has obtained that he believes offer concrete proof of veracity. Many of the judgments, and much of the background material, is drawn from the author's thirteen years of writing about financial matters, and especially from the seven years he spent in Detroit as a business writer for the Detroit *Free Press*. A *Free Press*-Agee feud began in September 1980, eighteen months after the author left Detroit. He has had nothing to do with the *Free Press* coverage of Bendix since 1979.

William Agee and Mary Cunningham Agee threatened in December of 1982 to sue the author and the publisher of this book for libel. At that point none of the manuscript had been written and the research was not even complete. In a letter to the publisher, the Agees' attorney, John Walsh, said his clients would not allow themselves to be interviewed by the author, who had made numerous attempts to reach them.

In April of 1983, when the manuscript was almost completed, Mr. Agee consented to be interviewed and spent approximately five hours in two sessions with the author. He said at the second interview that he would provide supplemental materials and would clear up several matters; at the time the manuscript was put into production he had not done so. Mary Cunningham Agee declined to be interviewed.

Chapter 1

The Game Board (I)

INTRODUCTION

The headquarters building of the Martin Marietta Corporation, a three-story, ultramodern structure in the Washington suburb of Bethesda, Maryland, is not the place one goes in search of humor. Marietta is a serious place for serious people. Visitors need not only a pass to get into the building, but also a Marietta employee to escort them while they are there. Visitors are supposed to be accompanied everywhere, even up to the doors of the restrooms, lest they swipe national defense secrets that are used for the guided missiles, warplanes and other weapons that Marietta helps build for the Defense Department.

The only outward sign that Marietta went through a war of its own not long ago is a subtle one—a new flagpole outside the building's main entrance. Flying on the new pole, between the United States and State of Maryland flags, is a replica of the famous old colonial flag with a snake and the motto, "Don't Tread on Me."

On the second floor, where Marietta's top executives work, is the office of serious Thomas Pownall, Marietta's chairman of the board. Pownall, who is not given to public displays of humor, ordered the pole built late in 1982 after his predecessor, J. Donald Rauth, gave him the colonial flag as a present. Pownall is very much like the company he runs: low-profile, low-key, quiet, very polite, exceptionally stubborn when crossed. A sixty-one-year-old physical fitness buff, Pownall is a passionate hunter: he loves to get up at ungodly early hours and shoot birds in the Maryland countryside. He does not make a public display of his hunting prowess, but for a while in late 1982 and early 1983, he displayed in the Marietta employee cafeteria a trophy commemorating the biggest game he ever bagged. The trophy, presented to him by one of his neighbors, is a large, framed blowup of a memorable picture that New York photographer Harry Benson took for People magazine in 1982 to illustrate a story about the "Most Intriguing Couple" of the year. The picture shows former Bendix chairman William Agee, whose behavior—including posing for pictures such as this—has made him one of America's best-known corporate executives. Agee is kneeling on his bedroom floor, while his equally or even more famous wife, Mary Cunningham Agee, is sitting on the bed, holding hands with him. Mr. Agee is staring at her. The caption on Pownall's picture: "But honey, I couldn't afford Martin Marietta."

Agee's company-buying days seem over for now. When he came hunting Pownall and Marietta, he found out that he had underestimated the fighting qualities of his prey. Instead of sitting by while Agee devoured his company, Pownall and his allies counterattacked with ferocity. In the end, Marietta's ripostes wounded Bendix so deeply that Agee had to make a quick deal to sell his company to Allied Corporation, a New Jersey industrial company.

Agee's move on Marietta, which began on August 25, 1982 and ended a month later when Allied acquired control of Bendix, set off perhaps the messiest corporate takeover battle ever waged: companies threatening to destroy each other; investment bankers devising ever-stranger moves; lawyers filling the courts with more than a dozen lawsuits, most of them irrelevant; banks willing to lend billions to finance the Bendix-

Marietta mutual cannibalism; the spectacle creating pressure in Washington to place some Marquis of Queensbury rules on corporate blood matches, which have been growing increasingly ferocious in the past few years.

What started out as a simple battle turned into the bizarre. Bendix, and to some extent Marietta, did not behave rationally. First, Bendix tried to buy Marietta. Employing the Pacman strategy—"I'll eat you before you can eat me"—Marietta offered to buy Bendix, but said it would drop its bid if Bendix dropped its bid for Marietta. When Bendix refused to back off, Marietta enlisted United Technologies to try to buy Bendix too, and made a deal with United to carve up Bendix. When even that did not scare Bendix off, Marietta set up its "assured second-strike capability"—a "doomsday" defense designed to destroy both companies if Bendix bought Marietta. Carefully showing Bendix that it was disconnecting the fail-safes, Marietta set up a situation in which it was obliged to buy control of Bendix if Bendix bought control of Marietta. The idea, again, was to make Bendix go away—the only way the "doomsday" machine could be turned off. Instead, Bendix bet a billion dollars and bought Marietta stock, apparently thinking that Marietta would desist and back off. Bendix also feared becoming someone else's takeover target if it backed away from the Marietta bid. But Bendix could not control Marietta's board of directors, even though it owned 70 percent of Marietta's stock. It became clear the doomsday machine was about to explode. To avoid the fallout, Bendix made a deal to sell itself and Marietta to Allied. Because Bendix had procrastinated in coming to terms with Allied, Marietta was able to take advantage of a one-minute loophole in the securities laws, make a separate peace with Allied and preserve its own independence. In all, hardly the type of calm, business-like behavior expected from top corporate executives.

Typical of the rather surrealistic quality of the battle was Bendix's "Unity Day" held on September 20. It was supposed to be a spontaneous demonstration by Bendix employees of their desire to remain independent. But at the same time the company was handing out Unity Day bumper stickers, hats and pins, William Agee was negotiating, filings with the Securities and Exchange Commission show, with Allied Chairman Edward Hennessy, Jr., to sell Allied a major interest in Bendix.

Before a degree of order was restored in late September, Bendix, number 86 on the 1982 Fortune 500 list of the largest industrial corporations in the United States, had spent $1.2 billion to buy 70 percent of Marietta; Marietta, number 130 on the Fortune 500, had spent $900 million to buy 50 percent of Bendix; and Allied, number 55 on the Fortune 500, had spent $1.8 billion to untangle the two by buying all of Bendix and 39 percent of Marietta.

The only company that did not get an opportunity to buy something was United Technologies, number 20 on the Fortune 500, which hovered over the battlefield as though waiting to pick off a wounded survivor or two at a cheap price. When none such emerged, United showed restraint and went home.

As Bendix, Marietta and Allied engaged in corporate frenzy, some $4 billion, much of it borrowed, was in play. A loose $4 billion is to Wall Street what blood in the water is to sharks. Like the remora fish that feed on the scraps sharks leave behind, the investment banking firms and lawyers representing the four companies in the fight picked off more than $25 million in fees. Wall Street arbitragers—professional stock traders who buy and sell multimillion-dollar blocs of stock during corporate takeover battles and for whom "long-term thinking" tends to mean "What will I order for lunch?"—are estimated to have earned between $100 million and $200 million selling Bendix shares to Marietta, Marietta shares to Bendix and more Bendix shares to Allied. The "arbs" would have earned much more, except the deal was so strange that it scared them off: they presumed the companies would act rationally and not buy each other.

While billions were circulating about Wall Street, ordinary people were finding it expensive and difficult to borrow money for such prosaics as new houses or automobiles. Small businesses strapped for cash often found a cold shoulder at local banks, which were more than happy to finance Bendix and Marietta so they could have enough money to buy each other. Bendix and Marietta executives also did not exactly distinguish themselves. The managements of both companies were apparently willing to risk the companies' futures if not their own. Top executives at the companies convinced their respective boards of directors to grant them "golden parachute" compensation packages. (A parachute is an employment contract providing for payment of several years of salary if new owners take over the company and displease the chuted employees by cutting their salaries, power or perquisites. The wholesale granting of parachutes is becoming almost scandalous, and is now a standard antitakeover ploy. In 1982, General American Oil granted golden parachutes to all its employees in a successful attempt to fight off a takeover bid by Mesa Petroleum.)

Bendix's William Agee, who four months after the takeover war ended declared in a speech at the Economic Club of Detroit that the Federal government should reduce social entitlement benefits paid people "above the margin," received a five-year parachute from the Bendix board of directors; no other Bendix executive got more than three years. In November, in the first known move of its kind, the Bendix board spent "approximately $2.5 million" to buy an insurance policy to cover Agee's parachute and severance arrangements for about two hundred and fifty other Bendix employees, in case the arrangements were not honored for any reason. That disclosure is made in a single sentence tucked into the 277-page document describing the Bendix-Allied deal; apparently not something either company is interested in publicizing.

The Bendix–Martin Marietta war was not one of corporate America's finest hours. Allied chairman Ed Hennessy, the presumptive winner, called it "a very sorry spectacle for American business."

The spectacle was made possible because of economic forces, and by application of business school theories that have made it respectable for executives to treat the companies they manage as assets to be milked rather than businesses to be developed and nurtured. This thinking is why many companies are run with an eye to the quick profit, which is not necessarily in the best long-term interests of shareholders and employees.

William Agee and Mary Cunningham, brilliant in games theory and scenario-drawing, apparently did not understand that people still act like people, not like made-up characters in a business school case study. A confusion of scenarios with life. To them Thomas Pownall was being irrational and thinking only of his own position when he had Marietta fight back so fiercely. Absent from their calculations, it would seem, was the likely consequence of backing a tough, self-made man into a corner and expecting him to submit. Not to mention that people in large reaches of corporate America—including many who had once admired Bill Agee—had grown disenchanted with the Agees and were willing to help Bendix's opponents.

On paper a case could be made for Bendix to try to buy Marietta—but life is not paper. Marietta stock was selling very cheaply in April 1982, when Bendix began accumulating shares. Marietta's very profitable aerospace operation would have fit in with Bendix's aerospace division—the two make many products that complement each other. Marietta stock was cheap because the company had poured the majority of its $1.6 billion of capital spending the previous five years into its troubled aluminum and cement businesses, which in 1982 were showing losses. Had Bendix been able to buy Marietta at a reasonable price, it would have been able to use profits from its other businesses to carry the cement and aluminum businesses until they became profitable, at which point either one or both could probably have been sold at high prices. But Mr. Agee apparently did not understand—nor, apparently, did his advisors—that Marietta was not willing to be acquired by William Agee, and probably not by anybody.

Agee—the name is pronounced *ay-jee*, with the accent on the first syllable—was in a position to launch the battle almost single-handedly, having managed to turn Bendix, a company with 62,000 employees and more than $4 billion annual sales, into what was essentially a personal fief. Most chairmen of giant companies have people they can safely talk candidly to and argue with: friends, senior executives or members of the board of directors. Agee seemingly had none of these outlets. One of the functions of a board member, in addition to controlling what the chairman does, is to give him a shoulder to cry on, or a wall to bounce ideas off. But in 1981 Agee had eliminated the board members who opposed him; he had fired, caused to resign, alienated or apparently frightened Bendix's senior executives; and he seemed to have few close friends in the business world. Instead, Agee relied heavily on advice from Mary Cunningham, who shared, it would seem, many of his strengths as well as many of his weaknesses.

Both Agees appear to be quick studies and to pride themselves on being "strategic thinkers." Both can make a very good first impression: they are handsome, bright, charming and know how to ingratiate themselves. Both are very ambitious, and move determinedly against enemies, real or perceived. They are both graduates of the Harvard Business School, and are the sort of people who tend to do well there. Harvard does not teach business management by giving its students an actual business to run and seeing how they do at it. Instead, it relies heavily on theory, analysis of situations and case studies. By its nature, that type of teaching is subjective rather than objective: how well you do depends on how your instructor perceives you. It puts a premium on gamesmanship and the ability to speak up quickly, which are not necessarily the attributes that make a good businessperson.

Agee spent his post-graduation years at the Boise Cascade

Corporation, which at the time was like an extension of business school: a place packed with bright young business school graduates who spent considerable time intellectualizing, but who ultimately helped run the company into the ground. Mary Cunningham went to Bendix immediately after graduation and captured William Agee's attention. For her, too, it seems that work was an extension of business school: much talking, little responsibility.

Agee was at a vulnerable time in his life. From talking to Agee's friends, relatives, family members and colleagues, a portrait of a troubled man emerges. In 1979 Agee was just past forty, bored and restless at Bendix, and aspiring to a cabinet position or the vice-presidency of the United States. At a minimum he desired a prominent job in a more glamorous place than Southfield, Michigan, the Detroit suburb in which Bendix has its headquarters, a place he is said to have never really liked. In June of 1979 Agee hired Cunningham, then Mary Cunningham Gray, to be his executive assistant. The job, despite its title, involves being a rather glorified go-for, with a chance to acquire insight and knowledge from the chairman. It is customary for many corporate presidents and chairmen to hire bright young assistants right out of business school with the goal of keeping them around headquarters for a year or two, then sending them to get experience actually running something. Mary Cunningham seems to have used her access to Agee to turn her job into a power base.

What happened after Cunningham was hired is by now a familiar story, but it bears some repeating. Agee, whose early career was aided greatly by his brightness and his ability to know what his superiors wanted, found similar qualities in his assistant. Little more than a year after hiring Cunningham, Agee had gotten a divorce, ending some twenty-two years of marriage, and had moved into an apartment across the hall from Mary Cunningham. He was spending a great deal of time with her; they went to lunch together on most days and often arrived at work together and left together. Executives began to complain that Mary Cunningham was blocking their access to Agee. And Agee promoted her twice—first to vice-president of corporate and public relations, a position for which she had no apparent qualifications, and later to vice-president of strategic planning, a job for which she had only her Harvard Business School degree as qualification. According to Bendix sources, her initial salary, about $35,000 a year, had tripled.

Mary Cunningham's rapid rise and the power she exhibited made enemies for her, especially among Bendix's female executives, who apparently feared their careers would be damaged by Ms. Cunningham. In September 1980, Agee told a meeting of about six hundred Bendix employees (and several reporters) in Southfield that he had been asked whether Cunningham's rise "has something to do because of a personal relationship that we have." Having raised the question—which members of his public relations staff had urged him not to do —Agee answered it: "It is true that we are very, very close friends, and she's a very close friend of my family," but that had nothing to do with her promotions. (When he called Cunningham a "very close friend of the family," Agee was already divorced—though few people knew that.) It is unlikely that any head of a Fortune 500 company had ever responded to office gossip with quite such a public statement in front of the press; it set off a predictable uproar. Members of the Bendix board of directors, who had already heard complaints from high Bendix executives that Cunningham was making Agee inaccessible, found themselves pressured to do something.

Cunningham, who as public relations vice-president had been the first person to recommend that some reporters be allowed at the meeting, was forced out of the company by the board. To soothe her pain, she was given a severance package that Harry Cunningham, who at that time was chairman of the board's compensation committee, said totaled $150,000. Jerry Roach, the head of Heidrick & Struggles, a top executive placement firm, helped place her at Joseph Seagram & Sons as a vice-president. Cunningham resigned from Bendix on Octo-

ber 8, 1980, and the Bendix board informally told Agee he
would be wise to break off contact with her. Bendix internal
documents obtained by the author show that Cunningham
called Agee and they talked on the telephone for hours a day
after her departure. The calls were charged to Bendix.

Later in 1980, when Agee was recovering at his resort home
in McCall, Idaho, from what he identified as mononucleosis,
Cunningham was spending six weeks in Idaho to establish
residency to qualify for an Idaho divorce from her husband,
Howard (Bo) Gray, Jr. Agee and Cunningham sent their
secretaries gold-foil-wrapped Idaho potatoes for Christmas.

Cunningham, meanwhile, had become the most publicized
businesswoman of the moment in America, thanks to the news
coverage of her Bendix situation and a widely syndicated five-
part newspaper series that the author Gail Sheehy had written
about her. The articles, supportive of Mary Cunningham, presented her as an innocent woman done in by male sexists at
Bendix. Large parts of the series, which depended heavily on
information from Cunningham, were either inaccurate or
questionable. Gail Sheehy now says Cunningham did not tell
her the whole story and that she wrote the series under such
pressure for speed that she did not check out Cunningham's
statements as she should have.

But in 1980, two years before Ms. Sheehy publicly acknowl-
edged this, Mary Cunningham had become something of a
feminist cause célèbre, and still remains one to some extent.
She has been on the cover of Fortune and Parade magazines,
has given speeches on topics ranging from "Why Corporations
Should be More Like Families" to the papal encyclical on
labor, and has been interviewed by Barbara Walters on
"20/20." Even after she left Bendix, Cunningham called the
public relations department to ensure that the scrapbooks of
clippings about her were being kept up to date.

By the time Agee launched Bendix's move on Marietta, he
was leaning heavily on Cunningham for advice. "I was and am
his strategist," Cunningham has said. But Cunningham had no

experience with a hostile tender offer. (She calls herself an "investment banker." She spent a summer as an intern at Salomon Brothers, a large New York investment banking house. But people at Salomon say she was a typical intern— someone who takes notes at meetings, makes Xerox copies and gets coffee. She was not invited back.) No one from Bendix accompanied Agee to crucial meetings with Marietta officials in Bethesda, but he took Mary Cunningham with him. The Salomon investment bankers representing Bendix regularly sent status reports to Agee's hotel suite at midnight or later, where he obviously shared them with Mary Cunningham, by then his wife.

According to members of Agee's family, in August 1982 he was no longer speaking to his parents or his two siblings. His two grown daughters were not speaking to him. (He did continue to speak to his young son.) Many of Agee's old friends from his native Idaho talk about how Bill is slipping away from them.

Agee, it seems, was bored by the humdrum business of running Bendix, a company that makes unexciting products such as air filters, engine starters and brakes. Encouraged by Cunningham, who told him publicly that he was a great man, and courted by Wall Street tycoons, who treated him royally because they wanted Bendix business, Agee moved for a major score on Wall Street. Acquiring companies tends to be considerably more fun than, say, slicing pennies out of the cost of making a brake. Agee had already made several impressive scores by astutely selling parts of Bendix at high prices; he was ready for the glamor of Wall Street. No one in Southfield, Michigan, can take one to famous restaurants such as New York's "21," where the power brokers dine, or book one into hotels such as the Palace or the Waldorf.

Agee, with $400 million of Bendix money to spend and bank guarantees to lend Bendix hundreds of millions more, ventured into big-time corporate finance. But although he had bought and sold companies before and had once bought a company that was fleeing another suitor, he had never been involved as the aggressor in a hostile deal, in which the company being pursued does not wish to be acquired and fights back. One of the ways Marietta fought back was by trying to take over Bendix. Agee's reaction to the pressure was to stop listening to his first set of advisors at Salomon Brothers and to shop around for a second set at First Boston; but he did not listen to them in crucial matters, and attempted instead to be his own negotiator. Not familiar with the game, he set off land mines. First, he went about Wall Street telling people he was worried because Salomon had gotten him into a position in which he might lose his company. This indicated weakness, and apparently encouraged United Technologies to bid for Bendix. Second, when he tried to negotiate a deal with Allied to delay Marietta, he handled matters himself. Allied chairman Hennessy said in an early 1983 interview with the author that he could not submit Agee's proposed deal to the Allied board of directors because he could never pin Agee down on what the deal was.

Bendix as an independent entity was in peril because of the defensive maneuvers of Martin Siegel, a director of Kidder, Peabody & Company, the investment banking firm that defended Marietta. Siegel has developed a talent for defending his clients against hostile moves by having someone buy the attackers—Bendix, he says, is the third time he has managed to do this. Playing against such a man means one risks one's own company when one attacks. That may, in the long run, act to inhibit hostile tender offers by scaring raiders off. In the short run, the tactics Mr. Siegel has developed, and other bankers will copy, mean a hostile deal is something only for professionals who think calmly. Amateurs should beware.

Just as he attracted a Mary Cunningham, who complemented certain of his weaknesses—such as an inability to admit error, and a failure to be totally candid with other people—William Agee on Wall Street attracted Bruce Wasserstein, thirty-five, a co-director of the mergers and acquisitions department at First Boston. Some consider Mr. Wasserstein the fastest mergers and acquisitions gun in the East—or in the West, for that matter. He is brilliantly inventive, exceptionally quick and supple in his tactics and can make a dazzling personal impression when the spirit moves him. Like Mr. Agee, he is bright, glib, sometimes arrogant and was successful at an early age. Both men tend to love the grand strategy and have relatively little patience with more pedestrian minds that want to move a step at a time. Both men also seem to be rather quick off the mark.

At the crucial moment when the Marietta-Bendix-Allied-United knot could have been cut with all four companies walking away intact and Bendix making a few million dollars of profit, Agee took a plunge and bought Marietta shares. Marietta then bought a majority of Bendix and, as part of a complicated three-way deal with Allied and Bendix, gave Allied the right to own the shares.

Bendix might still be independent and Marietta relatively debt-free had William Agee not decided to buy the Marietta shares. Mr. Wasserstein says that at the last minute he counseled restraint. Jay Higgins, Wasserstein's counterpart at Salomon Brothers, the firm supplanted by First Boston in the deal, lays a large part of the blame on Wasserstein. At a crucial Bendix board meeting, Higgins states, Wasserstein said, "Buy the shares, buy the shares, buy the shares, it's the deal of the century."

It was not—not for Bendix and Marietta.

Bendix, its cash spent on Marietta stock and with an additional $800 million borrowed from banks to buy more shares, is being absorbed by Allied. Allied's statements notwithstanding, financial data show that parts of Bendix will need to be dismembered or squeezed to make the acquisition work. It seems inevitable that the 500-member Bendix headquarters staff in Southfield will shrink greatly—there is no reason for Allied to have Bendix people doing jobs already performed at Allied. The inevitable firings in Southfield—and transfers of people from Southfield to Allied headquarters in Morristown, New Jersey—will hardly help the economy of the depressed Detroit area.

In addition to the expected casualties in Southfield, there are two financially troubled Bendix operations—machine tools in Cleveland, and automotive parts in South Bend, Indiana—that will probably be shrunk by Allied in the next year or so. Bendix was already moving some operations out of South Bend, but it had historical ties to Cleveland and South Bend that it was somewhat reluctant to sever. Bendix was also concerned about generating bad publicity close to home. No such inhibitions apply to Allied, which is trying to raise several hundred million dollars to help repay some of the costs of its Bendix-Marietta purchase.

Allied, which wanted to buy Bendix's profitable aerospace and automotive parts businesses to supplement its own troubled, low-profit-margin businesses such as chemicals, may have indigestion for a while. As will be seen later, income tax considerations played a substantial part in Allied's decision to buy Bendix, but Bendix's businesses need to be solidly profitable over time for the deal to work. Some of Bendix's businesses have been going poorly for several years; the company's profits were rising primarily because the income it earned on its huge cash holdings was rising. Now, of course, the cash is spent. Allied's most profitable operations, its oil and gas business, in early 1983 seemed about to become substantially less profitable because of drops in oil prices. Allied also has $300 million tied up in its Marietta investment, and the only way to get that money out is to have Marietta earn so much it can redeem the shares, as it is allowed to do under a Marietta-Allied agreement, or to have Marietta sold to a third party. Under its deal with Marietta, Allied cannot force the sale. These added financial pressures on Allied mean that some operations Allied or Bendix might have been tempted to nurse for a few more years may be cut off earlier because Allied cannot or will not continue to carry their losses.

Marietta, which borrowed $900 million from banks to buy Bendix stock to preserve its independence, has issued financial reports showing that the interest cost of the borrowed money used up the company's profits for late 1982 and early 1983, leaving Marietta with losses. With a large part of its borrowing capacity already used up to buy Bendix stock, Marietta is selling parts of itself and is raising money from investors by selling them new shares. In early 1983 Marietta sold two million new shares for $43.50 each—50 cents more than Bendix's original offer but less than the $46.66 it paid to redeem Marietta shares from Bendix-Allied. Ironically, Marietta may have become a better investment because of the Bendix-Marietta war. In early 1983, the company succeeded in selling some of its lower-profit operations at a handsome price. Because it now has far fewer shares outstanding than before, the company's profits per share could well reach record levels over the next few years. Had the company sold those operations before Bendix made its move, Marietta's stock price would probably have been so high that the company would not have been vulnerable to attack. By forcing Marietta into a "redeployment of assets," Bendix may well have spurred Marietta into becoming a more profitable company.

For Agee and Wasserstein the decision for Bendix to buy Marietta shares and then sell out to Allied was lucrative in the short run. First Boston earned a $5.5 million fee from Bendix for less than two weeks work—though it was difficult, all-consuming work, to be sure. That is about twice the fee First Boston would have gotten had Bendix settled on Marietta's terms. Agee, though forced out of his job as Allied president in early 1983, got millions of dollars as a consolation prize. Having Bendix taken over by Allied allowed Agee to cash in stock options worth $1.4 million (before income taxes), some of which otherwise would not have matured for years. The deal boosted the value of his other Bendix holdings to $4 million. He also has his $4.1 million—five years at $825,004 each —guaranteed-salary golden parachute, which he would not have gotten had Bendix not tried to buy Marietta, and which would not have been triggered had Bendix not sold to Allied.

For the long run, however, William Agee is a man without the power he has grown accustomed to wielding. He cannot summon the corporate jet or stay in a company-paid hotel suite or order the public relations people to get him on television. It is not likely that investment bankers and lawyers will court him, now that he is no longer chairman of a major account. He might settle in an investment banking house—he has an excellent sense of when to sell assets, and Wall Street firms might pay well for an opportunity to tap that expertise. His high visibility might get him hired for some grand-sounding if relatively powerless job. Either way, it is doubtful he will have the same ego gratification and power he got from being master of a multibillion-dollar company.

How did Bill Agee and Mary Cunningham get to the point where they could plunge Bendix into its remarkable venture on Wall Street? Why are companies such as Bendix raiding other companies in the first place? What really happens in the upper echelons of American business? How did William Agee's enemies get together against him and help do him in? What does all this tell us about the United States economy and the current state of American business management? A search for answers to those questions is what this book is all about.

Chapter 2

The Game Board (II)

WHY THE GAME IS PLAYED

The Bendix–Martin Marietta war, which featured four multibillion-dollar corporations slugging it out in public and several more in the wings waiting for a chance to fight, could not have happened in the good old days, say ten years ago, when corporate chairmen acted like gentlemen toward each other—at least in public. From 1929 to 1974, becoming involved in a hostile tender fight was something that a prestigious corporation just did not do. And even if an aberrant chief executive had managed to convince his board of directors to commence hostilities, no prestigious lawyer or investment banker would get involved.

Doing a hostile deal was "like spitting on the floor," says Martin Lipton, a New York City attorney who specializes in corporate combat cases. "It just wasn't done." Now, hostile deals, involving some of the proudest corporate names in the country and some of the most prestigious investment banking firms and law firms, are done all the time. The Bendix-Marietta-Allied Corporation-United Technologies Corporation four-way fight, with Combustion Engineering, LTV Corporation and several foreign companies all waiting for a turn, was the messiest tender offer ever.

But not the biggest. The early 1980s featured the biggest takeover deals ever, and three of the biggest started with hostile tenders. In 1981 Du Pont bought Conoco Oil for $7.5 billion after Conoco had suffered through three hostile tenders. In the first one, Dome Petroleum, a Canadian company, tried to buy a major bloc of Conoco stock as a weapon to force Conoco to sell its Canadian oil and natural gas holdings to Dome. Dome made a hostile tender for 20 percent of Conoco's stock and, to Conoco's horror, more than 50 percent of its shares were tendered. Which showed that Conoco's shareholders were willing to sell it out. Dome bought 20 percent of Conoco and traded that stock and several hundred million dollars for the Conoco Canadian holdings it coveted. The deal made with Dome made Conoco even more vulnerable, however. The company was now smaller—hence less expensive to buy—and a raider did not have to worry about getting the Canadian government to allow the transfer of Conoco's Canadian holdings to a new buyer. By Canadian law, the government must approve transfers of Canadian assets from one non-Canadian corporation to another non-Canadian corporation. Seagram then bid for Conoco. Seagram had sold its own oil company for $2.3 billion and wanted to buy oil properties cheap in a stock raid to replace the ones it had sold dear to the Sun Companies. Seagram had previously been involved in a losing battle for St. Joe Minerals, which went for $2.3 billion to the Fluor Corporation. Conoco went running to Du Pont for protection. Mobil Oil entered the Conoco sweepstakes, too. The Justice Department tied Mobil up on antitrust grounds long enough to ensure the company would lose, even though it was offering more money than Seagram or Du Pont. In the end Seagram bought the Conoco shares that had been tendered to it, and tendered them to Du Pont—which already had a clear majority of Conoco's stock tendered to it—and in turn ended up with 20 percent ownership of Du Pont. It is conceivable that some day Seagram will begin an even bigger battle by trying to sell its Du Pont holdings to a company like Mobil to use as the base of a takeover move against Du Pont.

In any case, in 1982 Mobil, smarting from its Conoco loss, tried to buy Marathon Oil. Marathon's executives decided they did not want their company taken over by another oil company—which might not need the expertise of Marathon's executive corps. Marathon went running to U.S. Steel for protection. U.S. Steel, which has complained for years that modernizing its steel operations was much too costly, somehow figured out how to scratch together $6 billion to buy Marathon, the second-biggest merger ever. For a while, Mobil threatened to make a hostile tender for U.S. Steel, but nothing came of it.

Also in 1982, in the third biggest deal ever, Cities Service Oil Company sold out to Occidental Petroleum for $4 billion. This deal also started with a hostile tender offer, and then got complicated. Mesa Petroleum, a small company that owned about 4.5 percent of Cities' stock and had a paper loss on the investment, threatened a hostile tender for Cities. Cities countered with a hostile bid for Mesa. Then Gulf Oil entered, bidding $4.5 billion for Cities. As part of the Gulf-Cities deal, Cities bought Mesa's Cities stock, giving Mesa a nice profit. Gulf got cold feet and pulled out of the deal. Cities, by then painfully aware that it could be taken over at any moment, succumbed to Occidental for $4 billion after Occidental threatened to start a battle if the company failed to submit.

It is against this background that the Bendix-Marietta war was fought. In 1982 there were about thirty hostile offers, according to the body-count kept by Kidder, Peabody & Company, an investment banking firm that is a major player in the merger field. There is a simple reason for this amazing number of hostile tender offers: there is money in it, both for the corporations doing the raiding and for the advisers that hold their coats while they slug it out.

Such raids do make economic sense during inflation, but there is almost no inflation now. It is the past inflation that has made these things feasible. When it becomes cheaper to buy *all* a company's shares than to buy its assets, a company is a candidate to be raided. It is not productive for society, but it can be a very profitable way for a company to expand.

Consider the case of Marietta. In April 1982, when Bendix began accumulating Marietta stock, the value of all Marietta's outstanding shares in the stock market was less than $1 billion. The company owed about $360 million in long-term debt. Thus, someone buying all of Marietta's shares at the prevailing price would own the whole company for less than $1.4 billion —the price of the shares, plus the obligation to repay Marietta's debts. This money would bring the ownership of a company that had spent $1.6 billion in the previous five years just to modernize its plants, and which owned an exceptionally profitable aerospace business that stood to benefit tremendously from massive increases in the defense budget.

Bendix, too, was vulnerable. Before spending its money on Marietta, Bendix owned cash and easily marketable securities equivalent to almost twenty-five dollars per Bendix share. Bendix stock was selling in the mid-fifties. At that price a raider buying all of Bendix could have paid about 40 percent of the purchase price just from Bendix's cash, and would be buying the company's collection of businesses at prices far below what they would have fetched in a private sale. One reason Bendix was so determined to buy Marietta was that if it didn't, Bendix felt it might become a takeover target itself.

It makes more sense for a company to pay $2 billion for Marietta—which would allow Marietta shareholders a price of some $1.6 billion, more than 50 percent above the April 1982 market value—than to try to build a new Marietta from scratch. It would take years, plus far more than $2 billion, to duplicate Marietta's assets and businesses. From a view of what's in the best short-term interests of its shareholders— though not in the best long-term interests of the country as a whole—it made better sense for Bendix to take over Marietta than to spend money building new enterprises.

Because it makes short-term economic sense for companies

to launch hostile tenders, Wall Street has evolved investment bankers and lawyers to handle these deals, and commercial banks have decided to make loans to finance them. To some extent, the availability of investment bankers, commercial bank loans and lawyers has allowed the tenders to flourish. But even though Wall Street now profits from hostile raids, it did not start them.

The reason for the raids is the stock market, which in many cases values a company's shares at much less than the company's assets would be worth to a willing buyer. Inflation has been largely to blame for that—and so have the changing patterns of stock ownership, as big institutional investors, who often buy and sell huge blocs on the basis of whim and caprice, have replaced more stable ma-and-pa stockholders.

As anyone who had money to invest during the 1950s or 1960s can recall, one of the big selling points of stocks was that they were an inflation hedge: their value would rise if inflation eroded the value of the dollar, and rising prices of shares would more than make up for the shrinking value of dollars. But there is no foolproof inflation hedge, as millions of small investors, and some very big ones, have painfully discovered. "Hard assets" like diamonds, gold and silver were the inflation hedges of the late 1970s—but they fell apart in the early 1980s. The value of a person's home was also supposed to be an inflation hedge—but in the early 1980s, a typical home was not rising enough in value to cover the cost of the mortgage to finance it. In many cases home prices were actually declining. Corporations decided in the late 1970s and early 1980s that oil companies and natural resource companies were the consummate inflation hedge; by mid-1983, resource prices and oil prices were down sharply from their highs.

Stocks failed as inflation hedges in the mid-1970s because interest rates rose much higher than expected. Interest rates are very important in stock analysis, because most forms of analysis try to determine a company's future levels of earnings and dividends. To relate those future earnings and dividends to today's values, one needs to crank into the equation the cost of money. If money costs 4 percent a year, a company whose dividend is 4 percent of its stock price—$1 a year for a $25 stock—is a reasonable buy. But if interest rates are 10 percent, that $1 dividend will support a stock price of only $10. The same thing happens when analysts try to translate the value of earnings in the future into a reasonable stock price today— trying to compare the value of a bird in the hand with that of two in the bush. At an interest rate of 4 percent a year, com- pounded, it will take eighteen years for one bird to grow to two. At 7 percent a year, compounded, it takes a bit more than ten years. At 14 percent, compounded, it takes just over five. So the higher the interest rate, the more a dollar today is worth compared with the prospect of having more dollars sometime in the future.

A security analyst tries to figure out how much a company will earn in the future, and how much an investor should pay for the right to those earnings. The higher the interest rate the investor can earn by putting money into things such as bonds or bank accounts, the less value he will place on corporate earnings or dividends that he won't see for several years.

But while inflation and its accompanying high interest rates drove down stock prices, they drove up the values of the prop- erties corporations owned. The high cost of money and the rising costs of labor and materials made it very expensive to build things, while the low stock prices made it relatively cheap to buy entire companies and take over their assets. An astute asset stripper could buy a company and sell the pieces off to eager buyers for more than he paid for the entire com- pany. Thus the merger boom—with its attendant surge in hos- tile takeovers—was born.

Wall Street historians date the 1970-80s merger boom to 1974, when the highly respectable Inco Nickel Company mounted a hostile attack on the ESB Corporation, a battery- making company that did not want to be acquired. To the astonishment of Wall Street, Morgan Stanley & Company, the very model of an old-line proper investment banking firm, represented Inco. Even though ESB tried to bring in United Technologies as a "white knight" to rescue it, Inco ultimately prevailed. Unfortunately for Inco's shareholders and ESB's employees, Inco did not conduct ESB's business with success, and ESB started to suffer losses. In 1982 Inco shut ESB down. Morgan Stanley did not refund its fee.

Morgan Stanley's willingness to take on a hostile tender offer made it instantly respectable for other investment bankers to do the same. Indeed, about the only major firm that does not want to be publicly attached to the aggressor in a hostile tender offer is Goldman, Sachs & Co. Goldman professes not to approve of such behavior. However, on several occasions Goldman has helped aggressors set their strategy, for which it was paid seven-figure fees. But when the offer was actually launched, another firm was the dealer-manager. Goldman has thus cultivated an image of being above the battle.

At the opposite end of the spectrum is the First Boston Corporation, which seems to pride itself on handling hostile offers, from which it makes huge fees. In the late 1970s First Boston almost failed. One of the factors that revived it was that its mergers and acquisitions department, headed by Bruce Wasserstein and Joseph Perella, suddenly began bringing in millions of dollars in fees. The sixty-five-person operation generated more than $40 million of fees in 1982 and was the firm's second-largest source of profit. Perella, who is unabashedly eager for fee income—"That's what we do [for a living]," he says—has a "street brawl" list to show potential clients. It shows First Boston's role in four of the more difficult hostile tender wars in the past few years. In the 1981 battle for St. Joe Minerals, in which Fluor Corporation outbid Seagram, First Boston represented St. Joe; it represented Cities Service in the Cities-Mesa Petroleum-Gulf Oil-Occidental Petroleum deal, in which Occidental probably overpaid; it represented American General Insurance in a 1982 war with the larger NLT Corporation, in which NLT countertendered for American General before First Boston came in, but in which American General prevailed; and it represented General American Oil, which was raided by Mesa Petroleum but ultimately sold out for a far richer price than Mesa was willing to pay.

Hostile deals, of course, carry much higher fees than friendly deals, which makes them far more lucrative for investment bankers. When the Bendix-Marietta war first broke out, First Boston worked all the possibilities. It helped a client, Combustion Engineering, analyze a potential friendly acquisition to rescue Marietta from Bendix. (Combustion decided not to do the deal.) At the same time, Perella was trying to get William Agee to hire First Boston as Bendix's investment banker, and had also tried to contact Allied Corporation to see if Allied wanted to buy Bendix. Clearly Perella did not especially care who First Boston's client was, as long as it had one.

But Perella's aggressiveness did not create the wave of deals. First Boston helped make some of the deals somewhat more complicated than they might otherwise have been, and may even have started one or two. But there are major economic forces at work here, just as there were in the three previous tender booms.

The first wave of mergers began in 1896, when the Sherman Act was passed, and it lasted until 1904. The Sherman Act, the first antitrust law passed by Congress, was designed to end the practice of companies conspiring to fix prices. But there was a big loophole in the law: conspiracies were outlawed, but monopolies were not. The result of this loophole was that financiers like Andrew Carnegie and Andrew Mellon put would-be collusive businesses into single companies, which had the potential to be far more profitable than if they competed with each other. Companies like U.S. Steel, Du Pont Chemical and American Telephone and Telegraph got their start during this period. Many mergers involved stock market manipulation, various forms of dirty dealing and stock raids. There were no special securities laws at the time, and almost anything went. This boom—which made a great deal of business qua business sense but little social sense, not unlike the current boom—was ended when the stock market collapsed in 1904, wiping out some of the primary players.

The second great merger wave took place from 1919 to 1929, the period in which companies like General Motors, Swift and Pullman took their current forms. It was also the period in which Chicago inventor Vincent T. Bendix started the Bendix Corporation, which expanded rapidly by buying companies in related fields. By then monopolies were illegal, thanks to the Clayton Act. But oligopolies were not. A monopoly is a situation in which a single company controls a market. An oligopoly is a shared monopoly—a small number of companies share the market. During this period General Motors, backed by the Du Pont company, which for years owned a controlling interest in GM, tried to buy as many supplier companies as possible, and also tried to buy up competitors. At one point GM was close to a deal in which it would have bought the Ford Motor Company, but that deal collapsed when Henry Ford insisted on being paid in cash rather than GM stock. Although some of the acquisitions made during this period were a little removed from companies' main line of business —GM bought home appliance companies and became involved in aviation, for example—most of the acquisitions made sense. A GM buying auto-related companies, or a Swift expanding its meat-packing businesses through acquisitions, was trying to make its basic business practices more efficient. But the 1929 stock market collapse and the advent of the Great Depression put a halt to the second wave of acquisitions.

The first modern-era merger wave lasted from about 1960 to 1968 or 1969, depending on who is doing the counting. These were the "go-go years," in which companies with profits of dubious reality bamboozled Wall Street analysts for a few years until the house of cards collapsed. The major fact that makes the 1960s boom relevant to the 1980s is that in the 1960s most mergers were done to show increasing profits, not to make businesses more efficient.

The 1960s were the decade in which the conglomerate—a company that owns many companies in different fields that have little or nothing in common—became a new factor.

The 1960s were a time in which the securities industry had begun to value stocks not on what the companies' businesses were worth or how large their dividends were, but on the basis of the profits the companies were reporting to their shareholders and what they could be expected to report in the future. A company that had rapidly growing earnings commanded a high value in the marketplace. A stodgy, boring company that ground out money and dividends but did not have an exciting story to tell commanded a low value in the marketplace.

In an era of permissive bookkeeping practices it was fairly simple for imaginative accountants to concoct high profits on paper. One way was to sell a small part of a company's holdings —say 10,000 acres of land out of a million-acre tract—to a friendly buyer at a ridiculously high price. On the basis of that sale the remaining 990,000 acres could be revalued upward. Even though that increase didn't produce a single extra penny with which to pay the bills, it made a profit for bookkeeping purposes. A second way was to take profits from deals that were not yet complete and report the profits as if they were. The most famous example is the now-defunct Stirling–Homex Corporation, which made modular houses. Stirling churned out houses, even though there were few buyers, and booked the profits from homes that were sitting around in its inventory, unsold. Sooner or later, despite reporting profits, the company choked on its bills. Another example—which was perfectly legal at the time it was done—was selling recreational land on time. A company would sell a $10,000 piece of property for $1,000 down and a $9,000 promissory note payable in seven to ten years. Even though the sale was not complete—the buyer could walk away from the note without having to make good on the balance—the transaction would be treated as a $10,000 sale and the profit booked accordingly.

Companies that did such things had rapidly growing earnings. Because their earnings were growing rapidly, the companies' stock carried exceptionally high prices. Because the stock carried high prices, it could be used to purchase companies with more solid assets but lower-priced stock. Using an accounting method called "pooling of interests," the conglomerate could show higher earnings per share after the purchase than before. Those rising earnings, in turn, made its stock soar even higher.

Because the conglomerates had to keep buying more companies in order to show ever-higher profits, they began to buy whatever was available. A special target was a company with large assets and low earnings—a steel company, or a meat-packing concern. The stocks of these companies would be cheap, because earnings were down, and managements were often stodgy. Once conglomerates got their hands on these assets, they could massage the balance sheet and income statement and show more and more earnings.

Tender offers were virtually unregulated at the time and the "Saturday Night Special" was born. A conglomerate would raid a big, stodgy, asset-rich company and give shareholders only a few days to decide whether to tender their shares. The idea was to stampede holders into tendering, lest they get left out. It worked well, and conglomerates were successful in raiding established companies, terrorizing managements.

Unlike the more current tender boom, in which most of the purchase price is cash, the Saturday Night Specials sometimes involved strange, often shaky securities. A company might offer to buy a second company for $75 a share of twenty-five-year debentures—secured only by the assets of the company being bought. In effect, the conglomerates were buying other companies with the companies' own assets. The functional equivalent is a mugger borrowing $25 from you to buy a gun so that he can hold you up and take everything you own.

This trend did not go unnoticed, and the Williams Act—the first federal legislation governing tender offers—was passed in 1968. Among other things the Williams Act ordered that most tender offers be open seven calendar days before any stock could be bought. That was changed to fifteen business days in 1980.

By then, pooling of interest accounting had become passé, and economic realities had caught up to the conglomerates. Higher interest rates in 1968 and 1969 did them in. Even though the conglomerates reported dazzling profits, they were chronically short of cash and depended heavily on borrowed money. When the money supply tightened and interest rates rose, the conglomerates could not meet their bills.

One of the best-known of the conglomerates was Ling-Temco-Vought, now LTV Corporation. LTV all but choked to death on the Jones & Laughlin Steel Company, which it bought to acquire cheap assets but which was losing so much money it almost sank LTV; LTV managed to scrape by and establish itself as a real company with help from its bankers. Ironically, LTV played a key role in the Bendix-Marietta war; its chairman, Paul Thayer, eventually helped put the Allied-Marietta peace settlement together because he was friendly with the chairmen of both companies.

The four main companies in the Bendix-Marietta war were all the result of extensive mergers. In its earlier years Bendix made numerous acquisitions, and in the 1960s and the 1970s it used acquisitions to branch into the forest products, machine tool and automotive replacement parts businesses. Marietta was formed in 1961 by a merger of the Glenn L. Martin Company, which made aviation products, and American-Marietta, a conglomerate which produced cement, among other things. Allied Corporation, formerly Allied Chemical, was formed in 1920 when Wall Street financiers put a group of chemical companies together. Since 1979, under Edward Hennessy, Jr., Allied has used acquisitions to diversify into the electronics and health businesses, and now, Bendix. United Technologies is the former United Aircraft, which over the past ten years has bought air-conditioning, elevator and semiconductor companies.

In several ways, however, the most recent merger wave is different from the previous ones—because the stock market is vastly different. Giant investors, such as insurance companies, pension funds and bank trust departments, now dominate the market in a way never before seen. The 1970s changed the nature of investing because many investors who bought and held stocks lost vast sums of money. The combination of big investors who have learned that long-term investing is not necessarily the path to long-term profit makes stockholders more willing than before to take a quick profit from a tender offer rather than to resist the lure of the immediate dollar and hang on for the long haul.

These trends have their origin in the post–World War II stock market boom, which ended abruptly in 1973. After World War II the market set off on an almost continuous boom. The Dow Jones Index of 30 industrial stocks rose from 250 in 1946 to 1051 in January 1973. Except for a few blips—such as the Korean War and President Nixon's flirtation with wage and price controls in 1970—there was little inflation, low interest rates and increasing prosperity. Millions of new investors were lured into the stock market, driving up share prices and producing comfortable incomes for almost everyone on Wall Street. No one had yet dreamed up money market mutual funds, double-digit interest rates were oddities found only in places like Brazil and Argentina, and tax-exempt bonds and tax-shelter partnerships were not feasible investments for anyone who was not exceptionally wealthy.

Although the stock market claims to be the ultimate in capitalism, there was very little competition on Wall Street when it came to the prices it charged buyers and sellers of securities for handling transactions. Minimum commission rates were set for all trades made on the New York Stock Exchange, an arrangement made under the jurisdiction of the United States Securities and Exchange Commission, which set the rates. The rates were high enough to afford Wall Street a comfortable living.

The minimum commission was based on the price per share of the stock being bought or sold. The higher the price, the higher the per-share commission. And commissions were almost the same per share for buying or selling 10,000 shares of General Motors as for buying and selling 100 shares. (A trade of less than 100 shares incurred a 12.5-cent a share "odd lot" surcharge.) The 10,000-share trade produced almost 100 times the commission revenues as the 100-share trade, and was far less than 100 times as expensive to handle.

Naturally brokers courted the big customers. Because customers could not shop for low rates—the minimum commission rule precluded that—they often steered business to specific brokerage houses in return for securities analysis or other services the houses provided. Securities analysis flourished, with the customers, in effect, picking up the tab.

Individual investors, however, began drifting away from the stock market, putting their money into such things as homes. The giant investors began growing restless at what they rightly perceived as price-gouging by Wall Street monopolists. Big investors began threatening to defy the New York Stock Exchange rules and buy their own exchange seats to avoid paying commissions entirely. Some investors began conducting business in places like the Philadelphia, Pacific and Midwest Stock Exchanges—the so-called third market—where the NYSE minimum commissions did not apply.

While this ferment was going on, the stock market collapsed. In January 1973 the Dow Jones Index was 1051.70, a record. By December 1974, after the Arab oil embargo and price-gouging by the Organization of Petroleum Exporting Countries set off massive worldwide inflation and a worldwide recession at the same time, the index had fallen 45 percent to 577.60. That decline, sickening as it was, was minor compared to the slaughter that took place among some of the stocks that had been the favorites of the big investors. These stocks, for a while called one-decision growth stocks, belonged to the "Nifty Fifty"—a group of securities that, for reasons which in hindsight have little validity, were favored by the big investors to the exclusion of other issues.

Shares of Eastman Kodak fell from a 1973 high of more than $151 a share to a low of $57.63 in 1974, a 62 percent decline. Avon fell from $140 to $18.63, an 87 percent decline. Polaroid went from $143.50 to $14, a 90 percent decline. Even International Business Machines—IBM—the big investors' all-time favorite stock, fell from a 1973 high of $91.25 to a 1974 low of $37.63, a 59 percent drop. The IBM example illustrates what inflation has done to the valuation of stocks. IBM is a fine company, with good management and healthy profits, and has produced remarkably consistent earnings growth. Yet in 1973, IBM had a price/earnings ratio of 28.5—each dollar of profits was valued at $28.50 in the marketplace. In early 1983, IBM was a vastly more wealthy and valuable interprise than it had been ten years earlier, but its price hovered in the high nineties, little more than in 1973. That is because investors had changed their standards, and as a result a company like IBM now had a price/earnings multiple of 13 instead of 28.5—each dollar of earnings supported only $13 of stock price. Over the course of a decade, then, IBM's price/earnings multiple fell almost as rapidly as its earnings rose, leaving anyone who had held the stock over that period a loser, compared to what the money could have earned in, say, a passbook savings account.

Under the pressure from the big investors, who were paying high commissions to lose money trading stocks, the Securities and Exchange Commission abolished the minimum commission system in stages. The final stage was May 1, 1975, when minimum commissions on even the smallest trades were eliminated. This led to a sharp fall in the commissions paid on large trades—some of them are 90 percent less per share than they were in the early 1970s. The abolition of minimum commissions on big trades led many stock brokerage houses to drastically scale back securities analysis—why pay expensive analysts high salaries if the customers care only about getting the cheapest commission rate? With fewer analysts around, there was a greater chance for stocks to be ignored and undervalued.

Entering the mid-1970s, then, big institutions did most of the stock trading (they now account for more than 70 percent), could wheel and deal in the market with very low commission expenses and had concluded that long-term investing was not necessarily good investing.

Even though there had been some hostile tender offers during the conglomerate era, hostile work was still not handled by the prestigious firms. However, there was plenty of expertise available, and some of the people with it became respectable.

A lawyer named Joseph Flom, now perhaps the most prominent takeover attorney in the country, worked on many early deals when there were no precedents to keep him out. That early experience served him well when the takeover wave began; he was already a blooded veteran. In the 1960s many of the long-established Wall Street firms were apparently not eager to admit Flom to a partnership, so he went out on his own. Much the same thing happened to Marty Lipton, who is a close number two to Flom in the mergers and acquisitions legal business.

Another player not afraid to do hostile deals was Felix Rohatyn of Lazard Frères & Company, an investment banking house. In the 1960s Rohatyn helped his friend Harold Geneen of International Telephone & Telegraph, at that point considered in some quarters to be a sort of rogue elephant of corporate America, to make a staggering series of acquisitions, many of them involving companies not overly eager to be bought by ITT.

Other veterans of the hostile takeover wars were Harry Gray, chairman of United Technologies, one of the first to realize the values the post-1973 stock market crash had produced, and Gray's partner, United's executive vice-president Edward Hennessy, Jr. Wall Street wits say a hostile deal is like sex—you don't know what it's like until you've done it at least once. Hennessy left United Technologies in 1979 to run Allied, and he and Gray are now rivals. Hennessy considers himself to be a protege of Harold Geneen, but in any case he has had the chance to study at the feet of two masters: Geneen and Gray.

In the Bendix-Marietta war all five of these experienced warriors ended up opposing Bendix and William Agee. Hennessy at Allied was technically on Agee's side, but the deal was far from friendly. Agee and Hennessy did not much like each other, and each seemed convinced the other was trying to mislead him. Flom was Hennessy's lawyer. Rohatyn and Lipton were working for Gray's United Technologies, and Lipton was also the lawyer for Kidder Peabody, Marietta's investment banker. Worse for Agee was that Marietta got an unusual amount of help, both in moral support and hard confidential data, from ex-Bendix employees who had little love for Agee. "I never got so much unsolicited help," says Martin Siegel, the Kidder Peabody director who headed the Marietta defense. "I had line-by-line results of some of their products. I knew the square footage of their plants." This information proved vital when Marietta and United Technologies set up their plan to divide Bendix—it helped Marietta figure out what specific parts of Bendix were worth. Not only did he get help, Siegel said, but he did not even have to run up much of a long-distance phone bill: "People called me."

Had Agee been a somewhat more conventional corporate chairman, it is unlikely that former colleagues would have behaved in such fashion. And one of the old Wall Street veterans—four of whom were not working for Marietta when the deal started—might have been willing and able to give him the candid advice he needed to hear: that Marietta was determined not to be acquired by Bendix. Had Agee hired any of these old pros, they might have told him the deal would not work. Instead he hired Salomon Brothers, which says it felt an obligation to serve the client, even though Agee was not taking Salomon's advice; First Boston, which claims that by the time it entered the fray that its job was to sell Bendix at a good price; and the law firm of Fried, Frank, Harris, Shriver & Jacobson, which told him that no court would allow Marietta to take control of Bendix at a specially called Bendix shareholders meeting if Bendix had bought a majority of Marietta's shares first.

Until it was too late, Agee apparently did not realize that with almost ten years of widespread experience with hostile tenders, defense had become a high art on Wall Street, and an attacker might now be putting his company at great risk when he tried a raid. In the early days of merger and acquisitions wars a target company's standard response would be a lawsuit to poke holes in the raiding company's voluminous filings at the Securities and Exchange Commission, and perhaps a public relations campaign. If that did not work the target might try to bring in a "white knight"—a company that would ride to the rescue by making the acquisition on terms the target company's management thought it could live with.

Such strategies, in which the aggressor's only risk was not getting the company it wanted to buy, are now to modern merger warfare what the two-engine bomber is to an intercontinental ballistic missile. Standard practice now is to attack the attacker, or to so ravage your own company that if the attacker wins, it will be a Pyrrhic victory, like Napoleon's seizure of Moscow. A favorite defensive strategy is Pacman, named after the game in which Pacman tries to devour power buttons so he can eat ghosts before the ghosts eat him. This move, also called a "biteback," means that the company being attacked tries to buy the company doing the attacking. One advantage of this move is that it puts the attacking company at risk, so that it has to spend time worrying about defense, which of course takes away from the time and energy it has to pursue the target. A variation of that is Pacman Plus Help, as in the Marietta case. The company being attacked not only countertenders, but it also brings in an ally. This makes the Pacman defense feasible for smaller companies being pursued by larger ones. Marietta's bid for Bendix was not taken seriously on Wall Street, and Bendix was not really at risk until United

Technologies entered. By bringing in partners to take the bulk of the attacker's assets, even small companies can now threaten to make a credible counter-tender. Another defensive move, which Marietta employed to the utmost, is the scorched earth policy. The point is to show the hostile raider that if he wins the battle, he will end up with only the hulk of the company he thought he was buying. When Marietta set up its if-you-buy-us-we-have-to-buy-you situation, it was telling Bendix that it was willing to risk destruction rather than be taken over. Because courts take a more lenient view of corporate moves than they previously did, scorched earth is a credible policy, though surely a distasteful one.

The crown jewels strategy is also a defensive strategy designed to make a company not worth taking over. The idea is to lure a white knight and to give the knight the right to buy a choice corporate asset at a price that is cheap but not ridiculously cheap. A ridiculously cheap price may be overturned by a court because it is a waste of corporate assets and thus illegal. The crown jewel strategy can be devastating to an attacker, who runs the risk of taking over a company that has been stripped of the asset he wanted most. A white knight often insists on a crown jewel deal to make sure he does not get stuck in a bidding war with the original raider.

Defensive strategies seem to have outstripped offensive strategies, at least for the most recent round of escalating tactics. The most effective offensive move is the two-tier bid, in which a raider offers a higher price to the shareholders selling early than to the shareholders selling late. This move is legal, though obviously unfair. It is designed to make certain that enough stock is tendered early for the raider to take control. Professional stock traders, who have Dow Jones ticker machines, assistants and messengers, can tender stock much more easily and quickly than small shareholders, who may not even know of the deal until something arrives in the mail, by which time there may be only a few days left in which to tender. If a stock certificate is in a bank vault somewhere, or the investors are away when the fight breaks out, they are out of luck.

War, they say, is a young man's game, and the people fighting the merger wars at investment banking houses tend to be very young. Like other investment bankers, the warriors generally have degrees from prestigious colleges, wear pin-striped suits with vests and sincere ties—altogether seeming the very image of gentility. But unlike their more pacific counterparts who spend their days thinking and taking clients out to lunch, the merger warriors are bred to kill.

Typical is a keen-eyed chap in his twenties or thirties. He spends long, long hours in the office working on deals or trying to concoct them. He is under enormous pressure, because he knows or senses that he will probably be a burned-out case by the time he is forty. If he has not made it big by then—generating enormous fees for the firm and acquiring a reputation for himself—he will probably never make it at all. Such pressure makes it hard for even the most noble-minded merger man to worry about what's in the best long-term interest of the client. For one thing, the merger man probably does not know very much about the client, except that his check won't bounce. To be sure, the banker has access to sophisticated financial data about the client, but that's nothing but numbers. To understand a company means understanding the people running it, knowing something about the businesses the company is in and knowing how the company got to be what it is. It is also helpful to have such information about the company that is opposing your client, so that you can predict what the other side will do. But this type of knowledge comes only through years of experience, and years are the asset a merger man is shortest of.

In addition to not knowing the client company well, many merger men know—or suspect—that their firm will never see the client again once the immediate crisis is past. So there is no long-term relationship to consider. In an increasing number of cases the merger man is like the specialist you hire to remove a growth from your intestines: you're not a patient, you're just another stomach to be cut. The merger man gets involved only for a short-term crisis: the client is trying to buy a target company, or a hostile buyer is trying to gobble the client up. Not surprisingly the merger man, perhaps subconsciously, tends to put the size of his firm's fee ahead of a client's long-term best interest.

In hostile deals the merger investment bankers operate on an incentive system. They receive a relatively small fee for taking an assignment; the real money comes from the incentive—successfully completing an acquisition (if the client is on offense) or foiling one (if the client is on defense). Which means it is in the banker's best interest to do the deal, regardless of whether it is in the client's best interest. The bankers' answer to this is that they are like lawyers, hired advocates whose job it is to do the client's bidding. But does not an investment banker also have a duty to the client: providing wise counsel? Investment bankers do merger work for a living; they are supposed to be experts at it. Most clients do only one or two hostile deals in a career, and often get carried away by the pressure.

Further, many white knight deals, in which a corporation snatches a company from the jaws of a raider, have turned out badly. Bendix's white knight acquisition of the Warner & Swasey machine tool company in 1980 was a $301 million case in point. Once Bendix bought the company it apparently could not figure out what to do with it. By the time Bendix sold out to Allied, the machine tool business was losing substantial amounts of money. And the two biggest white knight deals in history—Du Pont's 1981 purchase of Conoco, and U.S. Steel's 1982 purchase of Marathon Oil—both seem rather unwise in hindsight. Du Pont and U.S. Steel, cash-short, are now selling assets to raise money to repay some of the billions they borrowed to make the deals. Meanwhile the price of oil has fallen substantially since the deals were made.

To complete the picture, stockholders of some companies that successfully resisted being taken over might well wish they had another chance to sell out. In 1980, for instance, Standard Oil of California, which owned 20 percent of Amax Incorporated, a big mining company, offered to buy the rest for $78.50 a share, but Amax turned the offer down. At this writing, Amax stock was trading at about a third of that level.

The news media tend to make much out of the "winners" and "losers" in merger wars. The winner is someone who gets to buy the company; the loser is the person who did not get it. There are deals, of course, where the loser is better off than the winner. Gulf Oil, for instance, is probably grateful for the Cities Service purchase it didn't make for $4.5 billion. Occidental Petroleum, which paid "only" $4 billion, is having trouble staying profitable because of the cost of the money it borrowed to do the deal. Gulf, which was mocked in the press for pulling out of the Cities deal, now looks like a winner.

Harry Gray of United Technologies has been called a loser because he did not end up buying Bendix or Marietta. Yet what did United Technologies lose? Because of Allied Corporation's tax circumstances, which will be dealt with later, Bendix was worth far more to Allied than it was to United. Given that situation, Harry Gray would have been unwise to get involved in a bidding war.

Just as the Bendix-Marietta war was a breakthrough in the technology of merger wars, it was a breakthrough in fee structures. For the first time, some investment bankers received fees for both offense and defense from the same client. Bendix paid First Boston a double $5.5 million offense-defense fee, while Bendix's first investment banker, Salomon Brothers, got a mere $2.9 million. Marietta paid Kidder Peabody an estimated $6 million for offense and defense—in fairness to Kidder Peabody it should be noted that it tried all along to keep Bendix from buying Marietta shares; had Bendix accepted the Marietta peace offers that Kidder Peabody proposed, the Kidder Peabody fee would have been substantially less than it was —only $750,000. Lehman Brothers Kuhn Loeb got $5 million from Allied for offense, and Lazard Frères got $700,000 from

United Technologies for offense. Actually these fees were not record-setting for hostile deals. The biggest fee to date is the $17.4 million that First Boston got from Marathon in 1982; a one-way fee—defense only. It went as high as it did because First Boston was on an incentive basis: the higher the price Marathon was sold for, the bigger First Boston's fee. The Bendix-Marietta war, however, generated *more* fees than any previous deal—there were, after all, so many players.

A big investment banking firm that did *not* get a fee from the Bendix-Marietta was Goldman Sachs, which turned down Bendix's request that it consider supplanting Salomon Brothers. But Goldman profited anyway. Because it was not involved in the deal, its arbitrage department could speculate in Bendix and Marietta shares for the firm's account. Goldman Sachs' arbitrage department apparently argued with the investment banking department, which wanted to represent Marietta. The "arbs" are said to have argued that arbitraging the shares would be more lucrative for their firm. Wall Street arbitragers estimate that Goldman Sachs earned about $5 million—as much as Lehman was paid—trading in Bendix and Marietta.

Chapter 3

The King Of Bendix (I)

BILL AGEE IN IDAHO

In an age of giant bureaucratic corporations, few men, if any have risen as high as fast in the world of big business as William Agee did. Starting without inherited wealth, a prominent family name or political connections, Mr. Agee by the age of thirty-one had become chief financial officer at rapidly growing Boise Cascade Corporation, and by age thirty-eight was chairman of the board at Bendix Corporation, a Fortune 500 company. Despite his problems dealing with the question of Mary Cunningham, Bill Agee in August of 1982 was still generally considered by the news media and the public to be a boy wonder of American business. Then he launched Bendix's raid on the Martin Marietta Corporation. A month later Mr. Agee had lost control of his company, and his image had been transformed: an aging wunderkind remarkably influenced by young Mary Cunningham Agee, a man who had his company taken away from him by the Allied Corporation.

Bill Agee's meteoric rise and even more meteoric fall have a touch of Greek tragedy about them. His fatal flaw, for example, appears to be *hubris*—overbearing pride. Bill Agee seems to have been so successful for so long that he forgot that luck and chance had played a role in his life, and that like all mortals he could make mistakes. An examination of Mr. Agee's life and business career shows that instead of admitting error and learning from it, he tended to cover up—possibly even to himself. He began to believe in his press clippings, which proclaimed him a boy wonder with a magic touch. The arrival at Bendix of Mary Cunningham, who helped isolate Mr. Agee and flattered him, accelerated his fall, but did not cause it. Had Mr. Agee not been willing, neither Ms. Cunningham nor anyone else could have done it to him.

To most people, Bill Agee does not look like a fallen man. He is almost certainly a millionaire several times over; he has a guaranteed salary of $825,000 a year for five years; he is married to an attractive, intelligent, well-paid woman; he sits on the boards of directors of several prestigious corporations, among them Dow Jones and Equitable Life; he is famous and what is generally considered good-looking. But according to family members, since Ms. Cunningham arrived in his life Mr. Agee has become estranged from his sisters and parents, with whom he had been close, and from two of his three children. The roots that bind him to his native Idaho, where his friends are and where he sought refuge from the pressures of the business world, seem to be rapidly shriveling. His hopes of a successful political career in Idaho—he confided in people that he hoped to be an Idaho governor or senator one day—have almost certainly been destroyed by the notoriety generated by the Mary Cunningham situation and the Bendix–Martin Marietta war. "Anybody could run for office if he gets two thousand signatures on a petition," said Jim Goller, one of the state's most politically astute men and an assistant to United States Senator James McClure, "but could Bill Agee win? Absolutely not." With the loss of his power base in Bendix, Bill Agee suffered a decline in power and prestige.

To understand the true dimensions of Bill Agee's fall, it is necessary to understand where he had been. At the time of the raid on Marietta, Mr. Agee, then forty-four years old, was the chairman of the eighty-sixth largest industrial company in the

United States. He had been the top man at Bendix since January of 1977, when W. Michael Blumenthal resigned the Bendix chairmanship to become Jimmy Carter's Secretary of the Treasury. By 1982 Bendix was paying Mr. Agee more than $800,000 a year in salary and bonuses, and was supporting a lifestyle it would have taken him untold millions to duplicate: corporate jets to fly him almost anywhere; corporate helicopters to fly him to the airfields where the corporate jets were kept; company-paid hotel suites to house him when he got where he was going; company-paid limousines to ferry him about; company-paid meals in expensive restaurants. His power to command was impressive. In 1981, deciding that Bendix needed office space in New York City—where, possibly coincidentally, Ms. Cunningham had recently taken up employment—Mr. Agee rented 15,200 square feet in the General Motors Building just off Central Park and moved part of Bendix's international operation from Southfield, Michigan, to New York. The division had been moved from New York to Michigan a few years earlier, but Mr. Agee moved it back again.

Other corporate chairmen have perks too, but the combination of personal privileges that Bill Agee had and the corporate financial freedom that Bendix had was relatively unique. Further, in 1982 Mr. Agee had an unusually docile board of directors. In early 1981 four directors, disturbed at the chairman's actions in the Mary Cunningham matter and beginning to wonder whether he was telling the truth about his relationship with her, were considering taking action against him. Mr. Agee outmaneuvered them and elicited their resignations. Three of the ousted directors were prominent members of the Detroit business community.

Through shrewdness and luck Mr. Agee had sold three Bendix businesses—forest products, geophysical exploration and offshore drilling equipment—at the height of the 1980–81 natural resources boom. He also brilliantly timed the purchase and sale of a 21 percent interest in Asarco, a large mining company. Bendix bought its Asarco shares for $118 million in 1978 when mining stocks were depressed, and sold the shares to Asarco itself for $336 million in 1981 when metal prices were booming. Shortly after the sale mining began to decline again. The Asarco transactions enhanced Agee's boy-wonder image on Wall Street. What was not known outside Bendix at the time was that Mr. Agee had wanted to buy all of Asarco in 1978 but other top Bendix officials convinced him to stop at 21 percent. (By having 20 percent or more of Asarco's shares, Bendix could include that proportion of Asarco's profits in its own earnings statement.) After failing to buy all of Asarco in 1978 he tried again in 1980, and was fortunate not to have succeeded. Had Bendix owned Asarco in the early 1980s it would have been caught in the collapse of natural resource prices. "Bill used to come back and rail about the mossbacks running Asarco," one of his advisers at the time recalls. Mr. Agee, who was on Asarco's board because of Bendix's large holdings, tried to convince chairman Charles Barber to sell the company to Bendix. Later, Mr. Agee asked the Asarco board to approve a takeover by Bendix, but the board declined. Bendix needed the approval because it had promised that until 1985 it would not buy more than 21 percent of Asarco without the Asarco board's approval. Asarco was so pleased to be free of Bendix that it paid 13 percent above the market price of its shares at the time to induce Bendix to sell them.

In late 1980 Mr. Agee had begun talking publicly about turning Bendix into a "high technology" company through acquisitions—an answer to the question of what Bendix would do with all its money. But there appears not to have been any substantial high tech strategy. Wisely, Mr. Agee did not buy high tech companies in 1980 or 1981 when their prices were very high. Instead he bought high-yielding securities with the cash he had raised. Even after spending some $260 million in 1981 to buy four million Bendix shares, the company had $560 million of surplus cash and marketable securities plus hundreds of millions of dollars in borrowing capacity in the fall of

1982. Other executives—most notably Lee Iacocca, chairman of cash-strapped Chrysler Corporation—complained that Agee was acting more like a money manager than a corporate chieftain. But Agee could laugh all the way to the bank. With Bendix's surplus cash, he could patiently shop for companies the way most people shop for television sets. In 1982 Bendix bought sizeable positions in three big United States companies. It spent $101 million for 7.5 percent of RCA Corporation, which owns the NBC television network, Hertz rental cars and CIT Financial; about $35 million for 3.5 percent of Gould Incorporated, an electronic company that also has substantial landholdings in Florida; and $44 million for 4.5 percent of Martin Marietta, a defense contractor whose projects include the MX and Titan intercontinental ballistic missiles and the Space Shuttle and which also has large cement and aluminum businesses.

But Mr. Agee's personal image, in part tarnished because of his relationship with Mary Cunningham, was beginning to affect Bendix's business opportunities. The Cunningham matter gave corporate chairmen whose companies were being eyed by Bendix an easy reason to justify refusing Mr. Agee's overtures by calling his judgment into question. Corporate chairmen did not care about rumors that Bill Agee and Mary Cunningham had been having an affair during her days at Bendix. Their objection was what was considered the lack of judgment Mr. Agee showed in dealing with the problem, as well as the fact that he had left himself open to criticism by promoting her so rapidly. Instead of letting the "were they or weren't they?" coverage subside, Agee and Cunningham compounded the problem by talking about it. By the fall of 1982 the world of journalism would doubtless have moved on to other topics had the two of them just kept quiet. "They got a taste of ink, and they just wanted more and more," says a former Bendix public relations man.

Having announced that Bendix had a "high tech" strategy, Mr. Agee came under pressure to produce one. In 1982, in some of the first articles to criticize Mr. Agee's business judgment—as opposed to the articles about Mary Cunningham, which dealt with personal matters—the *Wall Street Journal* and Business Week questioned whether such a strategy existed. Buying any of the three companies whose stock Bendix had acquired—RCA, Gould or Marietta—would have given Mr. Agee an answer for them. When two of the three companies spurned his approaches, Mr. Agee attacked the third one, Marietta, in such haste that his advisers were not yet ready. Mr. Agee told the author that Bendix had planned all along to launch its bid when he did launch it, but two primary advisers, Jay Higgins of Salomon Brothers and Arthur Fleischer, Jr., of Fried, Frank, Harris, Shriver & Jacobson told the author the bid was not expected to be launched until after Labor Day.

Mr. Agee's first rebuff came in March of 1982 from RCA. Parts of the story are murky, but the general outline is clear. The shares of RCA were selling very cheaply in early 1982 because NBC's audience ratings were low and CIT Financial and Hertz, both of which depend heavily on borrowed money, were being hurt by high interest rates. In January of 1982, after meeting with RCA chairman Thornton Bradshaw, Mr. Agee began buying RCA stock—and did not tell Peter Peterson, Bendix's investment banker, about it. Peterson, chairman of Lehman Brothers Kuhn Loeb, was a member of RCA's board, where part of his role was to protect the company against being raided. After Agee met with Bradshaw, Lehman asked if Bendix were buying RCA stock, and Agee was not forthcoming. While Bendix was accumulating RCA shares without Peterson's knowledge, Mr. Agee apparently asked Peterson to send a letter to Fortune magazine to defend him —he had been criticized in a Fortune article ("The Boardroom Turmoil at Bendix," January 11, 1982). Mr. Peterson complied with the request, only to be embarrassed several weeks later, in March, when Bendix announced that it had accumulated more than five percent of RCA. That is a crucial number, because any person or company buying five percent or more of a company whose stock is publicly traded must disclose the fact within ten days by filing with the company and the United States Securities and Exchange Commission. The day Bendix announced that it would be filing, Agee met with Bradshaw, with attorney Martin Lipton, a takeover specialist representing RCA, in attendance. Lipton's presence was an indication of RCA's displeasure. Bradshaw was blunt in telling Agee that RCA did not want Bendix around. Later that day, in a press release, RCA in effect warned Mr. Agee that his personal life would become an issue if he pressed his bid. A statement issued in the name of RCA chairman Bradshaw said in part, "Mr. Agee has not demonstrated the ability to manage his own affairs, let alone anyone else's." Bendix backed off. The Bradshaw statement, used frequently in news accounts in August and September, haunted Bendix throughout its pursuit of Marietta. (Gershon Kekst, a financial public relations man, claimed to the author to have written that memorable sentence—and he said that after the release had done its job by making Bendix retreat, RCA declined to renew its contract with him because Mr. Bradshaw thought the language had been too harsh. RCA declined to comment.)

The RCA episode led some people to think that Bill Agee perhaps had a glass jaw, an impression that he apparently heard about. He took it on the chin again in July when he privately approached William Ylvisaker, chairman of Gould, and was told in coarse language that Gould was not interested in being acquired by Bendix. In August, Bendix sold its Gould stock, 1,550,000 shares, to Gould for $38,362,500—$24.75 a share. Because Bendix had never reached the five percent level, there had been no filing with the SEC or public announcement.

With two of his proposed targets reacting badly, Mr. Agee was out of options except for Marietta, unless he wanted to start accumulating stock all over again. So he never asked Thomas Pownall of Marietta about being acquired—he just attacked. Before giving the final go-ahead, however, Mr. Agee had Salomon do an analysis of a Bendix acquisition of RCA, despite the Bradshaw cold shoulder. RCA was code named "Wind" in Salomon's takeover scenario, Bendix was "Earth" (for Mother Earth) and Marietta was "Fire" (for the exhausts of guided missiles). "Wind" worked out to be an undesirable acquisition, largely because of accounting peculiarities having to do with the low value that RCA's television stations are carried at on its books. Which left "Fire," and the numbers looked very good, provided Marietta could be bought at a reasonable price. The lawyers and investment bankers for Bendix and Marietta agree that Mr. Agee had planned to make the Marietta bid after Labor Day of 1982, but hurriedly advanced the date to August 25 when the price of Marietta shares commenced soaring during the historic stock market rally that began in mid-August. The goal was to make the bid before Jay Higgins of Salomon's mergers and acquisition department told Mr. Agee it was unwise to attack Marietta without more planning, but Agee's mind was made up. Marietta's stock got too high. The haste was to cost Bendix dearly, depriving the company and Salomon of the opportunity to sit down for a long, frank discussion about tactics. Marietta, knowing that its high expenditures and low earnings from the cement and aluminum businesses made it vulnerable, had a preplanned defense package in place. With its military mindset, Marietta relied on the contingency plans and followed them. Bendix scrambled, and eventually found itself reacting to what its target was doing. In basketball they call that being taken out of your own game plan.

The first notice Marietta had that Agee had struck came early the morning of August 25, when a lawyer from a firm representing Bendix appeared at Marietta headquarters with a letter announcing the raid. Bill Agee had tried to call Marietta president Tom Pownall, but he was down the hall talking with public relations vice-president Roy Calvin. Before Mr. Pownall had a chance to return the call, the lawyer for Bendix presented Mr. Agee's letter. The lawyer, according to Marietta, had been stationed at a Bethesda phone booth near Marietta's headquarters building and was supposed to get a delaying call if Mr. Agee was unable to reach Tom Pownall. But the call was never made, and the lawyer turned up early. That set the tone for the battle that followed. A month after that first misstep, Bill Agee had lost the Bendix–Martin Marietta war, and seemed finished as a major force in American business.

This was not the ending that people had expected in Agee's hometown of Boise, Idaho, where he has been a celebrity for years. Boise, population 100,000, is a pleasant valley town with clean air, manageable traffic and a surprising number of large corporations. The Boise Cascade Corporation is based there, and so are Morrison-Knudsen, a large contracting company; Albertson's, a department store chain; and Trus-Joist, a building component-maker. Bill Agee's roots are deep in Idaho. Unlike many "local-boy-makes-good" stories, this one doesn't end with the boy leaving for the East or West and garnering fame and fortune. Mr. Agee gained that, to be sure, but never really left Idaho. He returned there frequently, to attend meetings or just to relax. In early 1977, after having been promoted to chairman at Bendix, Agee told a reporter from the Detroit *Free Press* that he frequently flew from Detroit to Boise for a weekend. It didn't take any longer to fly to Boise than to drive three or four hours from the Detroit suburbs to a vacation home in northern Michigan, Mr. Agee explained. Even though Bill Agee has not lived permanently in Boise since 1972, when he left to join Bendix, he has more friends in Idaho than in Michigan. "Bill has his roots right here," says Robert Hansberger, Agee's first sponsor in the business world. "Who gives a damn about him in places like New York and Detroit? He's a somebody here. His lifelong friends are here. Whenever he needs to refuel, he heads home."

For years, Bill Agee has owned a lakefront home in McCall, a vacation community about eighty miles from Boise, and has spent vacation and recuperation time there. When he and his first wife, also an Idaho native, were divorced in 1981, Mrs. Agee got the home in Bloomfield Hills, he got the home in McCall. It is one of the few places he can go and be left alone. Robert Hendren, a good friend—he was best man when Bill Agee married Mary Cunningham in June 1982—says he and Bill have had many conversations about life in the fast lane as compared to life in Boise. Mr. Hendren knows about success. His furniture business is very prosperous and he makes frequent trips to the East. Over a cup of coffee Bob Hendren mused about his friend. "I recall, specifically, one time Bill and I were having dinner in Manhattan," Hendren said. "I told him it must be exciting to be surrounded by all this energy and activity. He told me that so much of the life there [in New York] was facade. The good life, the genuine life, was back in Idaho." Among his Idaho friends, Agee could shed his chairman-of-the-board manner and indulge the more playful elements in his nature. "Bill and I have always goofed off together," says Sid Garber, an orthopedic surgeon in Caldwell, Idaho, and Bill Agee's "mad and crazy" partner in mischief for many years. In 1967, he recalled, he and Bill went to the Expo in Montreal without their wives. "God, we had fun," he says. "Bill has a wonderful sense of humor. He's one of my best friends." And even when they were both married, the presence of Mrs. Agee and Mrs. Garber did not stop Bill and Sid from acting like kids. "In Europe Bill and I were pranksters," he said. "In Paris, we pitched quarters at the cracks in the sidewalk. We'd play practical jokes on waiters."

Bill Agee grew up in rural Idaho with homely virtues: diligence, politeness, hard work, thrift. He is the third generation of Agees to live in Idaho. The family was originally Huguenot —Agee is from the French name Agé. The family emigrated to Virginia in the 1600s. The Agees moved to Idaho when Bill Agee's grandfather, a Baptist minister, was given his choice of parishes in either Texas or Idaho, and chose Boise.

Bill Agee's father, Harold, was a hard-working, self-made man with an aptitude for numbers. Bill, the only son—he has two sisters, one two years older than he, the other twelve years younger—inherited his father's facility with figures. Because Baptist ministers in Boise weren't paid very much, Harold Agee had to go to work directly from high school to supplement his father's meager salary. Harold, who graduated from Boise High School at the age of sixteen, became a clerk-typist at a local steel company. With his mathematical abilities and a flair for organization he worked his way up to general manager, but it took him more than twenty years. (It took Bill Agee only six years from the time *he* left school to become chief financial officer of Boise Cascade.) In 1953, when Bill was fifteen, Harold Agee moved the family ten miles to Meridian, Idaho, and bought a dairy farm there. The farm was successful, and Mr. Agee later became a political figure of sorts, serving in the Idaho Legislature from 1964 through 1970. On the farm Bill Agee helped milk the cows and clean the barn and performed his other chores. He was polite, respectful and diligent, a model brother, recalls Carolyn Agee Hjort. "Above all, dad taught us to be honest, to be straightforward," Mrs. Hjort, Bill's older sister, recalls.

In Meridian, Bill Agee was a big fish in a small pond. Many years later, associates recall, he still talked fondly about his days as an all-everything at Meridian High. His high school record was exemplary. According to the 1956 Meridian High yearbook, Bill Agee made the National Honor Society, was student body vice-president his junior year, class president his senior year, sports editor of the school paper, a member of the track, tennis and basketball teams, the lead in the school plays and cited for excellence in the oratory contest. His exploits fill three pages of the yearbook; his classmates voted him "hard worker." He was in every club except Chorus and Future Farmers. Young Bill also seems to have been a hit with the girls. In the "Wills" section of the yearbook the editors wrote: "Bill Agee leaves his 'line of bunk' to Al Evans; not that Al needs it, but we have to leave it to someone."

Meridian, present population 7,500, is now almost a suburb

of Boise, but in the 1950s when Bill Agee attended school there Meridian was rural. Only in his senior year at Meridian High were there as many as 100 students in a grade. After graduation Bill left Meridian High and plunged into the rougher waters at Stanford University. But just one year after leaving Idaho for Stanford he returned, and in September 1957, instead of starting his sophomore year at Stanford, he married Diane Weaver and enrolled at Boise Junior College (now Boise State University). Agee, whose *Who's Who* biography forthrightly lists Boise Junior College rather than the present Boise State University, has said that he dropped out of Stanford for financial reasons. As a newlywed, he explained, he couldn't afford tuition and living expenses at Stanford, and he didn't want to take money from his parents. His younger sister Jacqueline says that the elder Agees helped with the bills, and that the real reason Bill did not go back to Stanford was that he had worked very hard and achieved only mediocre grades rather than the *A*'s he made at Meridian High. "Bill cried when he got his grades," Jackie Agee says. "He got *C*'s, and he had never gotten a *C* in his life." Mr. Agee confirmed that his grades at Stanford had left much to be desired—he got a D in Spanish, he said—and that the difficulty of the Stanford program is one reason he did not return there. Married to a low-key, supportive woman—Diane Agee dropped out of Oregon State and never returned to college to get her degree—Bill Agee flourished at Boise Junior College. Not only was tuition a mere $70 a year, he told the author, but he could also work fulltime as a $1.50-an-hour controller at Albertson's. With an associate in arts degree from Boise Junior College and his Stanford problems behind him, he finished his degree work at the University of Idaho, another small pond, and flourished there too. He graduated with highest honors at Idaho, with a bachelor of science in business. His first daughter, Suzanne, was born the day he graduated. After Bill's graduation, the Agee family returned to Boise, where Agee worked as controller of Idaho Title Company and taught evening classes in accounting and economics at the Strategic Air Command base near Boise. Along the way, he became a certified public accountant.

In a crucial turning point, Agee was recruited for the Harvard Graduate School of Business by J. Leslie Rollins, an assistant dean. Until he left Harvard in 1966, part of Rollins's job was to scour the West for potential Harvard Business School enrollees. He challenged Bill Agee, who had excelled at the University of Idaho, to take on a tough assignment like Harvard. Rollins, Agee has said, told him not to worry about money because loans were available. Dean Rollins, seventy-eight, remained fond of Mr. Agee. "It's not just that he was great with numbers," Rollins says. "He knew exactly what to do with them and make them work." It would appear that Bill Agee was torn. On the one hand he was comfortable and secure in Boise with his wife and child. On the other hand he was ambitious, and Harvard presented an opportunity. A Harvard degree would make it easier to become president of a big corporation, a goal that would have been hard to achieve staying where he was. For such reasons, as well as perhaps to prove to himself that his Stanford problems had been a fluke, Agee went off to Harvard and he did well. (According to Agee, he was turned down once for Harvard because his grades on the verbal portion of the aptitude entrance examination were too low. The second year he applied, Mr. Agee said, he barely got in, and Dean Rollins apparently exerted pressure to get him accepted. Mr. Agee said he was spurred to excel by a Harvard dean who told him early in his first year that his verbal scores were so low he was unlikely to succeed. After graduating, he said, he thanked the dean for having given him the inspiration to succeed.)

When he graduated in 1963 he was a very marketable commodity. He had a master of business administration degree from Harvard, his CPA certification and a winning manner in interviews. Reenter Les Rollins: this time he recruited Agee for a job at an Idaho company, Boise Cascade Corporation. Boise Cascade was run by Robert Hansberger, another Rollins protege. (After he became chairman of Bendix, Mr. Agee re-paid Dean Rollins's kindnesses by hiring him to screen high-potential recruits for Bendix. Among the Rollins recruits—Mary Cunningham.)

The potential to rise rapidly at Boise Cascade was greater than at a more traditional corporation, so Bill Agee returned to Idaho. Bob Hansberger, a 1947 Harvard Business School graduate then in his early forties, took a liking to young Bill Agee and promoted him rapidly. "It's easy to keep your eye on someone you hired yourself," Mr. Hansberger says. So Bill Agee rose rapidly at Boise Cascade, and never seems to have been subjected to any serious form of adversity. When the company ran into trouble in 1971 he wasn't blamed for it even though he was chief financial officer at the time. And when the company almost failed in 1972 he had just gotten a job at Bendix Corporation.

In 1963, when Bill Agee came home to Idaho, Boise Cascade was one of the hot companies in the country. Bob Hansberger was impatiently trying to convert a small, sleepy lumber com-pany into a forest industry giant capable of competing with companies such as Georgia Pacific, Weyerhaeuser and Interna-tional Paper. In 1957, when Mr. Hansberger became chairman of Boise Cascade, the company had only $35 million a year in sales. In 1969, its peak year, it was up to sales of $1.7 billion and had a profit of $81.2 million. In the 1960s, Boise Cascade was growing rapidly, it was buying another company every few months, and Bob Hansberger was packing the place with bright young MBAs. In those days, by all accounts, Boise Cas-cade was like an extension of business school. Ideas were sought, concepts unveiled and many planning sessions were reminiscent of seminars. As in business school, being bright and quick was a key to getting ahead. Even among such com-petition, Mr. Hansberger remembers, Bill Agee shone. He was a native. He was bright, ambitious and had a good sense of humor. He worked long hours. He served on the Boise school board. And, of course, he was a devoted family man. With his quick wit and skill with numbers, Bill Agee, sponsored by Bob Hansberger, became one of the rising stars at Boise. He was one of the five leading candidates to succeed Hansberger, but was not number one. That was John Fery, one of Mr. Agee's rivals. It is frequently said in Boise that Mr. Fery and Mr. Agee are enemies; Mr. Fery refuses to discuss the subject.

At Boise Cascade Bill Agee got training not only in numbers, but in salesmanship. Mr. Hansberger was—and is—a fine promoter. He developed the image of a "humanist" who believed in open management and the promotion of young people who had untraditional ideas—themes Mr. Agee later stressed at Bendix. Mr. Hansberger was an expert at wooing the business press and securities analysts. Until 1971, when Boise Cascade was forced to announce that it had suffered severe losses, Mr. Hansberger convinced presumably skeptical writers and analysts that Boise Cascade was a sound, growing company. With Bill Agee, among others, at his side, Bob Hansberger made frequent trips to Wall Street. When analysts or reporters called Boise Cascade with financial questions, Bill Agee frequently answered them. It was an important job because it was vital for Boise Cascade to keep its stock price up—the higher the price, the fewer shares it had to issue to buy other companies; the fewer shares issued, the greater Boise Cascade's earnings per share, and the higher its shares would rise. Hansberger illustrated the benefits of being open, witty, progressive-sounding and quotable—up to 1971 Boise Cascade got nicely favorable publicity. Until the Mary Cunningham news coverage began, Bill Agee, too, was witty, progressive, open and quotable, and received favorable publicity as a result. A story about a rapidly rising, plain-speaking, good-looking, modern manager who made it to the top at age thirty-eight could be attractive to a business reporter looking for something interesting to write in the so-called human-interest area.

Had reporters taken the time to get beyond Bill Agee's charming facade they might have raised questions about exactly what his role was in Boise Cascade's problems. Boise

Cascade, not interested in rehashing ten-year-old bad news, won't talk. But old Boise financial reports and news releases, together with contemporary journalistic accounts, lead one to conclude that the chief financial officer may have played more than a minor role in the fiasco. The questions involve the accounting methods of Boise Cascade used under Bill Agee, and the disclosures—or lack of them—made to shareholders.

There were three problem areas that in 1971 and 1972 forced Boise Cascade to take almost $300 million of losses—losses which represented well over half the company's net worth at the time and were some of the largest that had ever been reported by any company. The three problems were land sales; a Boise Cascade joint venture with a black-owned construction company; and South American bonds owned by a Boise Cascade subsidiary, Ebasco.

Accounting for the profits on land sales is complicated. Suppose a company sells a piece of property for $10,000, but gets only $1,000 in cash and a $9,000 promissory note. And suppose the buyer can walk away from the note at any time by forfeiting what he has already paid. When the lot is sold, is it a $10,000 sale, or is it something less, because some buyers will fail to pay the full $9,000 note? Today, strict accounting rules require that the transaction not be counted as a full $10,000 sale because of the chance the note might not be paid in full. No such rules existed in 1970. It was a matter of judgment.

Under Bill Agee, Boise Cascade appears to have taken a most liberal view. A 1970 Forbes magazine story quotes him as saying, "We are about midway between the extremes of conservative and liberal accounting in the land sales business. However, we are getting more conservative all the time." A January 31, 1971, article in the Wall Street Journal quoted Mr. Agee as saying that after a review undertaken with the help of Boise Cascade's outside accounting firm, the company would make "no changes in its accounting method at this time." Despite these two statements, the footnotes to the 1971 Boise Cascade annual report show that the company counted the entire sales price as revenue in the year in which the land was sold, provided the down payment was 10 percent or more. There was a slight reduction given to the value of the note if its interest rate was relatively low, but no provision was established to cover the possibility that buyers would renege on their contracts. The lack of such a provision meant that Boise Cascade's profits in 1969 and 1970 were higher than they would otherwise have been. At the time, land sales were one of Boise Cascade's fastest-growing businesses, and the way the company reported its profits from the sales played a substantial role in Boise Cascade's increase in per-share profit. In 1971 and 1972 the company wrote off more than $250 million (some of which was offset by income tax credits), including sales that were reversed, when it pulled out of the recreational land business.

Boise Cascade also got into the then-glamorous urban renewal business in 1967 when it entered a joint venture with a black-owned construction company to form the Burnett-Boise Corporation. Boise Cascade, as part of its 44 percent ownership of Burnett-Boise, invested $600,000 in cash and assumed certain obligations of the venture. But those obligations—"contingent liabilities"—do not appear to have shown up in reports to shareholders. In 1971 Boise Cascade charged its earnings $37 million for Boise-Burnett obligations that it had been forced to cover. (Asked how it could lose more than sixty times the amount of money invested, Boise Cascade at the time declined comment, saying it did not want to affect race relations in the United States.) In fact, telling Boise Cascade shareholders about the contingent liabilities of Burnett-Boise would not have hurt earnings, but would have made Boise Cascade's balance sheet look weaker.

The Ebasco situation also involved balance sheets. In 1969 Boise Cascade bought Ebasco, formerly the Electric Bond & Share Company, in exchange for Boise Cascade stock. This move strengthened Boise Cascade's balance sheet because Ebasco's major assets were cash and bonds. The company had

United States government securities, which presented no problem, and $193 million of dollar bonds issued by South American countries. The countries gave Ebasco those bonds in exchange for Ebasco utility properties located there. The higher the reserve Boise Cascade set up to cover the eventuality that the countries could not or would not pay, the weaker its balance sheet would be. So Boise did not add to the $40 million reserve Ebasco itself had already set up. In 1970, when Ebasco traded its Chilean properties for $75 million of Government of Chile bonds, Bill Agee was quoted as saying that the bonds were sound enough to allow Boise Cascade to value them at face value. But unlike the United States government, which can, in effect, print dollars and use them to pay debts, South American governments cannot print United States dollars to pay off dollar-denominated bonds. In 1972, problems in Chile and other countries forced Boise Cascade to write off $50 million of its South American bonds.

Asked to respond to this analysis of his role in Boise Cascade's problems, Mr. Agee said he accepted responsibility, even though "as it related to all the accounting and the land business and all that sort of thing I was on the right side of those arguments internally from day one." And, "When you're the chief financial officer of a company, and you're one of the two or three chief spokesmen of the company, the good and the bad of whatever takes place at that company gets laid at your doorstep, properly or improperly, and you have have responsibility."

Bill Agee was not at Boise Cascade to answer questions about the 1972 write-off. In May, two months before the write-off was announced, Bill Agee accepted an offer from W. Michael Blumenthal and joined Bendix Corporation as an executive vice-president, director and member of the four-person office of the chief executive.

"The reason I think Bill left," Bob Hansberger says, "is simply because he saw some young men—young, but older than he was—ahead of him. Bill's timetable didn't allow him to wait

as long as he would have had to." Mike Blumenthal, who says
Mr. Agee was candid about the problems at Boise Cascade,
says, "The reason I was able to hire Bill was that he was really
anxious to get out of there."

Mr. Agee said he turned down offers to leave Boise Cascade
in 1971 because he felt obliged to stay and help Bob Hansberger cope with the company's problems. "As it was," he said,
"I almost waited too long."

By being fortunate enough to be able to leave Boise Cascade
in May of 1972, Bill Agee avoided being tainted by the second
writeoff. He also avoided the new regime at Boise Cascade. In
October of 1972 Boise Cascade's bankers forced Bob Hansberger, Mr. Agee's mentor, to resign as part of their price for
saving the company. John Fery, Mr. Agee's longtime rival, took
over. By then, Mr. Agee was already on his way up the ladder
at Bendix.

Chapter 4

The King Of Bendix (II)

BILL AGEE AT BENDIX

When he hired William Agee in 1972 Werner Michael Blumenthal, one of the world's renaissance men, was starting his reign as chairman of the Bendix Corporation. Bill Agee is a self-made man, but his impressive record pales next to Mike Blumenthal's. So far in his life, Mr. Blumenthal, fifty-seven, has been: a fugitive from Nazi Germany; a street urchin in Shanghai; a detainee in a Japanese internment camp; a translator; a licensed shill in a Nevada casino; a college professor at Princeton; an economist; a diplomat; secretary of the treasury of the United States; and chairman of two multibillion-dollar corporations—Bendix and Burroughs.

Despite an outwardly cool manner, one of Mr. Blumenthal's attributes is the ability to laugh at himself. When he was secretary of the treasury he tried to pay a dinner bill with his American Express card, only to be politely informed that it had expired. Finding himself short of cash, Mr. Blumenthal tried to pay with a personal check, but restaurant rules required two pieces of identification and Mr. Blumenthal had only his driver's license. Finally, inspiration struck, and he brought forth a dollar bill and showed the restaurant manager his signature on it. The restaurant took the check.

77

Nothing in Mr. Blumenthal's early history showed any indication that his signature would someday adorn a nation's currency—or even an American Express card. He was born in 1926 in Oranienburg, Germany, a suburb of Berlin, where his parents operated a women's clothing store. The store was looted and burned in 1938 during Hitler's campaign against German Jews, and Mr. Blumenthal's father was thrown into the Buchenwald concentration camp. Even though he had converted to Lutheranism years before, the Nazis considered him a Jew. (Mr. Blumenthal, the son of non-Jewish parents, is not Jewish.) Mr. Blumenthal's mother sold family possessions to raise the money to get her husband out of Buchenwald, and the family booked passage out of Germany and fled. Lacking visas, the Blumenthals in 1939 found themselves in Shanghai, China, which admitted people who did not have visas. Mike Blumenthal, who was just thirteen at the time, took odd jobs to help the family survive. He recalls wartime Shanghai as "a cesspool, a den of iniquity." He learned English in a British private school which was closed by the Japanese when they occupied Shanghai. The Blumenthals were then packed off to a Japanese internment camp for two years. When the United States Seventh Fleet arrived in Shanghai in 1945 it was met by seventeen-year-old Mike Blumenthal, who had hired a sampan and sailed up the Yangtze River to meet the American ships. Because of his knowledge of languages, Blumenthal worked for the Americans for two years, then booked passage to the United States.

In 1947 Blumenthal and his sister, with sixty dollars between them, arrived in California. Even though he had not gotten past the tenth grade in Shanghai, Blumenthal talked his way into San Francisco Junior College. After graduating, he attended the University of California at Berkeley. To support himself during his college years he was a truckdriver, a dishwasher, a theater ticket-taker, a night elevator operator and a licensed shill in a casino in Lake Tahoe, Nevada.

He got a doctorate in international economics from Princeton (where he is now a trustee), taught there, worked for the Crown, Cork & Seal Company for four years, becoming a vice-president, then labored in the United States State Department from 1961 to 1967. During his State Department days he met William Gossett, one of the most influential men in Michigan. Mr. Gossett is a partner of Michigan's largest law firm, Dykema, Gossett, Spencer, Goodnow & Trigg. Among other things, he has been general counsel of Bendix and the Ford Motor Company. As a result of his role in helping save Ford, which was on the verge of collapse when World War II ended, Gossett is a millionaire many times over. When Mike Blumenthal met him in 1962, Bill Gossett was an assistant secretary of state, the number two man in a United States trade delegation that was holding meetings in Europe with this country's trading partners. Gossett was running the delegation because the man in charge, Christian Herter, was on crutches and physically unable to do the job. Gossett then began to suffer incapacitating headaches—members of the United States delegation routinely had a drink or two together after work, and it was later discovered that he was allergic to whiskey—whereupon Blumenthal became the de facto head of the delegation.

After Gossett returned to practice law in Detroit, he told his friend, Bendix chairman A. P. (Jack) Fontaine, about the bright young man he had met in Europe. Mr. Fontaine was especially on the lookout for bright young men because of an age problem at Bendix—the top cadre of Bendix executives had grown old together, and the company was in short supply of young blood. In 1967, he hired Mike Blumenthal, who had just finished heading the United States delegation to the General Agreement on Tariffs and Trade negotiations. Because of the situation at Bendix, Blumenthal saw a chance to rise rapidly and accepted the offer. He was sent to New York to run Bendix International, and did a superb job of expanding International's operations and making them more profitable. In 1970 destiny, in the form of Jack Fontaine, tapped him on the shoulder. As Blumenthal tells it, Jack Fontaine and his wife went to Europe and spent time touring with Mr. Blumenthal and his wife (from whom he has since been divorced). Each couple had its own car, but one day Fontaine asked the wives to ride together so he could be alone with Mike Blumenthal. "We were riding from Barcelona to Pamplona," Mr. Blumenthal says, "and he told me, 'I'm going to be retiring in a few years, you're clearly a candidate for the number one or the number two job, but you've got to be in Detroit.' I said, 'Jesus Christ,' but I took the job." In 1970, Mr. Blumenthal became vice-chairman of the board and in 1972, chairman.

Mike Blumenthal was a man with an unusual history running a company with an unusual history. Bendix, which ended as an independent company with William Agee and Mary Cunningham running it, began with Vincent T. Bendix, a dealmaker also well known for his relationships with women.

A typical self-made millionaire of the early 1900s, Bendix was born in 1881, the son of a Methodist minister in Moline, Illinois, ran away from home at the age of sixteen to escape his father's discipline, gravitated to New York City, where he worked odd jobs, and wandered into the automobile industry, which was then young and vibrant and a rapidly evolving technology. Pioneers like William Durant (the founder of General Motors), Henry Ford, Ransom E. Olds and Walter Chrysler were just starting out. In 1907 Vincent Bendix also started an auto company—it produced a handful of cars, one of which is on display in the Discovery Hall Museum in South Bend, Indiana—but it was a flop.

Unable to make entire cars successfully, Bendix became interested in the problem of starting automobile engines automatically. He found a transmission device that would do the job, but he needed a special triple-thread screw which had to be produced in low volume and at high cost by hand. In 1913 he managed to find just the thing he needed at a bicycle show. The Eclipse Manufacturing Company of Elmira, New York, was mass-producing a triple-thread screw to make bicycle coaster brakes. Bendix licensed Eclipse to make his starter drive, and the money started to roll in. Then in 1923 on a trip to France, Bendix met Henri Perrot, an engineer, at an automobile show. Perrot had invented an internally expanding brake shoe, and gave Vincent Bendix a license to produce it in the United States. Because he was involved with starters and brakes, Bendix acquired the nickname of "Mr. Stop and Go." In 1924, during the stock market's giddy days, he raised $800,000 from investors and started the Bendix Corporation in South Bend, Indiana. He had no particular affection for Indiana; he picked South Bend because it was on a rail line about midway between Detroit and Chicago, which were competing to become the auto capital of the United States.

The Bendix Corporation was very, very profitable, and Vincent Bendix used the money to live very, very well. He bought a mansion in South Bend, renaming it Chateau Bendix. He became famous for conducting wild parties and having female movie stars imported for his amusement. The main Bendix plant had a special elevator reserved for his women, who were sent to South Bend by train. Occasionally he would adjourn important business meetings for a recreational interlude. "He would go downstairs and knock off a piece," recalls William Gossett, blushing. "He was quite a swordsman."

While Vincent Bendix lived the life of a roué, his company continued to grow, producing products no other company could match. Bendix used newly issued stock to buy more companies. He also did a large amount of business with General Motors, and in 1929 GM bought a major share of Bendix Corporation. It was a typical move for GM, which owned interests in many of its suppliers, and ultimately absorbed some— such as Fisher Body—into the company. It is not clear how GM acquired its Bendix shares. The closest thing to a Bendix corporate history, an article former chairman Jack Fontaine wrote in 1968, tells a complicated story about GM guaranteeing promissory notes the Bendix Corporation issued to buy another company. The Standard & Poor's corporate history sheet says that GM traded $15 million of cash, its Delco Aviation division and some licenses for 500,000 shares of Bendix stock in 1929. Neither GM nor Bendix can clarify the situation.

In any case, Vincent Bendix went happily along making deals. One of the acquisitions was the Pioneer Instrument Company, which made aircraft instruments. That marked Bendix's entry into the aerospace business, which had become glamorous in 1927 when Lindbergh flew the Atlantic. To cash in on the aerospace boom, Vincent Bendix changed the company's name to Bendix Aviation Corporation, even though well under 10 percent of Bendix's business involved airplanes. (The name was changed back to Bendix Corporation in 1960.) In 1931 Bendix sponsored the first transcontinental air race, from Los Angeles to Cleveland, a promotional gimmick. Major Jimmy Doolittle, a famous early aviator, won the first race with an average speed of 223 miles an hour. (The last race in 1962 was won by the crew of a B-58 bomber which flew at an average speed of 1,215 miles an hour.) Vincent Bendix was still having a good time. A 1930 picture at Discovery Hall Museum, taken at Chateau Bendix to honor the winner of the first race, shows Jimmy Doolittle, Vincent Bendix and about two dozen other men, plus a good-looking woman identified as "Miss Le-Tarte."

Bendix made other history too. Its South Bend plant was the site of the first sit-down strike in the United States. Inspired by a successful sit-in conducted by a French union, the United Auto Workers occupied Bendix's South Bend plant for six days in November of 1936, earning the UAW the right to be recognized as the sole bargaining agent for the workers. A later, much more famous sit-down strike at the General Motors facility in Flint, Michigan, won the UAW recognition at GM and helped the UAW to become an industry-wide union.

Ironically, the best-known product with the Bendix name—the Bendix washing machine—was *not* made by Bendix. In the 1930s two young inventors convinced officials at a Bendix Aviation subsidiary to allow them to use Bendix facilities to work on the development of an automatic washing machine. As the work progressed, Vincent Bendix became interested and allowed the inventors to use the Bendix name on the machine. In return, Bendix Aviation received 25 percent of the stock of Bendix Home Appliances, founded in 1936. For a while, Bendix had more than half the market for automatic washing machines, but as World War II approached, Bendix Aviation had other problems and in 1940 sold its Bendix Home Appliances stock. Ten years later Bendix Home Appliances was sold to Avco, which in turn was sold to Philco. The Bendix washing machine brand name no longer exists.

As long as things went well, General Motors, Bendix Aviation's largest shareholder, left the company alone. But in 1937 the company began losing money at the rate of $1 million a month. Alarmed, GM sent one of its bright young men, Ernest Breech, to South Bend to see what was wrong. Breech reported that to a large extent the problem was Vincent Bendix. Not only was Vincent the president of Bendix, he was plant manager at South Bend, where the biggest problems were. General Motors' Alfred P. Sloan, Jr., a business genius who had a strong moral code and abhorred waste, was undoubtedly none too fond of Vincent Bendix to begin with. Out he went. General Motors left Vincent Bendix with a seat on the Bendix board but gave Mr. Breech control over the company. Years later, a story was told that the War Department, alarmed at Vincent Bendix's ties with Europeans, had refused to allow the company access to secret information to produce war material unless Vincent Bendix was purged. William Gossett, who was involved in Bendix business at the time, says that was just a cover story for Sloan's deposing of the corporate founder.

Breech helped Bendix become profitable and successful as a government contractor during World War II, when its volume surged from $60 million a year to more than $1 billion. After World War II Ernie Breech left to become executive vice-president of the Ford Motor Company, which had been all but ruined as Henry Ford slipped into his dotage. Helped by his mother and his uncle, Ernest Kanzler, Henry Ford II wrested control of the company from his grandfather and brought in Ernest Breech to help save it. By bringing General Motors business disciplines to Ford, and by stocking its ranks with people he hired away from GM, Breech became the true savior of the company—though he never got much recognition for it.

Breech's vacancy at Bendix was filled by Malcolm Ferguson, an engineer whom Breech had spotted as a talented manager. In 1948 GM, which had moved Bendix's headquarters from South Bend to Detroit's Fisher Building across the street from GM's own headquarters building, sold the last of its Bendix stock (the sale netting GM just $25.90 per Bendix share, which appears to be less than the company had paid for the stock in 1929). Bendix's Jack Fontaine, who had succeeded Malcolm Ferguson, tried to change Bendix's nature. Recognizing that the company was overly dependent on sales to the auto makers and the federal government, Fontaine branched out into areas that he thought would be more stable. He bought a forest products company and the Fram Corporation, which makes replacement parts for the auto after-market. He also bought the nucleus of what became the Bendix machine tool business.

When Fontaine turned the company over to Mike Blumenthal in 1972, Bendix was at a crossroads. Blumenthal wanted to add to the diversification, to lessen the chance that Bendix's earnings could be wrecked by a slow year in the auto industry or the loss of defense contracts. He also wanted to show that a company could be both profitable and socially enlightened —shades of Robert Hansberger at Boise Cascade. Blumenthal, who was in his mid-forties, brought young people to Bendix and made managers' bonuses partly dependent on whether they promoted women and members of minority groups. He invited feminist Gloria Steinem to address the Bendix officer corps about sexism. He wanted Bendix to be an example of how management and labor could work together in harmony. While he preached this message, Blumenthal saw that much of Bendix's expansion in the United States took place in areas outside the UAW's reach. By explanation, he has said that the expansion took place in the most cost-effective sites, which happened to be outside the UAW-dominated Midwest.

In 1972 when Bendix's chief financial officer resigned, Mike Blumenthal had the opportunity to continue remaking the corporation in his image, and he seized it. "I got a headhunter and told him I wanted to interview the five or six most innovative financial officers in the country," Mr. Blumenthal says. "I was told there was a precocious wunderkind [Bill Agee]. I met him and liked him; he seemed mature beyond his years. I was concerned whether he'd had anything to do with the troubles at Boise, and I was told he hadn't." (Blumenthal told the author that his 1972 information was wrong, but he did not elaborate.)

Bill Agee could not have been more unlike Mike Blumenthal —which may well have been part of the attraction. "Herr Blumenthal," as Bill Agee playfully used to call him, had had to scratch for survival, while Agee came from a calm, stable home. Mike Blumenthal was an ardent Democrat and an internationalist; Bill Agee was a Republican and had never spent much time outside of Idaho except for school. But Mr. Agee *was* a superb numbers man and a very pleasant and charming fellow. Mr. Blumenthal, who seems to relish intelligent dissent, hired him. Just as Mr. Agee had been close to Bob Hansberger, he seems to have tried to get close to Mike Blumenthal. In Idaho the Agees had a resort home in McCall close to the Hansberger resort home. In his new job, the Agees began vacationing with the Blumenthals. The Agee and Blumenthal families, children in tow, got into the habit of spending their Christmas holidays together at Lost Tree Village in North Palm Beach, Florida. No one else high in the Bendix ranks did that. "Maybe he was playing up to me," Mr. Blumenthal said in an interview with the author. The two men played tennis together, Bill Agee, twelve years younger and a good athlete, consistently whipping his boss.

William Agee's first venture into the acquisitions business at Bendix proved an embarrassment, but possibly because he was new at the job and Mr. Blumenthal had a commitment to him he escaped adverse consequences. As part of its attempt to raise cash to satisfy its lenders, Boise Cascade put its profitable mobile-home and recreational-vehicle businesses up for sale in October of 1972. An investment banker suggested that Bendix buy the businesses. After some internal wrangling, Bendix made the purchase. Problems showed up during Bendix's pre-purchase audit of the Boise Cascade properties, but those difficulties were resolved by reducing the price Bendix paid by several million dollars, to $70.7 million. The deal was completed on December 31, 1972. In 1973, when the energy crisis hit, the bottom fell out of the recreational-vehicles market—an event no one could have foreseen. But there were also operational problems in the mobile-home business. Agee, having recently arrived from a high position at Boise Cascade, could have been expected to know about those problems. Though noting that, "I was the chairman, so I was responsible," Mike Blumenthal recalls that Bill Agee was in favor of the acquisition too. "He was very much involved," Mr. Blumenthal says. "He told me he knew the business; he was very positive about it."

It is impossible for anyone outside of Bendix to calculate the total loss Bendix sustained on that purchase, but it is reasonable to state that it exceeded $30 million. In 1978, following years of losses, Bendix sold one part of the old Boise Cascade operation for $25.8 million, taking a $17.8 million loss on the transaction. Other parts of the business have apparently been sold or liquidated over the years, but no details are available. Bendix declined to provide an overall loss figure.

Despite his role in the acquisition, which turned bad almost immediately, Bill Agee was very well thought of at Bendix. These were, for the most part, flush times in the automotive and forest products businesses, and profits were growing rapidly enough to easily cover the dent made by the mobile-home and recreational-vehicles missteps. Mike Blumenthal was viewed as a progressive, iconoclastic manager who hired good people and paid them very well, if they performed. Despite the problems that periodically ravaged the automotive industry, Bendix's profits grew steadily. Bill Agee, a member of the Bendix board, was a pleasant, open colleague. He impressed his fellow directors, spending long hours in the office and producing the information Mike Blumenthal asked for. His behavior and diligence were widely admired by other Bendix officers, and he was clearly in line for the number two job in the company. Mike Blumenthal, worried that his friend and colleague would jump to another company, recommended to the board that he be made president. On December 1, 1976, Bill Agee became president.

And then Bill Agee's good fortune struck again. Jimmy Carter made Blumenthal secretary of the treasury. Without ever having had to prove himself in the Bendix presidency, Bill Agee was made chairman on January 1, 1977. It was four days before his thirty-ninth birthday. He had never had a serious personal setback in his business career. He had made it to the top.

Agee inherited a company that had a reputation for being run very well. Despite the violent ups and downs of the auto industry, which accounted for about half of Bendix's sales volume, the company's earnings per share had increased every year since 1970. Because the company's earnings were more stable than those of other Detroit-area corporations, it was a more secure place in which to work. Other companies tied to the auto industry went through boom-or-bust cycles, but Bendix grew steadily. Such factors attracted a strong corps of executives to Bendix. Mike Blumenthal had encouraged dissent —it was said that if you didn't argue with him, you didn't get promoted—and Bendix executives were accustomed to speaking their minds.

In his early years at the top Agee did things that were overdue. He hired William Panny as the operating chief in 1977, and he and Panny cleaned up problems with the Bendix European operations, sold odds and ends, such as the remnants of

the recreational-vehicle and mobile-home businesses. Agee
spoke frequently of Blumenthal, and said he would like to
leave Bendix within a few years to pursue the sort of political
and teaching activities that Mr. Blumenthal had been involved
in before coming to Bendix.

But William Agee, as it turned out, was different from Michael Blumenthal in a fundamental way. Blumenthal, who had
never been to business school, believed that the way to increase Bendix's profits was by gradually expanding the businesses the company was already in, increasing those businesses' share of their markets and improving the company's
balance sheet. The Blumenthal approach produced year-after-
year of increased profits per share. Agee, a graduate of Harvard Business School, had more of a portfolio manager's approach. He seemed content to eliminate operations, provided
that the profit per dollar on the remaining assets was higher.
Blumenthal, who was fortunate enough to have spent most of
his ten years at Bendix at a time the auto industry was growing,
had, as mentioned, lessened the United Auto Workers' hold on
the company by expanding with new facilities located primarily outside the Midwest. Though he expanded away from the
UAW, Blumenthal still had amicable relations with the union.
Agee was convinced that the auto industry was in "the winter
of its life," as he often put it in public speeches. Rather than
merely expanding into nonunion areas, he began to talk of
moving operations out of the Midwest into those areas. Not
surprisingly, his relationship with the UAW deteriorated.
When Bill Panny came up with an idea to "deintegrate"
Chrysler's brake business by buying Chrysler's brake-making
equipment and turning Bendix into Chrysler's sole source of
brakes, Bill Agee rejected the idea. (This version, told by Bendix insiders, is confirmed by Paul Bergmoser, who was
Chrysler's president at the time.) Agee ultimately tried to sell
large parts of Bendix's automotive and truck businesses, but
could not find buyers willing to meet his price.

In 1980 Bill Agee was to make possibly the worst acquisition

in the history of Bendix. The company, which had a substantial
machine tool group, got into a bidding war with a Canadian
company, Amca, for Warner & Swasey, a Cleveland-based machine tool company that had a mediocre record. Kidder, Peabody & Company, Warner & Swasey's investment banker,
convinced Bendix to become a white knight. Bendix had already been eyeing W&S as a possible acquisition, so it made
some sense to bid for it. In the end Bendix won, but paid $301
million, an exceptionally high price. It was also buying a cyclical company in a cyclical business at the high point of the cycle.
The plan was for Bill Panny, the main force behind the purchase, to combine W&S with Bendix's machine tool division to
produce one large machine tool company capable of outfitting
the highly automated "factory of the future." Japanese machine toolmakers were already beginning to invade the United
States, but Bendix went ahead anyway. The Bendix board of
directors agreed that Warner & Swasey was worth having,
provided the price was not more than $70 per share, about
$240 million. But according to several people who were in-
volved in the Bendix end of the deal, during the excitement
of the bidding process Warner & Swasey's investment bankers
convinced Mr. Agee to make a "preemptive" offer of $83 a
share. After hurried telephone consultations with the directors
to get them to authorize the higher bid, Mr. Agee submitted
the $83 bid and was characterized in the press as winning the
fight. In September of 1980, Agee fired Panny and named
himself chief operating officer. But he left the W&S management in place, and the Bendix machine tool operation began
to drift. By all accounts except Bill Agee's and Mary Cunningham's, Warner & Swasey was Bill Panny's idea. With him gone,
no one paid much attention until Japanese toolmakers had
taken away much of W&S's business. The weak economy hurt
Warner & Swasey, too. In early 1983 Bendix was trying to
recoup by buying foreign technology to fill out its machine tool
product line, but the success of those efforts seems problemati-
cal. Bendix, with the second-largest machine tool operation in

the country, behind only Cincinnati Milacron, had a loss in the tool business in 1982—the first annual loss ever. The machine tool operation's future as an Allied Corporation subsidiary is at this writing unclear.

Warner & Swasey came back to haunt Bendix in another way. Kidder Peabody's Martin Siegel, who handled the W&S side of the tender offer battle, believed he saw that Bill Agee could get carried away in a negotiation—he was to exploit this perception in 1982 when he represented Martin Marietta. Mr. Siegel also made contacts with Bendix executives, who assisted him in finding vital information when Marietta was fighting Bendix.

In retrospect, some of William Agee's past and present colleagues, interviewed in late 1982 and early 1983, think that he began drifting, so to speak, after about a year in the Bendix chairmanship. After that, they say, he was rarely seen in the employee cafeteria, he was not as accessible or friendly as he had once been, he seemed to grow increasingly impatient, he seemed to tune out dissenting views and to surround himself with business school graduates whose philosophies were very like his own. He also seemed to some to be growing perhaps overly fond of the corporate jet and helicopter—he once ordered the Bendix financial staff to do a cost-benefit study to prove it was cheaper for him to take a helicopter to Detroit's Metro Airport than to be driven there in a car. No matter how the figures were viewed, the staff could not make them work out. Mr. Agee eventually stopped asking for the study.

To the outside world, however, things were as before. The favorable Bendix publicity that Blumenthal's unique background had generated was replaced by favorable publicity that Mr. Agee's unusual background generated. Just as Blumenthal had spoken out on social issues, Agee had articles written under his name on the plight of Social Security and other big-picture problems. He was still friendly with "Herr Blumenthal," who returned from Washington for a weekend and spent part of it soaking in the hot tub Bill and Diane Agee had installed as part of an addition to their house. The addition was valued at $87,000 for building permit purposes; it probably cost more than $100,000. But in the summer of 1979 Mary Cunningham Gray had come to work for Bill Agee at Bendix —and soon things began to change.

Chapter 5

The Queen Of Bendix (I)

THE RISE OF MARY CUNNINGHAM

"We really love swans and ducks, because they are monogamous."—Mary Cunningham, quoted in Monthly Detroit magazine, March, 1983

"I looked at the face of the Virgin Mary, and I saw the incredible pain as she held her son, who had been through the ultimate embarrassment, the ultimate in being betrayed by everybody . . . And all I could think of was a sense of identification with the pain . . . Who was I to be upset about the pain that had come into my life?"—Mary Cunningham, Parade magazine, April 25, 1982

"I was mentally raped, and that's no exaggeration."—Mary Cunningham, Washington *Post,* October 26, 1982

"Unfortunately, we're culturally bound by norms that preclude in many minds the existence of someone like myself."—Mary Cunningham, Detroit *Free Press,* September 25, 1980

A given: One of the essential attributes of any top corporate strategist for a large company is that he or she be a balanced, mature person. Major strategies affect not only companies and their shareholders but also the lives of employees, customers and suppliers. In the case of a $4 billion corporation such as

Bendix, strategies can affect entire cities and regions in which the company is a large employer. Drawing up and implementing strategies for such a company is no parlor game. Bendix strategies can affect thousands of jobs and hundreds of millions of dollars. In the case of Bendix pursuing a strategy to attack Martin Marietta, one company's strategy can have an important effect on a second company, which produces products vital to the national defense. The Mary Cunningham quotes cited above—selected from the dozens of articles that have been written about her since 1980—can reasonably give one pause about her qualifications as a corporate strategist. One may wonder, for example, about the balance and maturity of an individual who in effect compares losing a job to the sufferings of Christ on the cross.

The three years of debate about Mary Cunningham have centered about the role of women in business: Was Ms. Cunningham unjustly forced out of her Bendix job by sexist pigs? Is she a victim of sensationalist reporting in the news media? Is corporate America ready for a high-powered, brilliant young person who happens to be female? Those are large-scale important questions, to be sure. But there are other, more immediate questions to be asked, questions about personal power and responsibility: Who is this person, Mary Cunningham? What were her qualifications to wield the substantial power she derived in large measure from her closeness to William Agee? What did she do with her power once she got it?

Ms. Cunningham had a bachelor's degree in philosophy from Wellesley College and was Phi Beta Kappa, and held a masters degree in business administration, with honors, from Harvard. Ms. Cunningham arrived at Bendix in June of 1979 with a top-grade resume and a strong endorsement from J. Leslie Rollins, the former Harvard Business School assistant dean who had helped Bendix chairman Agee early in his career. Despite the 33-year age difference between them, the men are personally close. As a Harvard Business School student, Mr. Agee told the author, he did Dean Rollins' tax re-

turns and mowed his lawn. Dean Rollins helped ease Mr.
Agee's difficult, early days at Harvard. The two men, interviewed in 1983, spoke fondly of each other. Mr. Agee repeat-
edly called Dean Rollins "a wonderful man."

It must be reported that extensive interviews by the author
and his assistants with people who have known Ms. Cunningham over the years, including people who worked closely with
her at Bendix, produce an almost unanimous portrait of a person lacking in both practical business experience and emotional maturity. The portrait is of someone who radiated great
energy, who was not an original thinker but rather a synthesist
who would take other peoples' ideas and make them into her
own, a flatterer, a woman who was bright and quick, very good
with business jargon but who had considerable difficulty in
making decisions. An example several Bendix people cited was
the career plan she kept while at the company. This was a two
hundred-page document, frequently updated by Bendix secretaries as Ms. Cunningham changed her mind.

(An example of Ms. Cunningham's skill as a tactician can be
seen in the following anecdote, as related by Jacqueline Agee,
William Agee's younger sister. Ms. Agee said she was out of
work and ill and had fallen behind in her mortgage payments.
For the first time in her life she called brother Bill to ask for
a short-term loan. After hearing Jackie's request, Bill put Mary
Cunningham on the phone. Ms. Cunningham's solution, Jackie
Agee said, was, "Go to the local press and plant a story about
how the bank is taking advantage of a young woman with an
illness. I've dealt with banks and I know all about this." Ms.
Agee said she borrowed money from her parents instead.)

Ms. Cunningham seems to have generated a reputation for
brilliance. But in months of research and dozens of interviews
with present and former Bendix employees, the author could
not find a single project Ms. Cunningham completed at Bendix
that would demonstrate brilliance, at least on a corporate
level.

William Agee has frequently praised Ms. Cunningham's

work at Bendix, though there is some question about its nature. Mr. Agee told the author that Ms. Cunningham wrote "at least seven or eight speeches for him." Members of the public relations department at the time say that for the most part she took credit for speeches other people wrote. He also said Ms. Cunningham worked on two of Bendix's assets sales, did major analyses of eight potential acquisitions, critiqued the work of other people, and helped formulate the "high tech" strategy (of which more later). Bendix officials say that Mr. Agee lavishly praised Ms. Cunningham's work, but did not show it to the other executives.

Throughout her tenure at Bendix, Ms. Cunningham reported only to Mr. Agee. That is most unusual, even for a chairman's protege. It is common corporate practice for the chairman to promote his proteges to jobs in which they report to someone else. One reason for that, of course, is to see if other executives agree with the chairman's favorable assessment.

Even after Mr. Agee promoted Ms. Cunningham to vice-president of corporate and public relations—a full-time job— in June of 1980, she continued to be his executive assistant, which is also a full-time job. Mr. Agee said she could handle both jobs because she worked very long hours. In September of 1980, Mr. Agee promoted her to vice-president for strategic planning, another job in which she reported only to him. Her performance as public relations vice-president will be examined in the following chapter. She was the strategic planning vice-president for only a few days, so there is nothing to assess.

To the author's knowledge there are only two projects in which Ms. Cunningham was involved that produced results that can be measured. One is a study, produced in August of 1980, that discussed Bendix's brake business. The other is the acquisition of Warner & Swasey, the machine tool company.

Ms. Cunningham was chairperson of an eight-person group, nicknamed "Snow White and the Seven Dwarfs," that analyzed the brake business. But from the account of two "dwarfs" she played a minor role in the preparation of the report, which, based on excerpts that the author has seen, said little new. The only concrete suggestion was to move the production of drum brakes out of Bendix's South Bend, Indiana, plant unless costs could be cut sharply. Two "dwarfs" told the author that Bendix's automotive executives had long since realized this and were already trying to correct the problem.

In an August 1980 interview with the Detroit *Free Press,* and in discussions with Gail Sheehy, whose five-part series on Ms. Cunningham was syndicated in newspapers throughout the country in October of 1980, Ms. Cunningham professed a major role in the decision to buy Warner & Swasey. This was before it became clear that the acquisition had been an unsuccessful one. One of the major reasons that Warner & Swasey apparently lost money in 1982 is that Bendix did not take steps to deal with the Japanese threat to American machine-tool makers—a failure, presumably, of strategic planning. In fairness to Ms. Cunningham, however, she seems to have been only tangentially involved with Warner & Swasey. (Mr. Agee says the Warner & Swasey problem was his fault, for having left the existing managers in place too long. He predicted a comeback for the company.)

Mr. Agee announced in September of 1980 that the company was to return to its high-technology roots. He and Ms. Cunningham have said that she helped to formulate that strategy, though it is not altogether clear that there was a strategy. Mr. Agee told the author the strategy consisted of sharply increasing research and development expenditures, concentrating more assets on Bendix's aerospace operations and fewer on automotive, and concentrating on specialized products with high profit margins and decreasing the emphasis on commodity products with low profit margins. The company also made some minor acquisitions, which Mr. Agee said were part of the strategy. Such things do tend to seem more like rather obvious, basic business adjustments than a "high tech" strategy requiring restructuring the company. There was a decision to sell certain businesses at high prices—Bendix's forest product business, its geophysical exploration subsidiary and its offshore drilling equipment manufacturing subsidiary. The company also sold, and at the right time, its 21 percent interest in Asarco, the mining company.

Ms. Cunningham may well deserve credit for helping to influence these sales, which were brilliantly timed. (Of course the first half of the Asarco transaction—buying the stock—was done by Mr. Agee in 1978, before Ms. Cunningham joined the company.) Divesting some assets, though, is half a strategy. For a strategy to be complete, the assets must be redeployed and the strategist should make certain the redeployment is properly executed. In fact, the $800 million of cash that Bendix raised from its asset sales made the company a tempting take-over target—one reason it spent some $260 million in early 1981 to repurchase four million of its own shares, not a high-technology move.

In an interview with Monthly Detroit magazine Ms. Cunningham is quoted as saying: "I was and am his strategist," and Mr. Agee is portrayed as agreeing. If that is the case, then it is presumably Ms. Cunningham's responsibility that Bendix bought Warner & Swasey just as Japanese companies were beginning to move into U.S. machine-tool makers' markets. It also is presumably her responsibility that Bendix did not respond more effectively to the fundamental changes that have affected the automotive-components business the past few years. Because of the fuel economy standards mandated by Congress, U.S. cars are becoming almost identical to cars in other parts of the world. In previous years, U.S. cars were far larger and heavier. Because U.S. and foreign car designs are converging, components are converging too, which has made it possible for foreign component-manufacturers to compete with Bendix and other U.S. companies for the business of domestic automakers. Some of Bendix's most serious competitors for U.S. business are foreign companies to which the company has licensed a portion of its technology.

Mr. Agee and Ms. Cunningham have said that she was his

most valued and trusted advisor during the Bendix–Martin
Marietta contest. If such is the case, she presumably shares
responsibility for some of the missteps detailed in later chap-
ters. The one concrete accomplishment of the Agee-Cunningham Marietta strategy was to get Bendix sold at a reasonably
good price. That does not, however, seem to be the reason they
tried to take over Marietta. If Mr. Agee were principally interested in selling Bendix he might have been able to get a far
better price by selling the entire company or segments of it
under controlled conditions. As matters turned out, he had to
take what Allied Corporation offered at a time Bendix was over
a barrel.

Even after Ms. Cunningham left Bendix in October of 1980
she continued to have a substantive influence on Bendix, not
unrelated to her association with and influence on Bill Agee.
At the couple's June, 1982 wedding reception on the Bendix
grounds in Southfield, Bill Agee introduced his wife as "the
First Lady of Bendix," according to numerous, unchallenged
accounts. The 1982 annual Bendix management meeting, held
in Boca Raton, Florida, in November, was the first to which
executives' spouses were invited, according to an official Bendix spokesman, Berl Falbaum. Ms. Cunningham told an individual at a reception there that Mr. Agee had adopted the new
spouse-policy so that he could bring her to Florida. Ms. Cunningham also delivered the invocation at one of the dinners.

There is little or no reliable information about Mary Cunningham's youth beyond public and institutional records. As
she has told it:

She is the child of a broken home, her parents divorced
when she was about five. She was raised in Hanover, New
Hampshire, where Msgr. William Nolan, then the parish
priest, now the Catholic chaplain at Dartmouth, was her
guardian and surrogate father. She was a serious Catholic: "I
saw (my classmates) playing—you know, tattling and gossiping
—and I would use my time to read theology. They were talking

about the latest comic-book characters, and I was talking about St. Thomas Aquinas and proofs of God," she said in a Parade magazine story ("I'm Not Going to Let Them Change Me," by Lisa Bernbach, April 25, 1982).

She "suffered her greatest disappointment at seventeen. It was then she realized there was no way she could be a priest" (Gail Sheehy, five-part newspaper series, October 14–18, 1980). She worked hard at school and distinguished herself. She was an international Alpine ski racer and a classical pianist (the Detroit *Free Press,* August 25, 1980). At Wellesley she met Howard (Bo) Gray, Jr., a black man twelve years her senior, a Harvard Business School graduate who worked as a financial executive in New York City. They were married in December 1974. She graduated from Wellesley, Phi Beta Kappa, in 1973. She worked as a paralegal in New York City, according to biographical material she distributed in connection with a June 1982, speech in Detroit. She gave up her goal of becoming a lawyer and left Notre Dame Law School because, she has said, of Bo Gray: "She couldn't ask Bo to subject himself to living in the Midwest, where one night a motel owner had refused even to rent them rooms. So she gave up her law school to marry him." This was told to Gail Sheehy. "Her next step was law school at Notre Dame. She planned on becoming a judge . . . 'I made the decision to leave law school after one term,' she says, 'in order to minimize the difficulty that my being in South Bend, Indiana, was causing to my then-fiancé.' " This was told to Parade. Records at Notre Dame show that she was admitted on August 23, 1974, and withdrew voluntarily on September 6, 1974. She went to work at Chase Manhattan Bank in New York City, becoming an assistant treasurer, and decided to attend Harvard Business School, where she did very well. She declined attractive job offers in the $50,000 range from investment banking and consulting firms because she was impressed with Bill Agee, according to the Gail Sheehy account. She and Agee, she told Gail Sheehy, devised an extraordinary business strategy at Bendix, which produced tensions within the company. Agee's enemies struck at him through her, and she sacrificed herself for the well-being of the company and her friend, Bill Agee. She and Bill Agee were not romantically involved until after she left Bendix.

Harvard is the earliest point in Ms. Cunningham's career where the author and his assistants could find enough people willing to discuss her to allow the inevitable distortions and jealousies in individual accounts to be weeded out. Several dozen members of Ms. Cunningham's class were contacted, and about a dozen were interviewed at length. The people who had the greatest exposure to her at Harvard consider her average-bright—by Harvard Business School standards—but far above average in synthesis, packaging and self-promotion. She was well-known for going up to instructors after class and asking questions. "I counted once, and she had done it twenty-seven straight times," a classmate recalls.

Packaging is crucial at the Harvard "B-School" because grades are mostly subjective and almost everyone is bright and impressive. Unlike a math or engineering class, where it is possible for everyone to get A's by answering all the questions correctly, a Harvard Business School class is graded on a relative basis. There are three grades—excellent (the top 15 percent of the class); satisfactory (the middle 70 percent); and low pass (the bottom 15 percent). Class participation, which is completely subjective, counts for 50 percent of the final grade. Given the nature of the place, a premium is placed on quickness, self-promotion and the ability to draw conclusions from facts gathered from disparate sources—all Ms. Cunningham's strengths. Harvard Business School's course is a two-year, emotional, consuming experience in which few weaklings enter and from which almost none emerge. It has some aspects of religion: the students are told that they are the elite and that they have been chosen to spread the gospel of Harvard Business School among the unenlightened. The B-School women, who have had to overcome more obstacles than the men to get to Harvard in the first place, tend to be smarter than the men, who are no dummies. Most of the students have not only college degrees but work experience, and so are experienced competitors. Some people who have always excelled find themselves on the bottom of the heap for the first time in their lives, which can be a traumatic experience. The pressure is intense. A high class standing is worth many thousands of dollars over a student's work career; high-ranking Harvard Business School graduates are eagerly sought for the high-paying "fast-track" jobs that can lead to six-figure salaries in only a few years.

There are three degrees of intimacy at Harvard Business School: the class, the section and the study group. There are about eight hundred students in a class, many of whom never meet each other. A class is usually divided into about nine sections, each named for a letter of the alphabet. Mary Cunningham's was in Section E, Class of 1976. Section mates attend classes together and know each other, but not necessarily well. Study groups are more intimate. About half a dozen people, trusting each other, let their hair down and share ideas for the all-important class discussions. Study group partners usually come to know each other well, and a rough code of ethics generally prevails. While almost anything is acceptable at the B-School in pursuit of success, a convention appears to be that if one uses a contribution one has first heard in the study group from a colleague, one does that person the courtesy of mentioning that it was his or her idea.

According to several members of Ms. Cunningham's first study group, the group broke up because its members felt that she appropriated their ideas and presented them as her own. Members say the group re-formed without her, but Ms. Cunningham did not seem to notice. Several people, who say they were close to Ms. Cunningham during the first year but now do not care for her, say that by the end of the first year, people at Section-E parties, who had come to know her, would no longer speak to her.

People at Harvard, as well as at Bendix, say that in initial conversations with people who interested her, Ms. Cunningham would talk about Bo, her black husband; about Father Bill, her surrogate father; and about the sad circumstances of her childhood. "I had heard those stories the first day I met Mary," one of her classmates recalls. "She would say how nice it was to have a warm husband, how she had had an unhappy family life. Her mother married someone she wasn't happy with, and how she should have married Father Bill Nolan. When all those articles [about her] came out, I remembered it almost word for word."

A consequence of such apparent intimacy was that people, feeling that Ms. Cunningham was confiding deep personal feelings to them alone, would in return confide in her—which enabled her for a time to win over people at Bendix and to gain valuable insights from them about the company.

Among the people who claim to know Ms. Cunningham well there is an almost unanimous opinion that Bo Gray was a significant factor in her success at Harvard. Mr. Gray had already graduated from Harvard Business School and knew what the place was about. People who have met Mr. Gray say he is a calm, steady, smart man, an outstanding individual with a sense of perspective and balance. They say he calmed his wife, a high-energy, nervous woman given to overreacting to problems, working in binges and staying up all night to get her work done. Bo Gray tutored his wife on weekends—either he came to Cambridge, Massachusetts, to see her or she went to New York City to see him.

Mary Cunningham has said, in the Gail Sheehy series and elsewhere, that after she graduated from Harvard she was besieged by offers from investment banking houses to join their staffs. She has said that Goldman, Sachs & Company and Morgan Stanley & Company, two of the biggest-name firms on Wall Street, offered her jobs; neither company will confirm that. Some of her Harvard classmates say she told them she was taking the Bendix job only because she could not get the position she wanted on Wall Street, and that she planned to stay at Bendix only a year or two to establish her credentials.

J. Leslie Rollins, her Bendix connection, says: "In a million years, I never would have anticipated what happened." Dean Rollins and his wife, who have a farm in Athens, Ohio, were recruiters for Mr. Agee. Many high-potential hires and their spouses were sent to Athens for sessions on the farm with the Rollinses. Bill Agee had asked Les Rollins to recruit someone to become his executive assistant, and Rollins thought Mary Cunningham to be perfect for the job.

At this point in her life it would seem that Mary Cunningham had already had a taste of law and banking and did not much care for them. Her brief legal career has already been discussed; Dean Rollins says she told him that she was unhappy at Chase Manhattan Bank and was not sure that she wanted to return there after graduation from Harvard. He recalls: "I told her, 'With your energy, you shouldn't be in a bank behind a desk. You need something that will utilize some of your endless energy. You've got to be with the movers, shakers and leaders of the country. Why don't you go to work for someone like Bill Agee?' " According to Dean Rollins, Mary Cunningham's initial attraction for Bill Agee was the hours she put in at the job. "She would be up all night, writing position papers so they would be on his desk in the morning," Dean Rollins says. "Suddenly, he had a Girl Friday. He was fascinated that she took her job so seriously. He was astounded and delighted."

Ms. Cunningham and Mr. Agee have described her original Bendix job title—"executive assistant to the chairman"—as a position that involved advising him about acquisitions and other corporate strategies. Given the traditional nature of the job, Dean Rollins' "Girl Friday" description is rather much more likely. At Bendix, as at other large corporations, a chairman's executive assistant facilitates matters for him—arranging meetings, getting documents, making travel arrangements —but has little or no authority. The previous holders of those jobs under Mr. Agee and his predecessor as Bendix chairman, W. Michael Blumenthal, were typically given middle-management positions after their assistantships ended. Only Mary Cunningham jumped from assistant to vice-president.

In an interview with the author, Mr. Agee said that, in part, he hired Ms. Cunningham and gave her substantial responsibility because of his own history after graduating from Harvard. "We're all a little bit a product of our own background," he said. "Look at what I did when I was at Boise Cascade. I came in and worked as administrative assistant to John Fery (the number two man). In addition, part of the job offer was that I work as an administrative assistant to Bob Hansberger (the chairman). Within six months or less I was running a paper mill in Monroe, Michigan. I was also negotiating transactions in Guatemala and working on an acquisition that the company was entertaining in Portland, Oregon. At the end of seven or eight months, I was promoted to director of sales for the Kraft paper and paperboard business."

Mr. Agee contended it was not unusual for his assistants to move rapidly into powerful positions at Bendix. He cited one former assistant, Richard Breen, who became a corporate officer, and a second, Paul Slawson, whose next job was just below officer level. However, according to biographies of the two men provided the author by the Bendix public relations department, both were in their forties when they were Mr. Agee's assistants. They were not newly graduated from business school.

Mary Cunningham has implied that she had investment banking experience because she worked at Salomon Brothers in the summer of 1978 between her first and second years at Harvard. Jay Higgins, head of Salomon's mergers and acquisitions department, says that she was a summer intern—technically a "summer associate"—who performed routine tasks and was not invited back for a permanent job, as two-thirds of the summer interns were.

Ms. Cunningham has also implied that from the start she was to be Agee's strategic planner. Of interest is her description, as told by Gail Sheehy, of a meeting she had with Jerome

Jacobson, who was Bendix executive vice-president for strategic planning in June of 1979 when she joined Bendix:

". . . She ran suddenly into a bad omen. She has a vexing memory of . . . Jerome Jacobson, executive vice-president for mergers and acquisitions, [who] took her aside to give her some friendly advice 'for her own good.' He told her about several other 'feisty' women who had been broken and put away in back corridors of the company. And since she couldn't possibly know the meaning of confidentiality at her age, he added, he couldn't share information with her on any acquisitions he was doing."

At the time the alleged confrontation with Mr. Jacobson took place, he was a fifty-eight-year-old veteran of the merger business and of Washington consulting firms. He called the Cunningham account—as Gail Sheehy duly noted in her article— a "blatant falsehood," and reiterated that characterization in a telephone interview with the author.

At Bendix Ms. Cunningham drew on the expertise of others, and seems to have presented such expertise to Mr. Agee as her own. People who worked with her at Bendix recall that when Mr. Agee expressed displeasure with something, she disclaimed responsibility for it and blamed someone else. When he liked it, she took credit.

According to the Gail Sheehy articles, it was Bill Agee, against Mary Cunningham's advice, who insisted on promoting her to vice-president. It was also Bill Agee, against Mary's advice, who insisted on mentioning their relationship in the September 24, 1980 Bendix employees meeting: ". . . it was the only speech [of his] during a year and a half I didn't write" (Parade magazine).

It was because of disaffected, presumably male employees writing poison-pen letters (Gail Sheehy account) that the sensationalist press began writing about her. In fact, women in middle-management positions at Bendix interested the press in Ms. Cunningham. And until Mary Cunningham and Bill Agee themselves allowed Gail Sheehy to interview them,

much of the coverage seems to have been relatively restrained.

Though she has said she is Bill Agee's primary advisor, Ms.
Cunningham does not accept the responsibility for the outcome of the Bendix-Marietta war: Asked by Fortune magazine
—"Our Dream is to Work Together," an interview in the October 18, 1982 edition—whether she agreed with Mr. Agee
about going after Marietta, she answered: "I don't think that's
for me to answer . . . My position on the Martin Marietta deal
is irrelevant except to the extent it helped Bill refine his thinking."

As Mary Cunningham's influence grew, she appears to have
relished being able to wield power at Bendix. She scheduled
meetings for times that caused other people to interrupt their
weekends or work during vacations—meetings at which she
often either showed up late or failed to appear. One co-worker,
still at Bendix when he was interviewed, recalls sitting with
her in her office when she had nothing to do but, according to
him, simply felt like letting people with appointments wait to
see her.

According to numerous accounts she frequently dropped
Bill Agee's name in conversations, as in "Bill and I were talking
about the industrial group last night," or "Bill and I are going
to do" this or that. She flattered Mr. Agee in public, and
dressed down people who criticized him in her presence.
When there were people in Mr. Agee's office and she wanted
to speak with him privately she went to her office and telephoned him. People knew it was she, they say, because Mr.
Agee's secretaries had instructions not to interrupt his meetings except for her calls.

A meaningful incident occurred in January of 1980 at a party
marking Mr. Agee's forty-second birthday. Ms. Cunningham
arranged a party for him at the Renaissance Club in downtown
Detroit, inviting a dozen guests. Some of those invited were
not particularly close to Mr. Agee, and were surprised at the
form the party took. Ms. Cunningham assigned each guest a

month, and asked the guest to compose an original poem about the month and Bill Agee. She kept June for herself.

People who were there say that Ms. Cunningham's poem went along the lines of: "In June it will be a year / Since I've been here / And if nothing happens / I'll be gone." In June of 1980 Ms. Cunningham was made vice-president of corporate and public relations. There was nothing in her background that seems to have qualified her for this position—and subsequent events tended to demonstrate that her public relations judgment was not especially good.

Members of the Bendix public relations staff at the time she was in charge say that she spent almost all her time with Bill Agee and did not take an active hand in running the department. She frequently, they say, assigned three people to each write a speech for Mr. Agee, and would choose the best version and tell Mr. Agee she had written it. The staff members recall that despite Ms. Cunningham's statements about the need to overcome sexual and racial prejudices, when she was obliged to lay off two people as part of a companywide austerity plan in 1980 she fired the only black person in the department and a woman over forty.

About the time of Ms. Cunningham's arrival at Bendix Mr. Agee seems to have been going through a difficult passage in his life. He was forty-one years old and had been working hard for fifteen years. There was no higher post he could reach at Bendix, and he was getting a bit old to be a "boy wonder." As mentioned, he had told people that he hoped to leave Bendix within a few years to enter teaching, politics and public service.

The perception that Agee planned to leave the company, combined with the departure of a number of high ranking Bendix executives in 1980, combined to create an unusually high level of corporate politicking, as headquarters employees maneuvered for position in what they perceived as a power vacuum. Mr. Agee says this atmosphere—which did exist in 1980—along with the growing enmity of W. Michael Blumenthal toward him were the real problem, and that Mary Cunningham was not. "Many of the atmospherics predated Mary and predated the situation," he said.

Mr. Blumenthal's transformation from Mr. Agee's friend into something nearly the opposite cost Bendix dearly during the Martin Marietta war—some of Mr. Blumenthal's supporters helped Marietta with information about Bendix.

According to what Blumenthal told a number of his friends, the Blumenthal-Agee relationship appeared to have been souring before Mary Cunningham became a force at Bendix, but she accelerated the deterioration. Blumenthal told the author he preferred not to discuss his relationship with Agee. But the author obtained the information from Mr. Blumenthal's friends, some of whom have known the author for several years.

When it became obvious in mid-1979 that Mike Blumenthal's days as secretary of the treasury were numbered, he waited in vain for offers of office space or a Bendix directorship from his friend, Bill Agee. Other companies had made such offers, but Blumenthal wanted time to get his affairs in order before deciding which jobs to accept.

Not a man to suffer long in silence, Blumenthal called Agee and rebuked him for not having offered his former chairman the courtesy of the Bendix Washington office, and that apparently produced an offer of space, which was accepted. During his stay in Washington, Blumenthal met Ms. Cunningham; the two did not get along well. Blumenthal made his opinion of her known to Agee, who was not pleased. Agee began to hint that Blumenthal should accept some of the proffered directorships, implying—but not saying—that Blumenthal was not welcome on the Bendix board. Blumenthal fumed. Later in 1979 he was approached by directors of the Burroughs Corporation, a Detroit-based computer company, to become vice-chairman and heir apparent to the chairmanship. Burroughs, which was somewhat smaller than Bendix, was in need of strong top management. It had engaged in some creative accounting techniques to report continually rising profits but was finally beginning to show its problems. Agee told Blumenthal that he had put in a good word with him with Burroughs chairman Paul Mirabito, attorney Alan Schwartz and retired Kmart Corporation executive Harry Cunningham—all of whom were directors of Bendix as well as Burroughs. (Cunningham, no relation to Mary, conceived, planned and executed the S. S. Kresge Company's campaign to de-emphasize variety stores and plunge into discounting with Kmarts, a strategic move that probably saved the company.)

Blumenthal later discovered that rather than trying to help him get the Burroughs job, Agee had apparently tried to get it himself. An account of Bill Agee's attempt to head off Mike Blumenthal is contained in a letter Harry Cunningham later wrote to another Bendix director, Robert Purcell. Purcell, who unsuccessfully used the letter in an attempt to oust Bill Agee, showed it to the author. In it Harry Cunningham related an account of a Saturday morning meeting with Agee. Cunningham wrote that Agee telephoned in agitation and asked to come to his house. When he got there, Agee told Cunningham that he understood Burroughs was planning to hire Mike Blumenthal, and that he wanted the job himself. Cunningham wrote that Agee made clear "his discouragement with automotive, the limited potential of aerospace and automotive . . . and how badly he wanted to be involved in computers." When asked who would run Bendix if he left for Burroughs, Agee is said to have replied, "[Bill] Panny will be all right at Bendix, and I will be nearby to provide any consultation he needs." (Mr. Agee says that Messrs. Cunningham and Purcell are not being truthful about him, but declined to be specific. Cunningham and Purcell, who are both in their seventies and have distinguished business careers and personal reputations, say they are telling the truth.) In February of 1980 Mike Blumenthal joined Burroughs. In September, Bill Agee fired Bill Panny.

The Burroughs incident seems to have finished off the Blumenthal-Agee friendship. Blumenthal attacks Agee in off-the-record discussions . . . for example, Tom Pownall of Martin Marietta says that Blumenthal apologized to him for having put Agee in a position of power. "He wasn't like that when I made him president," Pownall quotes Blumenthal. But Blumenthal restrains himself in public utterances. Mary Cunningham and Agee have gone public: In September of 1980, according to Fortune magazine, when Agee was asked by the magazine if he had any enemies, Ms. Cunningham answered, "Mike Blumenthal."

In late 1980, having attempted a reconciliation with Agee after Mary Cunningham left Bendix, Blumenthal had a final break with him. Agee and Blumenthal are both directors of Equitable Life. The Equitable board was being asked to approve a $40 million loan to the corporation that was buying Bendix's forest products business for $425 million in cash and promissory notes. Blumenthal pointed out that the Bendix-Equitable relationship was an exceptionally close one, and could prove embarrassing to the company if anything went wrong with the loan. Mr. Agee and Equitable chairman Coy Eklund sat on each other's boards, and Jewell Lafontant, a Chicago attorney, was a director of both companies. And, of course, former Bendix chairman Blumenthal was on the Equitable board, too. The Equitable board turned down the loan request, forcing Bendix to accept $70 million in promissory notes from the purchasers rather than the planned-on $30 million. (Blumenthal was prescient. In 1982, according to the Bendix annual report, the borrowers could not pay, and Bendix had to take possession of the collateral backing the note. The report said Bendix suffered a $5 million loss on the deal.)

In an interview with the author, Mr. Agee asserted that Mr. Blumenthal's torpedoing of the Equitable loan was only part of what Blumenthal did "to cause problems as it relates to the implementation of our strategy." He declined to cite any other examples.

Mr. Agee contends that part of Mr. Blumenthal's trouble

with him stems from Mr. Agee's decision to hold up, on conflict of interest grounds, money due Blumenthal on a lifetime agreement with Bendix. Once again, Mr. Agee would not provide details. However, according to a 1977 proxy statement sent to Bendix shareholders, Mr. Blumenthal in 1974 accepted a contract giving him lifetime income in lieu of money that was due him. According to the proxy, he collected the payments due through the end of 1980 when he became Secretary of the Treasury. That would mean nothing would be due him until 1981—well after he and Mr. Agee became estranged.

The author asked Mr. Blumenthal to reply to Mr. Agee's assertion that the two men's falling out had to do with money. Mr. Blumenthal answered as follows. His stipend, which would now run about $30,000 a year, is adjusted annually for inflation. Part of it requires that he "consult" with Bendix. But in 1979, when Blumenthal joined Burroughs, Paul Mirabito, chairman at the time, felt uncomfortable with that relationship and urged Blumenthal to waive the money during his Burroughs tenure. Blumenthal wrote Agee a letter to that effect. But in September of 1980, when Blumenthal became chairman of Burroughs, the Burroughs board saw no conflict —"after all, we are in different industries"—and approved Blumenthal receiving the payments. When Blumenthal, who had voluntarily waived his right to payments, asked to have them reinstated, Agee refused on the grounds that Blumenthal was still at Burroughs. "This action on his part was both astounding and sad," Blumenthal said. "It was astounding, because he knew very well it was a payment I had earned and I had waived. I felt sad, because I felt his action showed a type of character trait that struck me, to put it mildly, as not overly attractive. Fortunately, the amount wasn't big enough to be of great importance, other than as a moral issue."

Further, according to information the author received, and Mr. Agee—inadvertently, it would seem—confirmed, Agee told John Fontaine of the law firm of Hughes Hubbard, and Peter Peterson of Lehman Brothers & Reed, that they could not have both Bendix and Burroughs as clients. When the author asked Mr. Agee why he cared who the clients of Hughes Hubbard and Lehman were, he replied briefly, "There were conflicts."

Mr. Fontaine is the son of former Bendix chairman Jack Fontaine, the man who hired and promoted Blumenthal. Hughes Hubbard declined to accept any further Burroughs business—and has since lost the Bendix account; Allied Corporation, Bendix's new owner, uses a different firm. Pete Peterson of Lehman is said to have told Mr. Agee that Bendix did not have the power to select Lehman Brothers' customers. (Neither Fontaine nor Peterson would respond to the author's request to discuss these matters.) On January 23, 1982, the New York *Times* carried a brief item reporting that Bill Agee said that Bendix had called off merger talks with Burroughs. A Burroughs spokesman, Jon Lowell, says that came as a surprise to Burroughs, because no such talks were ever held.

As the Agee-Blumenthal relationship worsened, the Agee-Cunningham relationship grew. Shortly after arriving at Bendix, Ms. Cunningham commenced having an after-work drink with the chairman in his office. They began to arrive and leave work together, and to eat meals together, frequently at the T.G.I. Friday's restaurant near Bendix headquarters. After several months of this visible closeness, when Ms. Cunningham asked for something in the name of the chairman it was no longer clear whether it was the chairman or his executive assistant talking.

According to numerous accounts, when Mr. Agee was away Ms. Cunningham flaunted her closeness to the chairman:

In the fall of 1979, a former co-worker says, she told him that Bill Agee had returned early from an Idaho vacation to take her to a rock concert.

She seems to have made a point of telling people that she and Agee took two-bedroom suites in hotels when they traveled together on company business. One co-worker, calling at the room number Ms. Cunningham had left, found it was Mr. Agee's room.

At a meeting at Mr. Agee's house in July of 1980, he being elsewhere, she displayed detailed knowledge of where the telephone in his bedroom was. As in all other such cases, the author heard this account from two people in separate interviews. Before this meeting, according to the same two people, she invited two out-of-town men who were to be at that meeting to stay in her apartment. At the time the Republican convention was in Detroit and there were no hotel rooms available for miles. Asked where she would go, according to these sources, she replied, "I'll stay with a friend."

Mr. Agee and Ms. Cunningham contend that their behavior was perfectly normal for a chairman and his executive assistant, who routinely is obliged to be with him on numerous occasions. They have also in effect suggested that both their marriages were breaking up by the time Ms. Cunningham came to work at Bendix in June of 1979. There is no evidence other than their word to support this, and Mr. Agee offered none.

Ms. Cunningham told Parade magazine in April 1982 that she "has been separated from her first husband since 1979," and told Gail Sheehy that "by January [of 1980], Mary had to face the reality that her marriage was finished." But in November 1979 she and Bo Gray, holding hands, appeared on a Detroit television station's show on commuter marriages and talked about how much in love they were. Ms. Cunningham spoke of going back to New York on weekends to see Bo. A former Bendix colleague recalls that Ms. Cunningham called Mr. Gray for advice, and a former neighbor in the Michigan apartment complex where Ms. Cunningham lived says he recalls seeing numerous pictures of Mr. Gray in the apartment. Mr. Agee told the author that Ms. Cunningham had had an on-again, off-again separation from Bo Gray for most of their marriage, including virtually all the time she was at Bendix.

Of his own marriage, Mr. Agee said, "It was not a sudden divorce . . . there is an inference that Mary was the cause of my divorce. That is absolutely not true. She wasn't at all. There were separations before that a lot of people didn't know about.

It was not a happy relationship, as far as I was concerned, for an extended time." In her articles, Gail Sheehy wrote that Bill and Diane Agee had discussed parting at an Aspen Institute session thirteen years before their divorce took place. Diane Agee, described by friends as a shy, withdrawn woman, declined to be interviewed, but Jacqueline Agee, Bill Agee's younger sister, said the Agee clan gathered in Idaho for Christmas in 1979 and that Bill and Diane had never seemed more in love. Ms. Agee and Caroline Agee Hjort, Mr. Agee's older sister, say Diane Agee has told them that she and Bill never had the discussion described in the Sheehy article. One of Diane Agee's oldest friends, who asked not to be named, said Diane has told her that as well.

Whether Bill Agee and Mary Cunningham were intimate while she was employed at Bendix is their own very private, personal business. The *only* reason it is an issue is that they have made it one. Mary Cunningham, intentionally or not, gave various people at Bendix the idea that she was indeed intimate with Bill Agee—and then inquired of some of these same people who was starting the rumors about herself and Bill. In August of 1980, before Mary Cunningham became a public issue, some Bendix board members had grown uneasy about the so-called Cunningham-Agee relationship and asked Agee about it. He told the directors that he had no romatic involvement with Mary Cunningham, that their relationship was strictly business. He apparently did not tell the directors that he was divorced and had moved into an apartment across the hall from Mary Cunningham's.

Mr. Agee and Ms. Cunningham deny there was anything romantic between them while she was at Bendix. During her tenure, however, the two were seen holding hands at the 1980 U.S. Open tennis tournament and the 1980 Republican presidential nominating convention.

The convention, which was held in Detroit, is an event in which Ms. Cunningham's actions appear to have adversely effected Mr. Agee's chances of getting a political appointment in the Reagan administration. Their behavior at the convention may have been influenced by the fact that at the time, Bill Agee was to all intents and purposes divorced, though few knew it.

According to public records, Diane Agee filed for a divorce in Idaho City, Idaho, on or before August 14. The divorce, which was uncontested, was granted on August 18. To qualify as an Idaho resident and obtain such a divorce, Diane Agee had to have lived in the state for at least six weeks prior to August 14—covering the time in July when the Republican convention was held. The Agee divorce is on file in Idaho City, the seat of Boise County. Idaho divorce lawyers say divorces are sometimes filed there to keep them out of the press. Boise County, population approximately 2,900, is off the beaten track of newspaper reporters.

It seems Mr. Agee had long desired a political appointment to high office, and in 1980 was in an excellent position to get one. The convention, being in Detroit, gave him an opportunity to host parties and dinners, and to provide manpower to help run the convention. As luck would have it, he was friendly with Jude Wanniski, a Morristown, New Jersey, writer and economist who was the foremost publicist of "supply-side" economics. Mr. Wanniski was a consultant to Bendix. As Ronald Reagan became ever more the likely Republican candidate, Mr. Wanniski became increasingly influential and promoted his friend and client Bill Agee, who had been farsighted enough to become chairman of a businessman's committee supporting the Reagan candidacy. In early 1980 Wanniski wrote an article for National Review, the prominent conservative publication, in which he suggested that Bill Agee should be director of the Office of Management and Budget.

Added on to the fortuitous Detroit and Jude Wanniski circumstances, Bendix had a Washington lobbyist, Nancy Reynolds, with close ties to Ronald and Nancy Reagan as well as to Bill Agee.

Mrs. Reynolds, an Idaho native and ten years older than Mr. Agee, had been his babysitter on occasion. Their families shared investments. She had been working for Bendix ever since 1977 when Bill Agee hired her away from the Boise Cascade Corporation, where she had been working for Agee's old rival, John Fery.

Nancy Reynolds went way back with the Reagans too. A mark of the esteem in which the president holds her can be seen in the handwritten note he sent Fortune magazine in 1981 when the magazine asked him for a comment as part of a profile story it was writing about Mrs. Reynolds. The note, written while Reagan was recovering from John Hinckley's attempt on his life, read: "Nancy Reynolds continues to be a much-beloved friend of Nancy and myself. She had always been willing to help in any way that is suitable for her in her present position. She has a sound PR judgment and can raise the morale of all around her just by saying hello."

But Mary Cunningham, it seems, had on occasion embarrassed Mrs. Reynolds, who told numerous people that she disliked Ms. Cunningham. Even though both Mrs. Reynolds and Ms. Cunningham were Bendix vice-presidents, Ms. Cunningham outranked Mrs. Reynolds because the Washington lobbying office reported to the vice-president of corporate and public relations. Mrs. Reynolds, who declined to be interviewed by the author, told people that Mary Cunningham obliged her to introduce the younger woman as her boss. Ms. Cunningham referred to Mrs. Reynolds, twenty-three years her senior, as "that older woman." If Agee had aspirations for political appointment from President Reagan, it would seem that in this instance Mary Cunningham did not help. (Mrs. Reynolds, now a lobbyist with her own firm, is still close to the Reagans.)

Nonetheless, Mrs. Reynolds was helpful at the convention. Introducing herself as Bendix's vice-president for corporate relations, Mary Cunningham, arm-in-arm with Mr. Agee, took him to meetings and parties that Mrs. Reynolds had arranged. Using her personal ties, Mrs. Reynolds arranged for Senator

Paul Laxalt, the Republican senator from Nevada who is one of Mr. Reagan's staunchest allies, to stay at the Agee home. Mrs. Reynolds arranged for Ronald Reagan to rehearse his acceptance speech at Mr. Agee's home, but when Mr. Reagan, the Republican nominee, delivered the speech, Mrs. Reynolds was unable to attend, Bendix insiders say. She was at a hotel, on Mary Cunningham's orders, attending to details of a party scheduled for later that evening.

Ms. Cunningham told people at Bendix she was promoting Bill Agee for the vice-presidency of the United States because it was obvious that Ronald Reagan needed a young, attractive, progressive businessman as his running mate. "Nancy Reynolds told us all about it, and laughed," one high Bendix official says.

Part of the Agee campaign was a party he gave at his home one night for Jack Kemp, the Buffalo, New York congressman who was the vice-presidential hopeful of the "supply-siders." Jerry Flint, Washington bureau chief of Forbes magazine, attended and remembers being struck by how attractive Mary Cunningham was. "I wanted to ask her for a date," Mr. Flint says, "but I saw her and Agee together and I figured she was private property." Thomas Pownall of Martin Marietta, a good friend of Jack Kemp, was introduced to Mr. Agee and Ms. Cunningham at the party by Jude Wanniski, the supply-side publicist.

The Agee-Cunningham public displays of affection apparently did not win Mr. Agee points with powerful Republicans, and given the way Mrs. Reynolds felt she was treated by Mary Cunningham, it is unlikely that she put in a good word for Bill Agee.

After the convention ended, Mr. Agee, with no political appointments on the horizon, returned to running Bendix.

Chapter **6** —.

The Queen Of Bendix (II)
THE FALL OF MARY CUNNINGHAM

Three months after the 1980 Republican convention, Mary Cunningham, Bendix Corporation's vice-president for corporate and public relations, was herself forced out of the company by publicity because she did not understand how the news media work.

The events that led to the coverage that ousted her began with an exceptionally favorable story about her. Another irony is that it was not, as commonly assumed, a disenchanted chauvinist Bendix male who leaked information to the papers; it was a Bendix middle manager named Elizabeth Howe, the previous executive assistant to William Agee, who felt that Ms. Cunningham's actions were bad for the company and bad for women in business.

The last straw, so to speak, Mrs. Howe told the author, was the laudatory story the Detroit *Free Press* printed about Mary Cunningham in August of 1980. It was one thing dealing with Ms. Cunningham inside Bendix, Mrs. Howe said, but she did not want the newspaper to continue to be misled, or misinformed.

The press's tale of Mary Cunningham began late in August of 1980, when the *Free Press*'s business news department found itself scrambling for a personality profile for the "Sunday Ticker," a regular weekly feature. Someone remembered that Bendix had appointed a twenty-seven-year-old vice-president in June. A summer intern, Susan Tompor, was dispatched to see her. Mary Cunningham talked for several hours. Among the matters discussed were the Warner & Swasey acquisition, in which Mr. Cunningham said she was "heavily involved"; her first meeting with Bill Agee ("It was like a meeting of kindred spirits, a meeting of the minds"); and Ms. Cunningham's job, which she described as liaison chief between Bill Agee and the Bendix Corporation, and between the Bendix Corporation and the rest of the world.

Susan Tompor returned with a glowing story. Indeed the resulting article, which ran in the August 24 *Free Press*, was on the order of panegyric. It read in part: "If Bendix chairman William Agee is the boy wonder, a phrase often used to describe the youthful, high-energy executive, then Mary Cunningham, Bendix's new vice-president for corporate and public relations, must surely be wonder woman . . . Together, the dynamic duo fought for mergers and acquisitions, battled bad investment and flew high above a gray-skied economy to insure Bendix shareholders' return in a recession."

After reading the article, "I was torn between amusement and outrage," Mrs. Howe recalls. A veteran of rough-and-tumble Michigan Democratic politics, Mrs. Howe, now the state's commissioner of licensing and regulation, understands how newspapers work. She sent another female Bendix manager, a friend of *Free Press* business editor Louis Heldman, to have lunch with Heldman and to tell him that the *Free Press* had, so to speak, been had by Mary Cunningham. (Mrs. Howe's emissary has asked the author not to reveal her name. She said she is afraid that she and members of her family may be vulnerable to retaliation by Bill Agee and Mary Cunningham.) Heldman may be a male chauvinist, but if so he has hidden it well. During his two years as *Free Press* business editor he hired three women for what had been an all-male reporting staff and hired a fourth woman as his assistant and eventual successor. Currently managing editor of the Fort Wayne (Indiana) *Sentinel,* Heldman is married to a woman who kept her maiden name and lives in a different city ninety miles away, where she attends law school.

Like other Detroit newspaper writers, Louis Heldman had always been impressed with Bill Agee, whom he found charming, disarming and smart. "You could talk to Agee as long as you wanted," Heldman said. "He acted like he had all the time in the world, and you [rather than he] would be the one to end the conversation. But when you looked at your notes you found there was hardly anything there." A year after he had written the story that led to the media coverage that led to Ms. Cunningham's departure, Heldman said, he was invited with other news people to an off-the-record supper with Bill Agee. At the supper, Heldman recalled, Agee poured a superb wine, sat with no aides around him and joked about the expensive Louise Nevelson sculpture that had just arrived at Bendix headquarters. The statue, ordered during Bendix's flush years, made its appearance during a lean year. "He said, 'They're calling it Agee's Last Erection,'" Heldman recalls. He also recalls Agee asking what the reaction would be if he got married.

Mr. Heldman was learning more about Ms. Cunningham's influence on Bendix, but he could not figure out what to do with the information. Newspaper stories traditionally rely on a "news peg," an event that provides a rationale for printing information that the reporters and editors know. Heldman had no peg. "I said, 'This is fascinating, but I don't see how you get it in the newspaper.'"

While Heldman pondered, matters at Bendix were coming to a head. On September 12, Agee announced a corporate reorganization, and the new stress on high technology. On the second page of the news release, Agee also announced the "resignation" of Bendix president William Panny.

Agee says he told Panny in early 1980 that he would have

to leave Bendix, and that after that, Panny became a "disruptive influence" and was one of the primary reasons for problems at Bendix. Mr. Panny indignantly denied that Mr. Agee had given him warnings in early 1980. "When he hired me (in 1977) his ambition was to get a little bit of money and go off into politics," Mr. Panny said. He said Agee fired him "because we had arguments over the girl. I told him she was a disruptive influence, and I talked to some of the directors about it." He said Agee put out the press release announcing his "resignation" before he resigned. (Harry Cunningham's letter, discussed in the previous chapter, referred to the "disgraceful firing of Bill Panny." Cunningham was chairman of the compensation committee of the board, which had the power to fire executives. He would presumably have been told of, and agreed to, the Panny firing had it been decided months before, as Agee said.)

At an employee meeting twelve days after Panny's departure was announced, Mr. Agee said, "Bill Panny was not fired." Asked by the author why he had made that statement, Mr. Agee seemed taken aback. His answer: "Had he mentally quit? Sure, or he wouldn't have been behaving" the way he was. Mr. Agee contends that South Bend radio stations carried items about Mr. Panny having gotten another job while he was still at Bendix. Agee said he would produce the stories. The Bendix public relations department informed the author that no such stories could be found.

The Agee-Panny relationship had always seemed strange. Mr. Panny, who had an intimate knowledge of plant operations, is burly, up-from-the-streets-of-Brooklyn and scatological. He spent his formative years at Rockwell International, a macho place in which battles are waged with bloody axes, as opposed to the stilettos used at Bendix. At Rockwell, according to one middle manager who had worked at both Rockwell and Bendix, "We had to teach some of the new hires how to curse. At Rockwell, people would say things like, 'We want this plant in balls-out production,' and 'Tell her to go suck on a tail-

pipe.' " Mr. Agee, of course, could not have been more different: slim, soft-spoken, urbane, he concentrates on finances
rather than operations.

It is well known that Mr. Panny had little use for Ms. Cunningham; his most polite characterization of her in private was
"the girl." When Mary Cunningham was in charge of the 1980
study of Bendix's brake operations, Panny considered her behavior at the Bendix South Bend plant to be disruptive, and so
told her and Agee, according to numerous accounts.

Another senior executive, strategic planner Jerome Jacobson, had quietly departed in August to join his old friend, W.
Michael Blumenthal, at Burroughs. The September 12 news
release announced his resignation as well.

To be sure, some of Bendix's operating people did not like
the way Panny conducted business. He ran operations with a
far heavier hand than the operating people were accustomed
to and insisted on detailed reports. He tended to browbeat
those who did not submit the requested forms. He did not fit
into the Bendix corporate culture. In any case, it seems likely
to the author that the September 12 reorganization—which
substituted a ten-person "chairman's council" for much of the
work Panny had been responsible for—was a smokescreen for
the firing of Panny.

Shortly after Mr. Panny's departure, according to an account
printed in Fortune magazine, Fortune called Bendix and
asked to be allowed the run of the premises for a story about
the company's "new strategy." Members of the Bendix public
relations staff say they warned Mr. Agee and Ms. Cunningham
not to allow Fortune in during such a delicate time for the
company . . . there was growing turmoil at headquarters; the
board of directors had begun trying to find out what was going
on; Bill Panny, Jerome Jacobson and Mike Blumenthal were all
estranged from Bill Agee. Any reasonably competent reporter
would call them for information in the course of researching
a Bendix company story. Nonetheless, Mr. Agee and Ms. Cunningham decided to let Fortune in.

Bill Agee then called a special meeting with Bendix head-quarters employees for September 24 to explain the new high-technology strategy and to discuss other matters, among them the departure of Messrs. Panny and Jacobson. Mr. Agee planned to announce Ms. Cunningham's promotion to vice-president of strategic planning. The PR staff warned against his mentioning his relationship with Mary Cunningham. The only way to deal with the Cunningham question, the PR people said, was to prepare an answer to a possible question on the matter, but not to highlight it by mentioning it in his opening remarks.

Louis Heldman, who was informed of the meeting by his growing source-network within Bendix, thought he finally might have a way to get the Mary Cunningham matter into the paper. If Bill Agee mentioned her, Heldman decided, he would have a news peg. When Heldman asked Bill Agee for permission to attend the meeting, he also said that if he were excluded, he would get the information secondhand and write the story on that basis. Because Fortune was going to be present, Mr. Agee allowed Louis Heldman in. Because Heldman was being allowed in, Bendix also invited his counterpart, Ken Ross, business editor of the Detroit *News,* though no one briefed Ross on the meeting.

Knowing that reporters from Fortune, the *Free Press* and the *News* were in the room, Mr. Agee made his now-famous comment: "It is true that we are very, very close friends, and she's a very close friend of my family." Louis Heldman at last had a peg for the story he had worked on for a month. "Someone told me later," he said, "that I looked so excited that he thought I was about to swallow my tie." Heldman wrote his story, "Bendix Boss Slaps Down Office Gossip, Denies Romantic Link," which was page one in the September 25 *Free Press.* Aware that he was dealing with sensitive material, and concerned about being viewed as a sexist, Heldman's second paragraph read: "It was an unusual moment in corporate America —a chief executive giving rumors the status of company con-

cerns that needed to be discussed openly with subordinates."
Much of the story dealt with Agee's comments about Bendix
business and his promise not to accept a job in Ronald Reagan's
administration if Governor Reagan defeated Jimmy Carter in
November.

(Because Ken Ross of the Detroit *News* did not fully understand the significance of Mr. Agee's references to Ms. Cunningham, he was "skunked" on the story. He told the author that
when he reported for work on September 25 he was chewed
out at length by his superiors for having missed a story of
national significance. To recoup, the *News,* engaged in a circu-
lation war with the *Free Press,* dug into the personal aspects
of the Cunningham-Agee relationship, unearthing that Bill
Agee had been divorced in August of 1980 and that he and
Mary Cunningham were living across the hall from each other
in the same apartment complex.)

At least twice, in 1982 speeches to the Women's Economic
Club of Detroit and the American Newspaper Publishers Association, Mary Cunningham has given her view of what happened. To quote from her Women's Economic Club speech,
given May 26, 1982:

"The plot thickens as only one day after the announced
strategy [on September 12], anonymous letters with the same
postmark start to arrive on [Bendix] directors' and [Detroit]
local editors' desks suggesting that the relationship between
the chairman and the vice-president be investigated. And a
few days later, the chief executive holds a routine employee
meeting to share the elements and implications of the new
strategy . . . Amidst the complimentary statements was included the sentence, 'It is true that we are very close friends
and she is a close friend of my family, but that has nothing to
do with the way I and others in this company . . . evaluate her
performance . . . ' " (Her quotation of Agee is different from
the author's. The author took his version from Bendix's official
meeting transcript, which says "very, very close friends" and
"a very close friend of my family," and shows the portion

beginning with "but" as a separate sentence.)

It is here that the sadness of this tale begins to unfold. Two rival papers in a community. Both had asked to be present at the meeting. One, the *News,* reported a major business story detailing the new corporate strategy, the layoffs and the promotions. The other, the *Free Press,* ran with a now famous headline: Boss Slaps Down Office Gossip, Denies Romantic Link.

Mary Cunningham's version seems in error in several respects. Louis Heldman was working on the story in late August, two weeks before the alleged September 13 arrival of anonymous letters. The September 24 Bendix employees meeting was not a routine meeting; it was a special one. The Detroit *News,* as Ken Ross said, missed the story. Later the *News* published information far more critical than anything Louis Heldman printed.

The original, balanced *Free Press* story was picked up and sensationalized by other news media. Remarkably, Mary Cunningham and Bill Agee on September 25 called from California, where they were visiting the Bendix forest products division, to ask if there had been any coverage. "You'll be a national story by noon," a former Bendix PR man recalls saying. He was right, and the massive coverage that followed helped convince the board of directors to ease Ms. Cunningham out. (Before resigning under pressure, she made and withdrew several resignations, according to unchallenged accounts published in, among others, the New York *Times* and Fortune magazine.)

In a brilliant tactical move Ms. Cunningham recouped her own position—if perhaps weakening Bendix's—by talking to Gail Sheehy, despite the no-comment rule the company had decided was the only way to limit the damage. If, however, she and Agee had not talked to Gail Sheehy and had refused all comment, the story would very likely have died well before the August, 1982 move on Marietta. Without fresh quotes and information from the principals, there was no way the news media could have kept the story alive over a period of two years.

At the time her articles were printed, Mrs. Sheehy was living with Clay Felker, editor of the New York *Daily News'* afternoon paper. That paper, which was to be closed down in 1981, was struggling, and Mr. Felker, seeing news accounts of Ms. Cunningham's travails, recalled that Mrs. Sheehy had formerly interviewed her for possible inclusion in a book entitled *Pathfinders.* Felker asked Gail Sheehy to do a quick series on Ms. Cunningham for his paper. Mrs. Sheehy called Ms. Cunningham and Mr. Agee. They agreed to see her. Writing against a tight deadline and predisposed to her hypothesis that the Mary Cunningham matter was a case of a bright, new-era woman being shot down by old-time, sexist male pigs, Gail Sheehy presented Mary Cunningham as a kind of martyr.

Mrs. Sheehy later said: "I had never had anybody, in the course of interviewing I don't know how many thousands of people over twenty years, look at me with her baby blue eyes and lie so boldly about Agee," in the February, 1983 issue of Interview magazine. "I think that she's been a disaster for well-intentioned, bright, honest, hard-working women in management. She's not, you know, their Joan of Arc or their standard-bearer. She is a betrayer of the cause. Mainly, I think, because she is what most women fear being thought of as."

In an interview with the author, Mrs. Sheehy, who said that she had been threatened by the Agees' lawyer, declined to elaborate on her Interview remarks, but she talked about how she came to write things she now regrets:

"I wasn't comfortable," she recalled. "There was something enamel about her face. Here was someone who had a hysterical obsession with success that could allow the mind to repress anything that might get in the way." Mrs. Sheehy went on to say she grew increasingly concerned when she called Mike Blumenthal at Bendix and he told her to check the Mary Cunningham story very carefully. She called some of the people Ms. Cunningham had presented in a bad light, and duly noted their comments. But the thrust of the stories she reported showed that she was convinced that Mary Cunningham was giving an accurate account. (One person Gail Sheehy did not call was Louis Heldman, although she attributed direct quotes to him: " 'Do you have a love affair going with Bill Agee?' Louis Heldman asked. Stunned, Mary replied, 'I will not dignify that with an answer.' " Heldman says Cunningham made that dialogue up, and his September 25 story would seem to support him in this. It contained quotes from Mr. Agee and Ms. Cunningham, including her quote—"Unfortunately, we're culturally bound by norms that preclude in many minds the existence of someone like myself"—cited at the start of the previous chapter. Louis Heldman says he now knows why people don't always believe what they read in newspapers.)

Asked why she ran the series if she had doubts, Mrs. Sheehy answered, "I must have just sat on my instincts instead of listening to them. I almost never do [write] anything really fast. I don't feel comfortable that I know what the story is."

But Gail Sheehy, faced with a tight deadline, wrote what she had. When the series started running, she says, she got lengthy calls from Mary Cunningham, who was in the LaCosta resort at the time. (Bendix telephone bills the author has obtained confirm that.) One problem, Mrs. Sheehy said, was that Mary Cunningham told her that her father had killed her brother in a car accident, but the brother had really died of disease. "One day, she'd be on the phone saying, 'How can you make up all this stuff?' " Mrs. Sheehy said. "The next day, she said she thought it was wonderful." Finally, Mrs. Sheehy said, she told Ms. Cunningham to let their lawyers argue; she heard nothing further from Ms. Cunningham. (Mr. Agee contended to the author that Gail Sheehy made up much of what she wrote in the five-part series. He said that Sheehy had taken information from an interview Ms. Cunningham had granted eighteen months earlier, on a no-name basis, and attributed it to her. He and Ms. Cunningham spent very little time with Sheehy, Mr. Agee said. Sheehy said she told Ms. Cunningham that information from the earlier interviews would be attributed to her, and that Ms. Cunningham assented to that. Sheehy says she quoted Agee and Cunningham accurately, and has tape recordings of their interviews to prove it.)

Though Gail Sheehy has changed her mind, the version of Mary Cunningham as a brilliant martyr, widely disseminated in her series, apparently lingers. Ms. Cunningham is in demand as a speaker; she has written guest columns in Newsweek and U.S. News & World Report concerning the burden of fame. She appears on television talk shows. She is also reportedly writing a book.

Mary Cunningham resigned from Bendix on October 8, 1980. She and Mr. Agee say there was no romantic relationship between them while she was at Bendix, and that their romance, which culminated in marriage on June 5, 1982, developed after she left the company.

After resignation from Bendix, "I wasn't sure I wanted to see Bill Agee again," she told Parade magazine. "I wasn't sure, if I did see him, whether I even wanted to be friends, let alone develop it beyond where we were," she told Savvy magazine. She apparently made up her mind rather quickly. Telephone bills obtained by the author indicate that she made two telephone calls to Bill Agee's McCall, Idaho home on October 9, made a fifty-minute call and a twelve-minute call on October 10 and on subsequent days made lengthy calls to Mr. Agee's office in Southfield, as well as to the Waldorf Towers hotel in New York, where he frequently stayed. Most of these calls were placed from the LaCosta resort, near San Diego, where Ms. Cunningham has said that she stayed. All the calls were charged to Bendix.

Not long after leaving Bendix, Ms. Cunningham was in Idaho commencing the process of obtaining an Idaho divorce from Bo Gray. The divorce was granted on January 6, 1981, according to records on file in Idaho City. To meet the six-week residence requirement Ms. Cunningham would have had to be in Idaho for at least the latter part of November and all of December 1980, a period when Mr. Agee, said by associates to have looked poorly, went to McCall to recuperate from what Bendix spokesmen have described as mononucleosis. Associates recall that the Bendix corporate jet, carrying Mr. Agee's mail, made frequent trips from Southfield to Idaho. Executives at the time recall him conducting business from McCall by holding Speakerphone discussions with executives in Southfield.

"She was in Idaho for that period of time," Mr. Agee said, "but she wasn't with me. I saw her during this period of time . . .She stayed with some friends of ours and hers." He declined to identify them.

Ms. Cunningham, whose divorce was filed in the same obscure Idaho county in which Mr. Agee's divorce was filed, was represented by Winston H. Churchill, a prominent Boise divorce attorney. Mr. Churchill has said that he is an old acquaintance of Bill Agee's but that Mary Cunningham contacted him herself about getting a divorce. Bo Gray's lawyer, Howard Manweiler of Boise, said that he was brought into the case by Mr. Churchill, and that Mr. Gray did not contest the divorce. According to the decree, Mr. Gray was awarded the couple's co-op apartment in New York City, and Ms. Cunningham forgave a loan that she had made to him while she was in Harvard Business School.

While Mr. Agee was recuperating in Idaho, some Bendix directors began to wonder what was happening in the company. With Bill Panny gone and Bill Agee out ill, it began to seem to some directors as though the management ranks at Bendix were a bit thin. In a secret struggle, first detailed in Fortune magazine ("The Boardroom Battle at Bendix," by Hugh D. Menzies, January 11, 1982), at least four directors decided to move against Bill Agee—but he forced three of them out first.

In an interview with the author, Mr. Agee said: "A large part of the Fortune magazine article is absolutely wrong and untrue." He declined to point to specific errors. Mr. Agee told the author that, "If you treat those [things] in the way they [Fortune] did, you've got very serious problems."

The author interviewed several people who say they were Mr. Menzies' sources. The author has also interviewed the four dissident directors: Harry Cunningham, Alan Schwartz, Paul Mirabito and Robert Purcell. They confirmed the Fortune story, with one minor exception that will be noted. Some of the following details are taken from the Fortune account, but most of them derive from the author's own research.

In late 1980 some directors were growing uneasy at what they considered Bill Agee's increasingly questionable actions. They had been surprised when Bill Panny had been severed and less than pleased when Mr. Agee had announced the board's "unanimous" support of Ms. Cunningham when two of the directors—Alan Schwartz and Jewell Lafontant, had been unreachable and had not been asked. A third director, Bob Purcell, said he had never been asked. When Bill Agee told the board there was no romantic involvement between himself and Mary Cunningham, the board supported him. At this point Mr. Agee had been divorced and rented the apartment across the hall from Ms. Cunningham's; he apparently did not tell this to the board.

Messrs. Cunningham, Mirabito and Schwartz, all respected members of Detroit's close-knit business community, were embarrassed when the so-called Mary Cunningham story became nationally prominent. Purcell says he began to wonder whether Agee had been telling the board the truth about his relationship with Mary Cunningham. Purcell further says that his concern was not with the relationship, if any, but with whether Agee had told the board less than the truth about it.

Harry Cunningham, considered one of the grand old men of Detroit business, had been on the Bendix board since 1965, longer than any other director. He had close relationships with many of Bendix's officers, who confided in him. Retired, he had the time to spend interviewing Bendix executives to find out what impact Mary Cunningham might be having on Bill

Agee's performance. In the summer of 1980 Mr. Cunningham had begun to hear reports that Mr. Agee was unduly favoring Ms. Cunningham.

When the Mary Cunningham matter blew up in September of 1980, the board forced Ms. Cunningham out. It also paid her a generous severance—Harry Cunningham says it was $150,000—and took no action against Mr. Agee, assuming the Agee-Mary Cunningham matter was resolved. But in late 1980 Harry Cunningham began to hear that the problem was not resolved—that Bill Agee was not in Southfield as often as he used to be and that executive morale was suffering.

As mentioned, Mr. Cunningham was chairman of the board's organization, compensation and nominating committee, which had the power to fire Bendix officers, including Mr. Agee. "Three directors—not including Mirabito and Schwartz —suggested we ought to have a meeting," Mr. Cunningham told the author. He scheduled a March 6, 1981, committee meeting to deal with the question of Bill Agee's performance as chief executive. The committee meeting was scheduled to precede the full board meeting set for March 6, and was to be in executive session—i.e., without William Agee present.

Harry Cunningham said that when he told Mr. Agee of the meeting, "he said, 'Oh my God, here we go again.'" Later, Cunningham said, Agee called him back and said, "Let's not wait, let's have a special meeting." That meeting was scheduled for New York City on February 25.

Before the question of Bill Agee's performance could be raised at that meeting, Mr. Agee announced that Bendix was in serious negotiations to acquire a high technology company, and therefore Alan Schwartz and Paul Mirabito, who were also directors of Burroughs Corporation, had a conflict of interest and should be asked to leave the board. Bob Purcell asked Mr. Agee to name the proposed acquisition; he refused. After the committee gave Mr. Agee the authority to request that Mirabito and Schwartz resign, Mr. Agee turned on Harry Cunningham, a former Burroughs director. It was true that Cunningham had left the Burroughs board eleven months earlier (not eighteen months, as Fortune reported), Mr. Agee said, but Cunningham had a conflict because he lived across the street from Paul Mirabito and was friendly with Mike Blumenthal, the Burroughs chairman. Agee suggested that Harry Cunningham also resign.

"That's where I made my mistake," Harry Cunningham told the author. "I said, 'Brother, you can have my damn resignation.'" After the meeting, when he had calmed down, other directors told Mr. Cunningham that he had been foolish to resign. When he returned to his hotel room, he says, he found a message to call a "very high" Bendix executive, whom he has declined to identify but who he said was still working for Bendix at the time of this writing. The executive, according to Mr. Cunningham, told him that Mr. Agee had rented a large amount of office space in New York City's General Motors Building, presumably to be near Mary Cunningham.

Cunningham now decided to withdraw his resignation, and to alert Mirabito and Schwartz. He called them on February 26, the day after the committee meeting, but was too late; both men had already submitted their resignations to Agee by telephone.

Mr. Mirabito told the author that Bill Agee had called him at his Florida home at 7:30 in the morning, waking him up, and gotten his resignation: "He said, 'Harry Cunningham has resigned because of a conflict.' I said if Harry thought there was a conflict, then I would resign too." Schwartz told the author that Agee had called him after talking to Mirabito, and that he had resigned because Agee told him that Cunningham and Mirabito had resigned for conflict-of-interest reasons. Apparently Mirabito and Schwartz took Agee at his word, assuming that no gentleman would try to rush them off the board.

All three men decided to withdraw their resignations, and Harry Cunningham called Bill Agee to tell him of their decision. Mr. Cunningham said Mr. Agee called back from a company plane "somewhere over the Rockies," and had the plane turn around and go back to Michigan after Cunningham told him that the three wanted to unresign. Later Agee told Cunningham that oral resignations were binding and could not be withdrawn. Cunningham said that Schwartz, a respected corporate lawyer, agreed that was true.

Bob Purcell remained on the Bendix board through August of 1981, waiting for the company to announce the high-tech acquisition that Mr. Agee had cited to obtain the resignations of Cunningham, Mirabito and Schwartz. On August 26, 1981, when no acquisition had materialized, Mr. Purcell tried to get the other "outside" directors—directors not Bendix employees —to move against Mr. Agee. When they did not do so, Purcell, who was nearing the mandatory retirement age for Bendix directors of seventy, resigned himself. Unlike the other three directors, who until now had not publicly explained how they came to resign, Purcell felt that he had an obligation to bring public pressure to bear on the Bendix board to discipline William Agee. Purcell has spoken to journalists, including the author, to tell his story. "There is a question about whether a corporate director should talk about his reasons for resigning from a board," Purcell told Fortune. "The tendency is to leave and shut up. But on matters like this, I think it is appropriate for a director to speak out."

Mr. Agee has a different version of the events. He says there was, in fact, a conflict—though he will not say what it was— that made it improper for Alan Schwartz and Paul Mirabito to remain on the board. He also said that Harry Cunningham had been exempted from the mandatory retirement age of seventy under a "grandfather" provision that allowed him to stay on because the retirement age was set after Cunningham was already on the board. He said that Cunningham had told him he would resign any time Agee wished. (Cunningham confirms this.) As for not allowing Cunningham to withdraw his resignation, Agee says: "When a decision is made like that and you agree that there's a problem that could arise, grown men sit there and say, 'This is it.'"

It is still not clear what the conflict of interest was based on that Mr. Agee invoked to obtain the three resignations. Though Mr. Agee did not say this was the conflict, he did tell the author that Bendix had held serious negotiations about acquiring Burroughs in 1979 "before Mike Blumenthal left the government." Asked with whom at Burroughs the negotiations were held, Agee said "the principals," and declined to comment further.

When the author told Paul Mirabito, Burroughs' chairman in 1979, that Agee said there had been serious negotiations that year, Mirabito replied: "That is not true at all." Harry Cunningham, who is close to Mr. Mirabito and was a Burroughs director at the time, said that Bill Agee had once asked in passing what he thought of a Bendix-Burroughs combination. Cunningham said he repeated Agee's remark to Mirabito, who said he was not interested. Cunningham said he delivered Mirabito's reply to Agee, and never heard of the matter again.

If indeed there were serious Bendix-Burroughs negotiations in 1979—which has been denied by Burroughs' then-chairman —one wonders why Mr. Agee would have allowed the Cunningham-Schwartz-Mirabito conflict of interest to linger until 1981.

It seems not unreasonable to speculate that Mr. Agee's real concern was Mike Blumenthal, with whom all three of the Detroit directors were close. The departure of the Detroit directors came after Mike Blumenthal's previously mentioned success at getting the Equitable Life board to turn down $40 million of financing for the company that purchased Bendix's forest products operation. The directors' departure was also, it appears, about the time that Mr. Agee told the Hughes, Hubbard law firm and Lehman Brothers investment banking firm that they had to choose between Bill Agee and Bendix and Mike Blumenthal and Burroughs as clients.

In any event, the departure of the three Detroit directors in February of 1981 gave William Agee essentially a free hand.

Until September of 1982, much too late to influence events, Agee's board of directors granted him virtually unlimited freedom. In September of 1982, when Agee lost the Martin Marietta war and sold Bendix to Allied, four directors resigned in futile protest.

In March of 1981, about a month after securing the resignations of the three dissident Detroit directors, Mr. Agee hired a new vice-chairman for Bendix: Alonzo McDonald, Jr., former chief of staff for the Carter White House. McDonald later brought in his own cadre of loyalists, some of whom displaced veteran Bendix officers who were opposed to the drift in the company. Agee kept the chiefs of Bendix's operating divisions reporting to him but did not seem to take great interest in running the company on a day-to-day basis.

Bill Agee's authority was now almost complete. The problem directors were gone. Most Bendix executives opposed to him were either gone from the company or kept their opinions to themselves. Alonzo McDonald was in charge of the headquarters operation, which allowed Mr. Agee to spend more time outside of Southfield. He was seen with increasing frequency in public with Mary Cunningham, but there was no one at Bendix to make adverse comment.

In early 1982 Mr. Agee, now a convert to Catholicism, obtained an annulment of his 1957 Presbyterian marriage to Diane Agee from the Boise Catholic divorce tribunal. (Mary Cunningham had obtained an annulment of her marriage to Bo Gray from the Brooklyn, New York tribunal. A member of the Boise divorce tribunal said that the Agee annulment was treated like any other. The tribunal member declined to say what the grounds for the annulment were. Members of Mr. Agee's family say that Diane Agee told them that the grounds were that Bill Agee had had an unhappy childhood, married Diane to get away from home, and that the marriage had therefore never been valid. (Mr. Agee said that reason was one of the "many" grounds cited in the annulment.) Diane Agee was notified that her former husband had requested the annulment, and of the grounds for the request. She chose not to contest it.

In June of 1982, William McReynolds Agee married Mary Elizabeth Cunningham in a ceremony performed by the archbishop of San Francisco. It was later that month that Bill Agee introduced Mary as "the First Lady of Bendix" at a reception on the company's grounds in Southfield.

Mr. Agee now had more than $400 million surplus cash at Bendix, with $100 million more tied up in RCA stock; his control of the board and the Bendix officer corps was virtually complete; and he was married to his designated strategist.

The stage was now set for the Bendix raid on Martin Marietta.

Chapter **7**___.

Offense's Opening Gambit
BENDIX ATTACKS MARIETTA

The Bendix–Martin Marietta war began in April of 1982, during one of Bendix chairman William Agee's "shopping trips" to Wall Street. With half a billion dollars of Bendix money to spend, he was again looking for an investment banker.

The Bendix account was being moved for the second time in two years. Until 1980 it had been split between Lehman Brothers and Morgan Stanley & Company. Mike Blumenthal had hired Lehman Brothers because Lehman's George Ball had been a patron of his while he was in the government and the two men were friends. In 1980 Bill Agee had moved the entire account to Lehman Brothers, whose chairman, Peter Peterson, had actively wooed him. Peterson, a former Secretary of Commerce, involved himself with the Bendix account, Bendix insiders say. The firm made Bill Agee feel very much an important client and bombarded him with suggestions about what to buy and sell. At Morgan Stanley, it would seem, the Bendix account had been treated as nothing special.

Lehman Brothers handled most of Bendix's asset sales in 1980 and 1981, and pointed to those sales as showing the firm's expertise in "redeploying assets." Having made commissions by selling assets, Lehman no doubt was looking forward to earning further commissions by making acquisitions for Bendix. But when Bendix bought 7.5 percent of RCA Corporation, an important Lehman client, without telling Lehman about the purchases, the relationship became terminal.

Mr. Agee told the author that he was thinking of buying more RCA stock for Bendix, and he could hardly ask Lehman Brothers to analyze RCA for him. He said that in early 1982 Lehman asked what he was up to with RCA and he had not told them. "There are some things you tell your investment banker, and some things you don't," he said.

In early 1982, Mr. Agee had meetings with Salomon Chairman John Gutfreund, whom he knew. Alonzo McDonald, Jr., Bendix's president, was a friend and Harvard Business School classmate (class of 1956, Section F) of Harold Tanner, chief administrative officer of Salomon's corporate finance department. Salomon was eager for the Bendix business—in early 1982 companies with $500 million to spend were indeed few and far between.

Mr. Agee was interested in Gould Incorporated, the electronics company, but Salomon declined to become involved. Salomon had handled a sale of Gould's financial subsidiary and felt close to the company. Several Salomon executives were also personally friendly with Gould chairman William Ylvisaker, and some owned condos in a Florida real estate devlopment that Gould ran.

Salomon was perhaps not the firm for Agee and Bendix. Salomon is exceptionally powerful and rich—on an average day in 1982 the company owned about $8 *billion* of securities for its own account—but the company tends to approach mergers and acquisitions as a benign part of business rather than an exercise in combat. The Salomon mergers and acquisitions department, run by Jay Higgins, thirty-eight, specializes in friendly, negotiated deals. The transactions of which Salomon is proudest tend to be such as BankAmerica Corporation's acquisition of Charles Schwab, the discount brokerage house, or the Xerox acquisition of Crum & Forster insurance company.

Bill Agee and Bendix would almost surely have to make an unfriendly deal; Salomon does not handle those especially well. A more aggressive firm with a taste for battle, such as, say, First Boston Corporation, would perhaps have been more promising.

Nonetheless, when Bendix came calling, Salomon trotted out its stars, including the Chicago office's Ira Harris, Salomon's best-known mergers man. Although Salomon said that Jay Higgins, rather than Ira Harris, would handle actual merger work, this does not appear to have been clearly stated to McDonald and Agee. "We might have been derelict in choosing them," McDonald said. "If Jay had been the only one attending the meetings and Gutfreund had not taken an interest in it and if Ira had not been there in terms of planning the tactics, we would probably have gone with another firm."

In April of 1982, during one of his several calls on Salomon, Mr. Agee ordered the firm, which specializes in buying and selling large blocs of stocks and bonds for its own account, to begin purchasing Marietta shares for Bendix. From April 1982 through the end of July, according to public records, Salomon bought 1,632,500 Marietta shares, about 4.5 percent of the company, without significantly running up the price. Bendix's average cost for the stock, including the commissions it paid Salomon, was $27.05 a share. At that price Bendix could hardly lose, thanks to Marietta's relatively generous dividend and the laws governing corporate income taxes. Unless Marietta reduced its dividend or its share price declined sharply, Bendix stood to make a handsome return: 85 percent of the dividends a corporation receives from another corporation are excluded from federal income tax; for a company such as Bendix, which pays a 46 percent federal income tax, the effective tax rate on dividends received is just 6.9 percent—the 46 percent tax rate times the 15 percent of the dividend that is taxable. An individual taxpayer, by contrast, has no such tax advantage from dividends. Individuals pay the full tax rate on dividend income above $100, or above $200 for a couple filing a joint return.

The Marietta dividend was $1.92 a year. That gave Bendix a 7.1 percent return, based on its average cost of $27.05 per Marietta share. After federal taxes Bendix's return from Marietta's dividends was 6.6 percent. To earn that same return from a fully taxable investment such as bank certificates of deposit required a 12.2 percent rate—and in April of 1982 interest rates were beginning to fall sharply. Buying the Marietta stock committed Bendix to nothing, and the dividend income would be no worse than what Bendix would have earned by putting the money into short-term investments.

There are several ways to begin a corporate takeover, and a secret acquisition of just under five percent of the target company's stock is a rather classic opening gambit. Five percent is a magic number because a company buying that proportion of a second company is obliged to declare itself by publicly disclosing the purchase within ten days by filing a 13(d) form with the target company and the U.S. Securities and Exchange Commission. At that point the buyer's interest becomes public knowledge, and arbitragers and other traders often rush in, thereby pushing up the target's price.

Buying just under five percent of an undervalued target company provides insurance, of sorts, to a would-be raider. If the raider acquires the target, having bought shares earlier at a lower price lowers the overall cost of the deal. If the target company succeeds in finding a white knight to make a friendly bid, the raider can often earn enough money by tendering his shares to cover all his expenses, and perhaps even make a profit. If no white knight appears and the acquisition bid is unsuccessful in any case, the target may agree to buy its stock back at a premium over the market price to induce the raider to go away.

But there are also risks involved. Secretly buying almost five percent of a company's stock is not always so easy. If, for example, the stock is bought too quickly the buying pressure may drive up the price and alert the target to the fact that it is being stalked. If the stock is bought too slowly the target's vulnerability may independently attract another suitor, or securities analysts may begin promoting the stock, running the price up. And there is always a risk that while the raider is amassing shares, news of the raider's interest will leak out, rumors will spread, the stock will rise and the advantage of surprise will be lost.

The investment bankers doing the buying register the shares in their own name rather than in the client's. The buyers are frequently playing cat-and-mouse with targets, some of whom have learned to monitor closely their stock transfer sheets. These sheets, available only to the company and the people it designates, show who has bought shares and who has sold them. To avoid showing a suspicious profile on the sheets, an investment banker will make purchases irregularly, staying out of the market for days at a time, and may make the transactions on several different stock exchanges. Martin Marietta shares, for example, can be bought not only on the New York Stock Exchange, but on the Pacific Stock Exchange in Los Angeles and the Midwest Stock Exchange in Chicago as well. A familiar ploy is for the investment banker to leave the stock in the exchange's central depository. In this fashion anyone watching the transfer sheets will need to acquire a second set of sheets from the depository itself to check the depository's own transactions.

Salomon purchased most of the Marietta shares on the Midwest Stock Exchange, and left the shares registered in the name of Kray & Company, the exchange's depository. (Some shares were also bought on the New York Stock Exchange.) Salomon kept the accumulation secret from other stock traders—the average cost Bendix paid was only a few dollars higher than the price had been when the buying had started in April. But according to Martin Siegel of Kidder, Peabody & Company, Salomon's purchases of Marietta shares triggered the distant early warning system that Kidder was manning.

"We knew about it in June," Mr. Siegel says.

Kidder, an old-line Wall Street investment banking firm, was watching Marietta's transfer sheets because that company was one of about one hundred that had hired Kidder to defend them, even though they had not yet come under attack. Under Mr. Siegel, Kidder had carved out a unique niche in the merger wars—tender defense. Realizing that most investment bankers concentrate on helping clients attack, Marty Siegel, the head of Kidder's mergers and acquisitions department, decided to concentrate on defense. Although Kidder had been known to help clients make hostile acquisitions, its reputation had been made by the successful defenses it had mounted.

One of Mr. Siegel's strategems was to find someone to take over the raider. Before the Bendix–Martin Marietta war, Mr. Siegel said, he had managed twice before to get the raider acquired and the target saved. When Brascan tried to buy Woolworth in 1979, Brascan itself was acquired by Edper Investments, a branch of the Bronfman family. In 1980, when Daylin tried to buy Narco Scientific, Siegel helped arrange for W. R. Grace to buy Daylin instead.

Although he seemed to relish the hand-to-hand combat of the merger wars, Mr. Siegel was one of the warriors who understood that the recent wave, like others before it, would crest and recede. Anticipating that, Mr. Siegel for several years had been selling a Kidder tender-defense package to corporations that felt vulnerable to being taken over. If they did not feel vulnerable, Mr. Siegel often attempted to demonstrate to them that they were, if he so believed. By corporate standards the Kidder service was inexpensive. The basic fee was $75,000 for the first six months and $25,000 for every six months after that. The bigger the company, the bigger the fee. Mr. Siegel has asserted that Kidder makes no profit on the money clients pay for the service, that Kidder uses it as a loss-leader to get an opportunity to land other business, such as underwriting stock or bond offerings, from its tender-defense clients. Underwriting fees are not as large as those earned in contested mergers, but most corporations have far more underwriting than tender deals. As Martin Siegel has put it, "The M & A (mergers and acquisitions) business is cyclical, and when it all goes away we'll have a stronger client base." Given this setup it stands to reason that a defense-package customer will hire Kidder, at a six- or seven-figure fee, should a raider strike, and when Bendix attacked Martin Marietta, Marietta hired Kidder for defense rather than using its traditional investment banker, Goldman, Sachs & Company.

Part of the Kidder defense service is monitoring client companies' transfer sheets. The monitoring has become more difficult in recent years because raiders have learned to take evasive action to avoid being identified. "There has been a constant escalation in the tactics," Mr. Siegel says. "When raiders found that Cede (the depository of the New York Stock Exchange) was being monitored they moved to Kray & Company (the Midwest Stock Exchange) and Pacific & Company (the Pacific Exchange). When defenders used only the monthly transfer sheets, the raiders began timing purchases so that nothing suspicious would show up on the monthly sheets. Now the defenders have gone to weekly sheets."

Reading transfer sheets is an educated-hunch business, not a science, but in June of 1982, Martin Siegel says, it began to seem to Kidder that Salomon was accumulating Marietta stock for someone, and was attempting to hide the fact by registering the shares to Kray, the Midwest depository. A bit earlier, by coincidence, Kidder found that a different firm, Bridge & Company, was using Cede to accumulate shares of Gould, another Kidder tender-defense client. (Bendix never told Salomon it was accumulating Gould stock with another broker at the same time that Salomon was accumulating Marietta stock, Salomon's Jay Higgins says.) Some digging by Kidder later unearthed the fact that both blocs were being bought for Bendix.

In the middle of July Bill Agee called William Ylvisaker, Gould's chairman, to discuss a possible acquisition of Gould by

Bendix. The antitakeover doctrine, as preached by Marty Siegel, requires that in a circumstance such as this the target company use the clearest possible words to tell the raider no. In August Bendix approached Gould about buying Bendix's Gould stock, and Gould bought the stock from Bendix at $24.75 a share, the prevailing market price. At that point, Mr. Siegel says, he began to warn Marietta that Bill Agee on behalf of Bendix might soon turn his affections toward Marietta. "We ordered an antitrust review done, and there was no legal impediment on antitrust grounds to a Martin Marietta–Bendix combination," he says.

While Salomon bought Marietta shares Bill Agee and Alonzo McDonald continued to request Bendix-RCA-Marietta scenarios from Salomon—or "Earth," "Wind," and "Fire," as they were referred to. Providing such studies is, of course, part of the way an investment banker earns his fee. The Salomon studies showed that Bendix had picked a fine target in Martin Marietta. The numbers checked out well, and the fact that Marietta's aluminum and cement businesses were troubled, Salomon concluded, would probably make it difficult for the company to attract a white knight. Further, if the acquisition did not work, Salomon said, Bendix would probably be able to earn enough by selling the Marietta stock it already owned so as to show a profit on the deal.

Bendix was considering trying to take over RCA in a hostile raid, according to Jay Higgins, despite the rather forbidding public relations and bookkeeping consequences. He said that RCA's main attractions to Mr. Agee seemed to be its television stations, the NBC network, and the power and prestige that would have accrued to him if he ran NBC.

But RCA was not a realistic acquisition prospect. It was clear that RCA was prepared to make Mr. Agee's personal life an issue, and that the company could have effectively used the "freedom of the press" argument that McGraw–Hill Incorporated used successfully in 1979 when American Express Company tried to take it over.

Had Bendix somehow managed to overcome these problems and acquire RCA, Bendix would have had to deal with RCA's troubled businesses, Hertz and CIT Financial. Had either business been salable at a reasonable price, they would have long since been sold. And buying the TV stations would have produced an accounting nightmare. The stations, which are RCA's most valuable asset, are carried on the books at a very low value. This is because the stations' most valuable asset—their license to broadcast—is an intangible one. Buying RCA would have forced Bendix to pay as much as $1 billion above the value at which RCA's assets were carried on its books. Over a period of time, Bendix would have had to charge that $1 billion against its earnings. Were Bendix able to spread that charge over forty years, the most favorable treatment it could hope for, its earnings would be hit for $25 million a year, more than one dollar per share, into the twenty-first century. Bendix finally abandoned the RCA notion.

According to several people on Bendix's side of the war, Mr. Agee said in August that Bendix would make a go or no-go decision about whether to pursue Marietta sometime after Labor Day. But in August the stock market started to rally. Rumors surfaced that Bendix was going to make a "pass" at Marietta, and the price of Marietta stock rose. Bendix hurriedly advanced the date. To keep Marietta stock from rising further, which would have forced Bendix to pay a higher price for it, the tender offer was announced on August 25 even though it did not formally start until August 26. Announcing the offer before the stock market's 10:00 A.M. opening on August 25 prompted the New York Stock Exchange to suspend trading in Marietta shares, thereby making it impossible for the stock price to continue rising.

While the emergence of the Bendix bid was not much of a surprise to Martin Marietta, it apparently came as a shock to the Bendix corporate planning staff. The staff routinely prepared studies showing dozens of companies as possible acquisitions, but nothing much seemed to come from most of them.

One former planner—at the time of this writing he was still on the Bendix payroll—who visited his colleagues on August 25, the day Bendix announced that it would tender for Marietta, recalls watching the planners hurriedly looking up Marietta in their Standard & Poor's handbooks so that they could see what their own company was going after. Says this former planner: "What happened was in keeping with Bendix's approach to large acquisitions—keep as few people involved as possible, for reasons of secrecy. Small projects could involve dozens, but large ones might involve only a handful, with any number-crunching passed on to the worker bees in disguised form."

Although Bendix had lined up lawyers, public relations firms and Salomon Brothers for its Marietta bid, it had never tried the simplest approach of all: asking Martin Marietta's management or board of directors if the company were willing to be taken over on a friendly basis. Mr. Agee has told people that before the move on Marietta, Peter Peterson of Lehman Brothers had tried a friendly approach on Bendix's behalf but had been rebuffed by Marietta. None of the documents the author examined indicated that Bendix had made a friendly approach—and such approaches are customarily disclosed in filings at the Securities and Exchange Commission. Some people the author interviewed at Marietta said they think Peter Peterson mentioned Bendix in passing during a 1981 telephone call he made to Marietta President Tom Pownall, but that no one at Marietta was interested. (Agee told the author that Peterson asked him whether he would be interested in having lunch with Marietta and that when he said he would, Peterson did approach Marietta but the company was not interested in a meeting.) Shortly after the Bendix attack on Marietta began, Marietta says, Mr. Peterson did call—to tell Tom Pownall that Lehman Brothers was not involved.

Once Bendix attacked in haste, it never got a chance to repent at leisure. Although discussions between Salomon and Bendix had gone on for months, there was never a long talk about strategies and fallback positions. There were two prob-

lems that later haunted Bendix, and they were both obvious
ones. The first was that Marietta could countertender for Bendix, which at that point did not have "shark-repellant" provisions in its corporate charter to make a hostile takeover difficult. The second was that in the case of a countertender,
Bendix might be at a disadvantage because it is incorporated
in Delaware. Under Delaware law a majority shareholder can
call a special meeting and vote in the board of directors of his
choice without giving notice. Marietta, on the other hand, is
incorporated in Maryland, where state law requires that ten
days notice of a special meeting be given. These weaknesses
were discovered by Marietta's lawyers the day after Bendix
announced that it would tender for Marietta, and Marietta was
to exploit them to the fullest even though in the end their
importance turned out to be more apparent than real.

The Delaware-Maryland disparity became irrelevant; Bendix obtained a court order on September 22 barring Marietta
from voting any Bendix shares it might acquire as the result of
its countertender. But in the early days of the battle the disparity was important. It gave the Marietta board of directors
grounds on which it could predict victory, and so encouraged
the board to adopt the Pacman strategy. The disparity also
convinced some investors that Marietta was serious about its
tender for Bendix, making these investors more willing to tender their shares. And the prospect of Marietta taking over
Bendix, rather than the other way around, was a morale-
booster in Marietta's headquarters.

Arthur Fleischer, Jr., of Fried, Frank, Harris, Shriver &
Jacobson, Bendix's lead lawyer, said his firm, hired on August
18, just a week before the bid for Marietta was launched, had
told Agee of the Delaware-Maryland problem but it made
little sense to hold up the deal to move Bendix's charter to a
different state.

In any event, Bendix gained a head start on Marietta, which
few Bendix strategists had expected, by getting rapid approval
of the tender from the Federal Trade Commission. Bendix

needed approval under the Hart-Scott-Rodino Act. Because Bendix presented a clean case and had prepared well for the F.T.C, it got F.T.C approval quickly. Normally, Hart-Scott-Rodino clearance took longer than the fifteen business days that companies had to wait before buying tendered stock. Bendix strategists expected that if Marietta countertendered, the F.T.C would clear the Bendix bid for Marietta and the Marietta bid for Bendix the same day, so neither company would have an advantage. It was pleased with the head-start (though in the long run it did no good).

In a deposition, taken as part of a lawsuit in U.S. District Court in Baltimore in which Marietta tried vainly to block Bendix's bid, Jay Higgins said under oath that Salomon had warned Bendix about the possibility of Marietta employing a Pacman defense. "We had told the [Bendix] board to anticipate that our offer to Martin Marietta would be rejected as inadequate and that we couldn't predict the specific response of Martin Marietta, but it could do a number of things, one of which would be a tender for Bendix," he said.

It would have been almost unthinkable for Salomon *not* to have warned Bendix about the possibility of a countertender, because Jay Higgins had been burned by a Pacman maneuver only a few months earlier. Mr. Higgins represented American General Insurance Company, which attacked NLT Corporation, which countertendered and almost won. Partly because Salomon had tried to sell a savings and loan association owned by NLT, American General called in First Boston Corporation to help, and Salomon, unhappily, had watched First Boston finish the deal.

Bendix management had been worried since early 1981 that it was vulnerable to being taken over at a cheap price by a raider eager to strip its assets. At the September 24, 1980 Bendix employees meeting at which he discussed the Mary Cunningham matter, Bill Agee had also discussed the possibility of being raided. In response to a question, the official Bendix transcript shows, Mr. Agee said that having hundreds of millions of dollars of cash ". . . makes you a little more vulnerable than when you have only $30 to $40 million in the bank." In a speech he delivered to the Atlanta Downtown Rotary Club on October 11, 1982, Bendix president McDonald said, "Frankly, Bendix has been a potential takeover target for more than a year now. With our attractive businesses and our strong cash position during a period of extraordinary illiquidity for American industry, we watched a number of companies moving closer to us, looking over our shoulder."

But despite these fears, Bendix took no steps to reduce its vulnerability until the Marietta countertender started—a lapse in strategic planning. At the company's 1981 or 1982 shareholders meeting it would have been a relatively simple matter to gain shareholder approval of "shark-repellant" measures designed to make it difficult for a raider to take a company over. Typical repellants are requiring a "supermajority" of 75 or 80 percent of the stock for takeovers, or electing directors to three-year staggered terms so that it takes a raider with a majority of the shares at least two years to gain control of the board of directors.

After the Marietta countertender began, Bendix tried to have a special, hastily called shareholders meeting adopt repellants, but it never got them passed. Calling the special meeting tended to show weakness, and distracted Bendix from its business at hand—buying Marietta.

Marietta, by contrast, had had defense plans in place since August of 1981 when Martin Siegel had convinced the company to buy the Kidder Peabody tender-defense package. Mr. Siegel, who had been working on a potential acquisition for Marietta, says that he noticed that Marietta itself was vulnerable and sold Marietta on the defense package.

Marietta was vulnerable not only because its stock was inexpensive in August of 1982 but also because its various businesses were not integrated and were run on a decentralized basis. This in turn would allow a raider to sell portions of the company, such as aluminum and cement, without disturbing the parts he wanted to keep, such as aerospace. (Marietta has itself since proved that point. In 1983, to help repair its balance sheet, the company sold cement plants for about $175 million and Sodyeco, its textile dye division, for $72 million. Its remaining businesses were not affected. A company of only one or two products, or whose plants provide material for each other's operations, could not so easily be split up.)

One of Marietta's defenses was to become friendly with its lender banks, so that there would be a good prospect that they would provide, say, some $900 million in credit on short notice. Arranging large credits was and is a complicated matter, involving negotiations of terms, fees and interest rates. Many banks require that their loan committees or even their boards of directors approve large new credits. By informally arranging credit before it was needed, Marietta was able, in a single weekend, to tie down $930 million of bank credits, giving it sufficient borrowing power to buy the Bendix stock for which it tendered.

Marietta's board, Martin Siegel says, had also accepted the need to offer "golden parachutes" to members of management, so there was no last-minute soul-searching over whether to grant them. Mr. Siegel is one of the few people willing to say a good word publicly about parachutes, which he claims are necessary to keep good people. "When a hostile takeover starts," he says, "the only people who call more than the arbitragers are the executive recruiters."

A traditional tender defense is to use delaying tactics in the courts, but Marietta did not rely on such moves. Indeed it was fortunate for Marietta that it was not counting on judicial intervention, because despite some fifteen separate lawsuits, neither Bendix nor Marietta could hold the other up for more than a few hours. In an afterword written on September 29, 1982, Wachtell, Lipton, Rosen & Katz, the law firm that represented Kidder Peabody, concluded that "the courts are growing more and more reluctant to interfere in tender offers, the countertender offer can be an effective defense by a target that wants to remain independent, and the state takeover statutes are dead." Bendix, on the other hand, placed great reliance on the courts. The company built its strategy on an assumption that even if Marietta countertendered, no court would allow Marietta to buy Bendix shares if Bendix already owned a substantial majority of Marietta. That assumption turned out to be incorrect.

Perhaps the biggest advantage of all to Marietta was that Martin Siegel and other Kidder people had been dealing with Marietta executives and directors for more than a year and had had time to establish a rapport with them. "We get involved, we bleed with these guys," Mr. Siegel says. "When they bleed, we bleed. You've got to have the sensitivity to understand the motivations of the players."

Because of the rapport, the Marietta defense went smoothly. Not so the Bendix offense. The personalities of the Salomon and Bendix teams did not seem to mesh. Jay Higgins and Bill Agee, who never sat down to talk privately at length, never understood each other. Client and banker were barely speaking during the latter stages of the takeover operation.

The low-key Mr. Siegel and the low-key Tom Pownall meshed well. Mr. Siegel is unusual in the high-powered, nervous world of mergers and acquisitions: he does not look older than his age, which is thirty-five. He goes home to Connecticut, where he lives with his wife and their young daughter, rather than socializing with the other merger men. Some people call him the Monk of Wall Street because he does not smoke or drink. He says he is in bed by 10:30 when he is on the road. A few years ago, deciding he was too portly, he lost weight, and is proud of being slim. When he eats at his desk, which he commonly does, he has one of his secretaries order him a lunch that never varies: frozen chocolate yogurt with sliced bananas. Dissipation is a diet soda to wash it down. "I used to have hamburgers every day until I heard they caused cancer," he says with a smile. Until he remarried three years ago Marty Siegel was a divorced man with a high income, a house on Fire Island and an Alfa Romeo sports car. He sold the house when it was suggested to him that it made him look faintly the swinger. Mr. Siegel and his wife, the former Jane Day Stuart, live in a cedar-and-glass house on the Connecticut shoreline, complete with a private beach. The home, which the Siegels designed themselves, includes a gymnasium, tennis court and swimming pool.

Mr. Siegel speaks tenderly of his wife and daughter, but he leaves his compassion in Connecticut. Even though his Kidder office is furnished with cartoons on the wall, Mr. Siegel makes sure that visitors understand that to him, mergers are no laughing matter. No visitor is allowed to overlook the tarantula that lurks in the papers that cover his desk. The tarantula, safely dead and encased in plastic, is the color of dried blood. It is a gift from a grateful client. Siegel will not say which one. On the bottom is the inscription: "Bites only when annoyed. Bite is painful."

The Bendix raid on Martin Marietta annoyed Martin Siegel. It annoyed Martin Marietta even more.

Chapter 8

The Marietta Defense

WHY MARIETTA FOUGHT BACK

If one had to select two companies whose management philosophies were incompatible even though the companies engaged in similar businesses, one could scarcely find better examples than Bendix under William Agee and Martin Marietta under Thomas Pownall. Outwardly the companies appeared to be similar, but in reality they were opposites in management styles and "corporate cultures." Such distinctions seemed to have been missed by Bendix when it launched its raid on Marietta—which helps explain why Marietta fought so hard to stay independent.

On paper Bendix and Marietta were indeed similar. They both had substantial aerospace operations supplemented by cyclical businesses: auto parts and machine tools for Bendix, aluminum and cement for Marietta. The Bendix and Marietta aerospace operations appeared to complement each other nicely. Marietta is a prime contractor, handling entire projects, while Bendix is a sub-prime contractor, handling parts of projects.

But almost everything else about the companies was in conflict. Under Bill Agee, Bendix had become the epitome of the short-term-oriented corporation of the 1980s. Mr. Agee talked

153

frequently of his devotion to long-term thinking and the need to spend heavily on research and development; his actions were otherwise. In 1980 he wanted to buy all of the mining company, Asarco Incorporated, but instead sold Bendix's 21 percent Asarco interest because he was offered a good price for it. That same year Mr. Agee was shopping for acquisitions to expand Bendix's forest products division—until a buyer appeared and offered a good price for the entire division; Mr. Agee then sold it. In 1980 Bendix even had its automotive operations up for sale, but found no buyers willing to pay what the company considered a suitable price.

In late 1980, when "high technology" was becoming a buzzword, Mr. Agee said Bendix would become a "high technology" company. In early 1980, when the "reindustrialization of America" was a popular theme, Mr. Agee bought Warner & Swasey, a machine tool company whose chairman professed no interest in robotics, the high-tech aspect of machine tools.

William Agee demonstrated no long-term devotion to any of Bendix's businesses. If he was offered a sufficiently high price, he sold. If he saw assets cheap, as in the case of Asarco in 1978, he bought. If he had a concrete vision of Bendix, other than the "high technology" strategy he talked of but never implemented, it did not become apparent.

Agee's approach to building value for Bendix's shareholders reflected the belief that he was capable of steering Bendix into the businesses with the highest profit potentials. He did not build, he traded. To concentrate on trading successfully over an extended period means having to outsmart all the other people trying to do the same thing. Bendix, under Bill Agee, was successful in selling assets—they fetched high prices unlikely to be seen again soon—but was not so successful in redeploying the money generated by the sales.

By the time Bendix moved to take over Martin Marietta, the profits from Bendix's operations were eroding. Part of the problem was a weak economy's effect on the company's automotive and machine tool businesses; another was Agee's ever-

changing management styles. After becoming chairman of
Bendix in 1977 he brought William Purple, head of Bendix's
aerospace business, from aerospace headquarters in Virginia
into Southfield, intending, Bendix people say, to give Mr. Purple added administrative duties. When that did not work out,
Purple went back to aerospace and Agee hired William Panny
as operating officer. Panny brought with him the Rockwell
International method of management, much more report-ori-
ented than the Bendix way, and implemented the new
method. In September of 1980 Agee fired Panny and announced a new, decentralized regime. He would be in charge
of operations. Panny was not needed under the new regime,
Agee said. In March of 1981 Agee hired Alonzo McDonald, Jr.
as vice-chairman of the board and later made him president.
McDonald has never run an industrial company; one of his
previous jobs had been chief of staff for Jimmy Carter's White
House, which was not known for being especially well
managed. McDonald was put in charge of headquarters operations; Agee was to be in charge of running the businesses.

While Bendix shifted approaches, apparently according to
what it perceived to be prevailing business styles, and occasionally succeeded, Marietta went to another extreme. It ignored trends. It did what it had always done: build up the
businesses in hand without much thought to selling them or
buying different ones. By historical accident rather than de-
sign Martin Marietta is a collection of unrelated businesses. It
is equally devoted to all of them. Instead of concentrating its
spending on consistently profitable operations, such as aerospace, and deemphasizing problem operations such as aluminum, Marietta operated on the assumption that everything it
owned was a sound business and in due time would recover
from the recession.

The company is an unusual combination of aerospace, aluminum, cement and aggregate (crushed stone) businesses, along
with data processing and chemicals. Its approach is to try to be
the low-cost producer in its fields. Bendix talked about taking

this Japanese-like approach to its businesses, but Marietta really *is* that way. Even though the aluminum and cement businesses are generally considered far less attractive than aerospace, aluminum and cement accounted for the majority of Marietta's capital spending from 1978 through 1982, some $860 million of the $1.63 billion spent. By contrast, aerospace, Marietta's most consistently profitable business, got only $316 million, or less than 20 percent of the spending. The more usual corporate approach is to put the most money into the businesses with the promise of the highest returns, and the least into the businesses with the lowest returns. Instead Marietta invested some $630 million in aluminum and $230 million in cement, which are subject to cyclical ups and downs, and which lost more than $75 million (before taxes and interest costs) in 1982. By contrast, aerospace earned $162 million (before taxes and interest) in 1982.

When the Bendix attack focused interest on Marietta, "We looked like we were deranged for spending all that money on aluminum," Thomas Pownall said in an interview with the author. The problem, he contended, was that Marietta upgraded its facilities just in time to have them ready for the worst aluminum market in memory. Had he known what the market would be like, Mr. Pownall said, he would not have spent the money.

Money was poured into cement and aluminum from 1979 through 1982, he said, because both operations were in danger of becoming outmoded due to changing technologies and rising energy costs. It takes huge amounts of energy to produce cement and aluminum. "Aluminum," Pownall says, "is like frozen electricity." Much of the spending went to convert plant boilers from oil to coal and to reduce the energy the plants consumed per unit of output. Because there were no buyers for the aluminum or cement divisions at what he considered reasonable prices, Pownall said, the choice was to upgrade them or face the possibility of having to close them as obsolete in a few years. "It's like driving your car to work," he says. "Let's say the car breaks. It's the only damn way you've got to get to work, so you fix it or you don't get to work. So we had to fix it."

Unlike Bendix, which had no discernible vision of what it wanted to be, Marietta's goal was clear: to be the lowest-cost producer of the products it made so that it would be among the highest-profit producers when the economy picked up.

Marietta prides itself on taking a long-term approach to its businesses, especially to aerospace. Says Pownall: "We began to work on trying to get a spacecraft to Mars in 1963. We got a contract in 1969, we launched in 1975, we landed in 1976 and we got paid in 1977. Things that are worth doing don't typically happen in an overnight sort of way, unless you're betting on the cheap or on the come or on something. If you're buying and selling companies all over the place, you may make a helluva lot of money overnight or lose a helluva lot of money overnight. But if you're *operating* a company, the likelihood is that your're not going to make a helluva lot of money overnight."

Marietta, proud of its role in building weapons for the military, believed—possibly arrogantly, Mr. Pownall acknowledges—that Bendix could not do the job. Even though Bendix has a sizeable aerospace business, Mr. Pownall says, "It's like saying two guys are both in the transportation business, except that one guy drives a taxi and the other guy runs a railroad . . . We concluded that they probably couldn't handle our business without screwing it up. We even screw it up once in a while ourselves . . . We are engaged in some very significant projects for the benefit of the entire U.S. of A. If those contracts were to be executed successfully, we had better be around."

Unlike Bill Agee, who seemed to be remaking Bendix in his own image, Tom Pownall and his associates considered themselves to be the conservators of the businesses built by their predecessors, beginning with Glenn Luther Martin, one of the nation's earliest aviators.

Glenn Martin was to the Martin Marietta Corporation what

Vincent T. Bendix was to the Bendix Corporation—a founding
father who stayed too long at the firm he started and had to
be eased out.

Glenn Martin produced his first airplane in 1909, six years
after Wilbur and Orville Wright made the first airplane flight
at Kitty Hawk, North Carolina. Martin, twenty-three years old,
built his plane in an abandoned church in Santa Ana, California. Deciding that the airplane business had more promise
than selling cars, his profession at the time, the young Martin
became a combination aerial pioneer and huckster. To promote aviation and raise capital, he flew aerial exhibitions. According to the official Martin Marietta history, at one point
Glenn Martin and his plane appeared in a Mary Pickford
movie, earning $700 a day for him and getting valuable public-
ity.

His military orientation surfaced early. He started making
training planes for the military, and one of his first air shows
involved attacking a mock fort near Los Angeles. In 1912,
according to the company, Glenn Martin scored a number of
firsts: first to deliver newspapers by plane, first to drop a base-
ball into a catcher's mitt from a plane, first to drop a bouquet
from a plane into a May Queen's lap, first to drop department
store advertising from a plane, first to take motion pictures
from a plane. He even became the first flier to take his mother
in an airplane, a trip they both survived. He also helped develop the parachute and the seaplane.

Along the way, Martin merged his company with Orville
Wright's to form the Wright-Martin Aircraft Corporation,
which broke up when the two men disagreed. In 1917 Martin
moved his plant from Los Angeles to Cleveland because Ohio
financiers backed him. They lost interest after World War I
because they lacked faith in the future of nonmilitary aircraft.
In 1929 Martin bought almost two square miles of land near
Baltimore and opened a large factory near Chesapeake Bay.
The bay allowed him to experiment with seaplanes. He sold
bombers to the militaries of the United States, Britain and
France, and it was one of his MB-2 bombers that sank the

derelict German battleship *Ostfriesland* in Billy Mitchell's famous exhibition that bombers could destroy warships.

With World War II approaching, sales of the Glenn L. Martin Aviation Company, which had gone public in 1937, soared. A Martin bomber, the *Enola Gay,* dropped the first atomic bomb on Japan. But when the war ended, the Martin company did not succeed in building civilian aircraft. It produced an unpressurized airliner at the request of Howard Hughes and Trans World Airlines, but it didn't sell. The company's 404 passenger plane suffered crashes, not surprisingly causing order cancellations. Several military contracts proved unprofitable. In 1951 the company was saved from insolvency only by the forebearance of its bankers and an infusion of capital from the Reconstruction Finance Corporation. Martin retired to hunt ducks, and the bankers' man, George Bunker, took over.

Bunker eliminated the company's civilian aviation business, cut costs and improved the company's financial and managerial controls. When the navy chose the Polaris submarine-launched guided missile over a new generation of naval military aircraft, the Martin company was out of the airplane business and into aerospace. It built the Polaris, the Titan ICBM, various air-to-air missiles, the Pershing ground-to-ground missile and the Vanguard satellite launching missile. The company was consistently profitable, but George Bunker, knowing the risks of depending on government contracts for 99 percent of the Martin company's business, tried—and failed —several times to diversify into nongovernment fields.

In 1961, by luck, he got his chance. As Martin Marietta tells it, Grover Hermann, seventy years old, was looking for a strong manager to take over his American-Marietta Company when he read in the *Wall Street Journal* about the Martin turnaround and George Bunker's attempts to attract nongovernment business. He told his people to get in touch with the Martin company's people, and in 1961 the companies were merged.

American-Marietta was an eclectic collection of businesses

that had evolved from the Hermann family's combination lumber yard-construction business-Buick dealership in Callicoon, New York. One of the Hermann's best-selling products was an asphalt paint. When the paint manufacturer went broke in 1913 the Hermanns gambled $5,000 to take over the company so they would still have a product to sell. They hired a chemist to develop new colors—for years the paint was available only in black—and the business prospered. In another technological breakthrough the Hermanns discovered that mixing powdered aluminum into the paint gave it better weathering and adhesion properties. In 1933 the Chicago World's Fair built clusters of temporary buildings covered with a new type of siding that did not take conventional paint well. American Asphalt Paint's new product, however, worked beautifully. American Asphalt proceeded to buy other paint companies, and after World War II expanded into unrelated businesses that included concrete drainage pipe, cement, aggregates, lime, O'Cedar mops, printer's ink, electrical equipment, tobacco processing and farm silos. It's not surprising that Grover Hermann felt the need for a strong manager to make sense out of what he had built.

After the new firm, Martin Marietta, was formed in 1961 there was a brief argument about whether the firm should be based in Chicago (American-Marietta's headquarters) or Baltimore (the Martin Company headquarters). They compromised on New York City. (The company moved to Bethesda, Maryland, in 1974). Hermann served as chairman of the new corporation for a time, then drifted out of the company. Trying to bring some order to its operations, Martin Marietta sold a number of its businesses in the 1960s, including O'Cedar mops, household chemicals and American-Marietta's original business, paint. The Federal Trade Commission forced the sale of some of the company's aggregate operations, concrete plants and lime plants. In 1963, flush with cash from those sales, Marietta bought back 2.4 million of its own shares and spent most of the remainder of its cash to buy the Harvey Aluminum Company.

For the balance of the 1960s and in the 1970s Marietta went quietly about its business, building weapons and churning out cement, aggregates, aluminum, concrete and chemicals. The company was low-key and very conservatively managed. It boasts that it has never omitted or reduced a dividend. The aerospace operation has dominated the company because all the chief executives have made their way up through aerospace. Unlike Bendix, operations rather than finance are emphasized. The company has a militaristic corporate culture—Tom Pownall, himself a graduate of Annapolis, has said on numerous occasions that he is sorry he left the navy to enter private business.

As mentioned, if Bendix is open to criticism for being somewhat eager to hop aboard trends, Marietta is open to criticism for ignoring them. In the 1960s and early 1970s, when money was cheap, Marietta did not borrow to expand or to acquire companies the way other technologically oriented corporations, such as United Technologies, did. Marietta stuck to its businesses and kept a low profile. The company did not borrow substantial amounts of money until 1981, under Tom Pownall. That year Marietta borrowed $194 million, more than doubling its long-term debt to a still-conservative $360 million. Marietta borrowed the money because it wanted to continue spending heavily to modernize the cement and aluminum businesses and its operations were not producing the money needed to accomplish that.

Marietta was vulnerable to a takeover largely because the aluminum and cement businesses, which had consumed so much of its resources, were losing money in 1982. And the company's major hope for a multibillion-dollar defense contract was the MX missile, whose future in 1982 was unclear. The MX uncertainty and the losses in aluminum and cement drove down the price of Marietta shares. In the second quarter of 1981, when defense stocks were briefly in fashion, Marietta's price reached over $50 a share. A year later, with defense stocks again out of fashion, Marietta's price was down by more than 50 percent—and Bendix began buying. Because, also as mentioned, Marietta was a decentralized company, Bendix could have sold off pieces of it (though it denied having that intention), covering the bulk of its purchase price and having Marietta's lucrative aerospace business for a very low net cost.

In a short-term-oriented world Marietta's long-term approach had long since fallen out of favor with investors, especially institutional investors. When faced with the choice of trusting Marietta's managers to increase value over the long term or taking Bendix's tender offer money in the short term, the shareholders overwhelmingly took the money. About 70 percent of Marietta's shares was ultimately tendered to Bendix, and normally the Bendix-Marietta war would have come to a cease fire then and there.

Except no one at Bendix—its advisors included—took into account the distaste that Tom Pownall and the Marietta board had for William Agee and Bendix. To be sure, Tom Pownall had his job to consider. He earned more than $600,000 a year at Marietta and at the age of sixty-one, was not too likely to find an equivalent position elsewhere. But when Bill Agee offered to make Tom Pownall the vice-chairman in the combined company, with the proviso that Marietta drop its opposition to Bendix, Pownall turned him down. "I told him, 'We're not here to talk about a job for me, we're here to figure out a way out of this mess,'" Mr. Pownall says.

The stubborness of Tom Pownall and his like-minded board of directors did not show up in the decision-trees or scenarios that Bendix used to plan its operation against Marietta. It would appear that no one on the Bendix side actually knew what Tom Pownall was like, and that no one made the effort to find out. Jay Higgins of Salomon Brothers says that Bill Agee ordered him not to deal with the other side once the war commenced. Bendix's lawyers were plotting legal moves, not reconciliation. Marietta's advisors told Pownall not to talk to Agee, and he took their advice. Jude Wanniski, the New Jersey writer-economist who had introduced Bill Agee and Tom Pownall to each other at Bill Agee's house in 1980, says no one from Bendix called him.

Although Tom Pownall is polite and soft-spoken—in a two-hour interview with the author, he did not say a single derogatory word about Bill Agee, either on or off the record—he is unusually determined. On New Year's Eve of 1978, for example, he engaged in an arm-wrestling match with his friend Congressman Jack Kemp. Jack Kemp, former star quarterback with the Buffalo Bills of the National Football League, has a right arm that threw a football sixty yards in the air. He is an experienced arm-wrestler and stated that he has never been beaten. Tom Pownall, six feet, one hundred ninety pounds, does not appear muscular. He sat down at the table with the ex-pro. "I thought I could do some tricks to him," Mr. Pownall said. The two men struggled for about five minutes before Kemp finally prevailed. Pownall, who had shown no sign of pain during the match, went to a hospital a few days later to have his arm ligaments repaired. He had torn them from the shoulder to the elbow. "I'm old, but I'm strong," he says. "I milked cows for twenty years. I have muscle—it's old muscle, but it's still muscle." Pownall, despite his equable public manner, grits his teeth so badly that he has had to be hospitalized to have them repaired.

He grew up in Moorefield, West Virginia, where his father was a strong Republican in a heavily Democratic area. Tom wanted an appointment to the Naval Academy at Annapolis, but no local Democratic politician would waste an appointment on the son of a Republican. Tom's mother, however, was a good friend of the wife of Jennings Randolph, a Democratic congressman, and Randolph appointed Tom Pownall to Annapolis. Pownall played on the football team, graduated in 1946 and returned to civilian life in 1949, though "I always liked wearing a uniform."

During the Korean War, Pownall served on a destroyer in the Pacific. Afterward he had a variety of civilian jobs. In 1960 he took a leave of absence to become an advance man for

Richard Nixon's presidential campaign. He lived in California at the time, Mr. Pownall has said, and was friendly with Herbert Klein, Nixon's public relations man. After a call from Vice-President Nixon himself, Pownall joined the campaign, working in New York City, Buffalo, Chicago, Alaska and Los Angeles. It was his fling, he says. In 1963 he joined Marietta, and moved steadily upward. In 1977 he became president, in 1982 chief executive officer, chairman in 1983 when J. Donald Rauth, his friend and sometime hunting companion, retired.

Above all, Tom Pownall seems to be a team player who operates by the book, and he seems surprised to have discovered that Bill Agee did things differently. "I never believed that his wife was the force she really turned out to be," Pownall told Time magazine ("You're Going to Kill Us Both," April 25, 1983). "They were the action advocates totally. . . . Agee was operating with the investment bankers, largely outside the Bendix corporation."

By contrast, Pownall kept his executives close to him. During the takeover battle, he says, four Marietta men—Charles Leithauser, chief financial officer; Frank Menake, Jr., general counsel; Laurence Adams, head of the aerospace division; and James Simpson, the former general counsel who was then running the chemicals division—were with him most of the time. He also figured that Marietta had paid Martin Siegel good money to represent Marietta, so he let Siegel do his job. When the Bendix attack came, Tom Pownall played by the book. Bill Agee played a lone hand and improvised.

Chapter 9

Defense's Opening Gambit

MARIETTA ATTACKS BENDIX

When Bendix announced on Wednesday, August 25, that on the following day it would begin a $43-a-share tender offer for Martin Marietta, Tom Pownall, as befitted a man with military training, took out the takeover contingency plan and followed it. The first step was to assemble the troops for an emergency meeting, which Pownall called for Wednesday afternoon at Marietta headquarters in Bethesda.

Because Bendix had launched its bid hurriedly, to keep Marietta's stock from rising on the basis of takeover rumors, Tom Pownall had a day of grace. Even though the Bendix announcement was made on Wednesday, the tender offer itself could not begin until Thursday, when Bendix filed the necessary papers with the U.S. Securities and Exchange Commission (normally, papers are filed and the offer announced simultaneously.)

Because Marietta had bought the Kidder Peabody tender-defense package in 1981, it did not have to waste precious time lining up investment bankers, attorneys and financial public relations men. They were already on retainer, waiting to go. As Martin Siegel of Kidder Peabody had suggested, Marietta had already reached informal understandings with its bankers

165

about borrowing some $900 million on a short-term basis.

By Wednesday afternoon Siegel, members of Marietta's
management and attorneys from Dewey, Ballantine, Bushby,
Palmer & Wood, the New York City law firm that represents
Marietta, were meeting with Tom Pownall in Bethesda to plot
strategy. The approach was simple: ask Bendix for peace, prepare for war.

First, though, came certain routine opening moves by both
sides. The initial steps in a contested takeover are almost as
predictable as the ritual moves in Japanese Nohi theater; the
Bendix-Marietta battle was no exception. Making the time-
honored approach, Jay Higgins of Salomon Brothers, speaking
for Bendix, telephoned Marty Siegel and told him that Bendix's Bill Agee wanted to meet with Tom Pownall to negotiate.
In the ritual response, Siegel said that his client was angry and
that the only way to negotiate was for Bendix to withdraw its
tender offer so Marietta would be talking "without a gun at our
head." In the next ritual move, Higgins consulted his client
and called Siegel back, saying that Bendix would not withdraw.
It was an understandable response. Without the threat of a
tender offer, Bendix had no leverage to force Marietta to negotiate seriously. And if Bendix announced the tender offer, then
withdrew it while negotiations went on, it could not expect to
have credibility if it decided to launch the tender again in the
event the talks with Marietta failed.

Dewey Ballantine attorneys were going through the ritual
moves prescribed for lawyers handling contested tenders.
They began to think about the lawsuit Marietta was almost
certain to file, alleging violations of the securities laws by Bendix. Courts, as seen, were and are growing reluctant to inter-
vene in tender offers, but it was and is standard at least to try
a lawsuit; it just *might* work. If the client should get lucky, the
lawyers might find something incriminating about the other
side, thereby inducing a judge to delay the tender offer or even
to block it entirely.

Attorneys representing Bendix were already performing

their ritual moves by showing up in court in states with antitakeover statutes and seeking injunctions to have the state statutes knocked out. After the federal Williams Act was passed in 1968 some states adopted takeover regulations of their own, the motive usually being to keep out-of-state corporations from raiding companies with headquarters or important production facilities in the state in question. The fear was that the out-of-state corporation, if successful, might move headquarters or production jobs elsewhere. In 1982, though, in *Edgar* v. *MITE*, the United States Supreme Court ruled that the Williams Act preempted state takeover laws. The *MITE* ruling has nearly eliminated the use of state takeover laws as a delaying device, but Bendix's lawyers, not wanting to overlook any possibility, went about the country obtaining injunctions. Before the Bendix-Marietta battle had finished, there had been court actions in ten states with takeover statutes: Delaware, Missouri, New Jersey, Maryland, Nebraska, Utah, South Carolina, Oklahoma, Louisiana and Michigan. Ultimately none of these suits had any impact on the result. Bendix almost managed to catch Marietta napping in late September, after Bendix had bought a majority of Marietta and Marietta was getting ready to buy a majority of Bendix. At almost the last minute, Bendix persuaded a federal judge in Detroit to issue an injunction barring Marietta's purchase of the tendered Bendix shares on the grounds that such a purchase would violate the Michigan Takeover Act. But Marietta convinced the federal appeals court in Cincinnati to override the Detroit injunction, and the Marietta effort to purchase Bendix went on without delay.

There were two obvious responses by Marietta to Bendix's takeover, and both presented difficulties. The first response was to find a "white knight" to buy the company for more than the $43 a share Bendix was offering. But the Marietta board did not want to sell the company at a time when its aluminum and cement businesses were depressed. Bringing in a white knight meant that the company was for sale, and the struggle became a matter of price, not a matter of principle. If a white knight offered more than $43, and Bendix then topped the white knight's bid, the Marietta board would have virtually no choice but to sell the company to Bendix. And, as Jay Higgins of Salomon Brothers had predicted, Marietta would have had trouble finding a white knight to pay a high price for it because the aluminum and cement businesses were cyclical and capital-intensive—the sort of operations many companies want to sell and few want to buy.

Because Marietta and Bendix were of roughly equal size, a countertender, or Pacman strategy, was possible, but on the surface not probable. Marietta had spent so heavily on its cement and aluminum divisions that there seemed no way the company could raise the money needed to tender for Bendix. Although Salomon and Bendix had discussed the Pacman possibility, they did not think it likely because they felt Marietta lacked the financial resources to pull it off.

Even if Marietta began a countertender, the time element would put it at a severe disadvantage with Bendix. After the Bendix tender for Marietta was announced, arbitragers were purchasing Marietta shares with the purpose of tendering them to Bendix for $43 or even more if Bendix, as the "arbs" expected, increased its bid. Marietta had to act quickly or the game would soon be over. Despite the time problem, the Marietta board acted very conservatively. The standard response when a company is faced with a raid on its stock is to have a board meeting within a day or two of the offer, declare the offer "inadequate" and authorize the chairman or a small committee of directors to take whatever steps they deem appropriate.

Not so the Marietta board. Tom Pownall scheduled a board meeting for Monday, August 30. By that time, he told Marty Siegel and the Dewey Ballantine lawyers, everything had to be set to launch the countertender. Which meant the Marietta tender for Bendix could not start until August 31—Marietta could not possibly file the documents with the Securities and

Exchange Commission until the day after the board meeting. The Bendix offer for Marietta had started on August 26, so Marietta would be starting out with a five-day handicap.

The time element was crucial because of the federal securities law in 1982 that tender offers be open for at least fifteen business days before the tendering company could buy the stock proffered to it. Unless Marietta could delay the Bendix offer for at least five days without having its own offer held up, *Bendix would be free to buy Marietta stock before Marietta would be free to buy Bendix stock.* Because Bendix could buy first, it looked as though it could take over Marietta, end the Marietta countertender for Bendix and emerge victorious.

But in the course of routine legal research in Marietta's law library, Dewey Ballantine partners found one of those legal loopholes that so often brings joy to a lawyer's heart. Owning a majority of a company's stock is usually considered to give the owner control—but not so in this case. To exercise control the majority owner must control a majority of the board of directors. To gain control of the board, the majority shareholder must call a special shareholders meeting and vote in the directors of his choice. Normally this is a mere formality. Not in the case of Bendix and Marietta, which were incorporated in different states. Bendix was incorporated in Delaware, Marietta in Maryland. (Companies must be incorporated in states because there are no federal incorporation laws.) As Leonard Larrabee, Jr., of Dewey Ballantine explains it, under Delaware corporate law a special shareholders meeting can be called by a majority shareholder without giving notice to other holders, while in Maryland ten days' notice are required. This distinction raised the possibility that even though Bendix could buy Marietta stock five days before Marietta could buy Bendix stock, Marietta might still be able to vote its Bendix shares and take over Bendix's board of directors before Bendix could vote its Marietta shares and take over the Marietta board of directors. According to lawyers on both sides, the law on this question is uncertain because the matter has never been litigated.

There were all sorts of complications, including whether Marietta would be considered a subsidiary of Bendix and thus unable to vote its Bendix shares under Delaware corporate law. (Bendix's lead lawyer, Arthur Fleischer, Jr., of Fried Frank, said he is certain that Bendix would have prevailed. Matters, though, never got to that point. In early 1983 Delaware was considering eliminating the ten-days' notice requirement out of fear that companies would move their incorporation sites to other states.)

True, the matter was far from clear, but the Delaware-Maryland difference raised at least a possibility that if both companies bought majorities of each other, Marietta might prevail. Which allowed Tom Pownall and Marty Siegel to tell the Marietta board that there was a good chance a countertender would frighten Bendix off—Marietta's only goal. "Everything we did was designed to make Bendix go away," Marty Siegel says. And *if* the companies were to be combined, Marietta wanted the deal on its terms, not Bendix's.

The weakness of the Pacman strategy was that it was a bluff. It could not stop Bendix from buying a majority of Marietta if Bendix was determined to press its bid. If Bendix bought a majority, the only way to find out which side would win the ensuing legal battle would be for Marietta to buy a majority of Bendix and see what happened. If each company bought a majority of the other, the combined corporation would have had about three dollars of debt for each dollar of net worth, a financial ratio that one investment banker said would produce a company with "a triple-Z credit rating."

But even to get to the countertender stage, Marietta had to ante up nearly a billion dollars in cash. In a tender for Bendix it could buy the second half of the company in exchange for newly issued Marietta securities, but it would have to pay cash for the first half to get its offer on the table rapidly enough to have any chance of influencing events.

Over the August 28–29 weekend, Marietta met with its bankers in Dewey Ballantine offices in New York City. Marietta had to convert its $900 million understanding into $900 million of loan commitments that were legally binding on the banks. In a move that surprised many people, including some on the Marietta side, the company did just that. "I never thought bankers could be moved like that," Len Larrabee of Dewey Ballantine says. By 3:00 A.M. Monday morning, August 30, in time for that day's Marietta board meeting, which was held in New York City, $930 million of loan commitments were in place. Marietta was ready for step one in its counter-attack.

While Marietta was getting its act together during the early days of the Bendix attack, the Bendix-Salomon Brothers act was falling apart. Tom Pownall of Marietta and Marty Siegel of Kidder Peabody understood each other and established clear lines of authority. Bill Agee of Bendix and Jay Higgins of Salomon never seemed to understand what the other wanted.

The Agee-Higgins combination was an artificial one to begin with. John Gutfreund, the head of Salomon, and Harold Tanner of Salomon's corporate finance department, had been involved in the wooing of Mr. Agee. Alonzo McDonald, Jr., the Bendix president, was a friend of Harold Tanner, head of Salomon's corporate finance department. Even though Jay Higgins was the head of Salomon's mergers and acquisitions department he was not the best-known Salomon mergers man. That was J. Ira Harris of Salomon's Chicago office. Ira Harris' picture has been on the cover of Business Week magazine, and he is frequently quoted in the press. Jay Higgins is low-key, unfamous, rarely quoted, and is little-known outside the merger business.

Not only was Jay Higgins not well-known outside the merger business, but there seems little doubt that he and Mary Cunningham did not much care for each other. Mary Cunningham, as mentioned, worked as an intern at Salomon in the summer of 1978, and Mr. Higgins and his associates have told people that she did not make a sufficiently good enough impression to be invited back for a permanent job. Ms. Cunningham's opinion of Jay Higgins is not known, but given the history, the speculation seems reasonable that it is unlikely that he was a favorite of hers.

Although Jay Higgins looks and acts like someone born to wealth and power, he has worked himself up from humble origins. He is the son of a steelworker from Gary, Indiana, a tough mill town where, he says, "They just come up and hit you alongside the head." Jay got a grant from his parish to help pay the cost of attending the local Catholic high school, where he starred in academics and was on the football, swimming and track teams. He was accepted by Princeton, Harvard and Yale, he said, but wanted to go to the Naval Academy. After winning a competitive appointment—he came out number one among five contestants, he says—Higgins changed his mind and asked the Ivy League schools to reactivate his applications, and went to Princeton, which offered him the largest scholarship. After Princeton, Higgins managed to obtain a position in the army Reserves, but three days into basic training, army doctors told him that a shoulder injury he'd suffered during his high-school football days made him medically unfit. Instead of serving in the armed forces he went to graduate school at the University of Chicago, joined Salomon Brothers in 1970 and has been head of the firm's mergers and acquisitions department since 1978. "I guess you could say I'm competitive," he says.

Mr. Higgins is also wealthy. He was a partner in Salomon Brothers when the firm was sold to the Phibro Corporation for $550 million in 1981. He declines to say how much of that money was his, but the partners averaged $12 million apiece. Mr. Higgins, however, is not flashy, does not wear his wealth on his sleeve. Other investment bankers talk about how much money they are paid. Jay Higgins does not.

It would appear that Jay Higgins and Bill Agee could not agree about who was running the show. Like Marty Siegel, Jay Higgins was accustomed to being allowed the latitude to search out possible white knights, to help plan strategy and—

most important—to handle negotiations with outside parties. The chairmen of client companies tend not to be professional negotiators. Investment bankers can also be somewhat more frank in discussions with each other than clients can. "The idea of intermediaries has existed for thousands of years," Mr. Higgins says. "The intermediaries can say terrible things to each other, while with the principals, it's sweetness and light."

Mr. Higgins, as mentioned, says that from the start he urged Bill Agee to make a friendly approach to Tom Pownall before making a tender for Marietta but that his client declined to do so. After the Bendix-Marietta battle began, Mr. Higgins says, Bill Agee ordered him not to talk to Marty Siegel or other representatives from Marietta. (First Boston Corporation's Bruce Wasserstein, who later supplanted Jay Higgins as Bendix's banker and saw few things in the Bendix-Marietta matter the way Higgins saw them, says that he too received instructions not to negotiate with "the enemy.")

Jay Higgins says that Bill Agee did not tell him until almost the last minute in August that Bendix had already lined up lawyers and public relations firms, and that plans for a Marietta tender were already well along. During the Bendix-Marietta battle, he said, Bill Agee was holding discussions with possible white knights without telling Salomon what was going on, and paid no attention to information that Higgins gave him about the possibility of a Marietta countertender and the difference between Delaware and Maryland corporate laws posing problems. "As long as I told him what he wanted to hear, we got along great," Higgins said.

While not allowing Jay Higgins, and later Bruce Wasserstein, to conduct negotiations, Mr. Agee, who had never before been the attacker in a hostile tender offer, attempted to negotiate himself. He talked privately with executives of Esmark Incorporated and Allied Corporation, and approached at least one Marietta director, John Byrne.

Mr. Byrne, a friend of Tom Pownall, tells of having a lecture he was giving at the University of Chicago interrupted by a telephone call from Bill Agee. The call, which took place in September, after the Marietta countertender was launched, came a day after a mutual friend, whom Mr. Byrne declined to identify, had asked whether Byrne would talk to Agee.

In the middle of his speech Byrne, who says he had never before met Bill Agee or talked to him, received a note saying Agee was on the phone and wanted to talk. Byrne says he sent a note asking if the matter could wait twenty minutes until his speech was over; the answer was that Agee wanted to talk immediately.

Byrne interrupted his speech and talked to Agee. "As I remember the conversation, we didn't accomplish very much," Byrne said. "I told him, 'Please, do not underestimate the Martin Marietta board's willingness.' One of the errors Bendix made is that they didn't believe we meant it. I said, 'Mr. Agee, with all respect, we thoroughly intend to buy your stock.' He was saying, 'Please get them to talk to me.' He asked if I would use whatever influence I had to get Tom Pownall and Don Rauth (Marietta's chairman at the time) to talk to him. If it were me, I would have talked to him, but Pownall was getting advice from bankers and lawyers not to do it."

At their meeting on Monday, August 30, the Marietta directors turned down Bendix's $43 offer as inadequate, announced a countertender for Bendix and gave Tom Pownall and certain of his colleagues golden parachutes.

Tom Pownall also got a lucky tie, courtesy of Jack Byrne. During the meeting Byrne sent Pownall a note on a folded piece of lined, legal-size paper. When Pownall opened it, expecting a message, he found a tie and a note explaining that the tie was being "tendered" to him. It was Jack Byrne's lucky tie, decorated with blue pennants and emblazoned with the motto, "Don't Give Up the Ship." Byrne had worn the tie during a stock raid on Geico Corporation, the automobile insurance company he heads. He advised Tom Pownall to wear the tie night and day. After all, it had worked once and might work again. In return, Byrne took Pownall's tie. Pownall wore the tie all through the Bendix-Marietta affair. (After it was over, he said, he had the tie cleaned, encased in glass and sent back to Jack Byrne. He also attached a little hammer, so that in case of emergency Byrne could break the glass and put the tie on.)

The countertender was shrewdly conceived. Unlike the Bendix offer for Marietta, which provided $43 in cash for the first half of Marietta and $43 of Bendix stock for the second half, Marietta's tender for Bendix was front-loaded: Marietta offered $75 a share in cash for just over half of Bendix, which was then trading in the middle 50s, and offered Marietta securities that it valued at $55 per Bendix share for the second half. In retrospect, the second half of the offer was probably not worth much more than $50.

A two-tier offer is a standard offensive strategy, designed to stampede shareholders into tendering their stock early lest they miss out on the higher half of the offer. If holders do not tender early they miss the opportunity to get into the "proration pool." If, for example, a company is offering cash for 10 million shares of the target and 15 million shares are tendered, the acquiring company will buy two-thirds of the tendered shares on a prorated basis. Someone tendering, say, 150 shares will receive cash for 100 shares and will have 50 shares returned to him. If someone misses the proration pool entirely he will be stuck with the lower, second half of the offer.

(Two-tier offers seem unfair, because professional investors nearly always get into the proration pool and many small investors get left out. A small investor who may not even keep his stock certificates in his house may find it difficult to find his certificates and mail them in on time in response to a complicated offer. Even though the tender offer had to be open for fifteen business days in 1982, the proration pool could close in only ten. As of this writing, two-tier offers are still legal. Perhaps the most famous two-tier offer was U.S. Steel's 1981 acquisition of Marathon Oil. U.S. Steel paid $125 a share in cash for half of Marathon, but paid securities valued only at about $80 a share for the second half. Some large Marathon stockholders talked about taking U.S. Steel through a complicated legal process called "appraisal" to increase the second half of the offer, but nothing came of the threat.)

The fine print in the Marietta countertender made many professional investors wonder whether the company was serious. There were numerous escape clauses that allowed Marietta to withdraw the offer. One involved Bendix: If Bendix withdrew its bid for Marietta, Marietta would withdraw its bid for Bendix. When Bendix had tendered for Marietta, the value of Marietta shares rose and the trading volume soared, a sign that professional investors were betting the deal would go through. When Marietta announced its bid for Bendix, the investors were so skeptical that Bendix's price scarcely budged and volume did not surge. Bendix, however, announced plans for a quick shareholders meeting to adopt shark-repellant amendments to its corporate charter.

The Marietta board and Marty Siegel realized that the countertender did not seem credible to many people on Wall Street. "They thought we were crazies," Tom Pownall says. In any event, Marietta did not really want to buy Bendix anyway. It just didn't want to be swallowed up by Bendix. At the August 30 board meeting Marty Siegel had presented the idea of finding a partner to help split up Bendix if the Marietta countertender itself did not drive Bendix off. It was a smart move. A big mean partner would give Marietta's offer credibility on Wall Street, which meant that arbitragers might tender their shares to Marietta. If enough arbitragers tendered enough shares, Marietta felt, Bendix might call off the bid and go home. If worse came to worse, having a partner gave Marietta a much better chance of prevailing. "It evened things out," Tom Pownall says.

Meanwhile Jay Higgins, who had warned earlier about the possibility of Marietta's countertender, was nonetheless among the professionals who did not take it too seriously. He began calling it the Jonestown defense, after the eight hundred cultists in Jonestown, Guyana, who committed mass suicide in 1978 by taking poisoned soft drinks. To make his point, Higgins had one of his subordinates buy packets of KoolAid, which he distributed as souvenirs. "I thought 'Pacman' didn't capture the essence of what they were doing," Mr. Higgins explains. "Their defense was to leave dead bodies lying out in the sun."

Although the stock market and Jay Higgins did not take the countertender as a mortal threat, Bill Agee and Al McDonald seem to have been considerably upset by it. Three people who were involved in Bendix's planning sessions say that whenever the possibility of Marietta making a two-tier countertender was raised, Mr. McDonald—Jimmy Carter's former chief of staff—said that if that happened, "I could get Congress to knock it out in a minute," or words to that effect. In his previously mentioned speech in Atlanta on October 11, 1982, he called two-tier offers "inherently unfair," and added: "Over time, I believe [they] can discredit our capital/equity markets in the United States and undermine public confidence in the fairness of our pricing mechanisms." (He also said that one of the "great appeals" of the Allied Corporation offer that ended the war was that the second-stage offer for Bendix was $10 a share more than the first stage. He did not mention that Bendix's original deal with Allied, which he had voted for, had a second stage that was $10 lower than the first stage. The second stage turned out to be higher only because Allied, as will be seen later, made a separate peace with Marietta and changed the deal.)

Mr. McDonald, Mr. Agee and numerous Bendix employees would have been especially hurt if a Marietta tender with a $55 second stage succeeded. Some twenty percent of Bendix's stock was held by the Bendix Salaried Employees Savings and Stock Ownership Plan, or SESSOP. Bendix's management, which at that point thought it controlled the SESSOP shares, obviously would not tender that stock. Nor would the managers tender the stock they personally owned outside the SES-SOP. So if Marietta's bid were successful, the SESSOP and the managers' personal shares would all be stuck with the $55 second half, and many stock options would have become worthless, or virtually so.

According to Bendix's filings with the Securities and Exchange Commission, Agee had stock options on 42,000 Bendix shares at a weighted average exercise price of $52.64 a share. In a $55 second-stage deal, they would have been worth a total of only about $100,000. McDonald was even worse off. His 40,000 options had an average exercise price of $58.90, and might all have become worthless. (Some of McDonald's options might have had an exercise price below $55 a share, but there is no way to tell.)

When the Marietta countertender was announced, Bill Agee apparently decided he had had enough of Jay Higgins and Salomon Brothers and began looking for a new investment banker. "Ira Harris [the noted Salomon merger man] was never involved," says one Bendix insider, who favored dismissing Salomon. "We were all dealing with the second string. They were not very good at talking big-picture stuff with Bill. When it became clear things were getting dangerous, we began casting around."

Alonzo McDonald told the author that on Wednesday and Thursday, September 1 and 2, he and Bill Agee and other members of the Bendix executive corps talked to numerous investment banking houses seeking a replacement for Salomon.

No one the author interviewed during the research for this book could recall a similar incident in which a client openly shopped for a new banker in the middle of a difficult, contested tender-battle. Higgins said Agee never told him he was looking for a new banker, that he found out only when people telephoned him to ask what was going on.

One of those that Agee talked to was Joseph Perella, a co-manager of First Boston's mergers and acquisitions department. When the Bendix-Marietta news broke, Mr. Perella says, he spent considerable time and effort trying to find a client willing to pay a fee for First Boston to represent. Investment bankers in such circumstances generally tend to be somewhat more diffident. But according to Mr. Perella, "Whenever a situation develops in breaking news, we try to get our firm involved one way or another. It's what we do [for a living]. We've been very successful at getting in."

When the deal broke, Mr. Perella said, he tried to reach Bill Agee to see if First Boston could represent Bendix, and also tried to convince Marty Siegel of Kidder Peabody to accept First Boston as a co-investment banker on defense. (Siegel declined the help.) Also, Mr. Perella said, "We made on the order of thirty phone calls to companies that might want to buy Bendix or Martin Marietta. I called Siegel at Kidder Peabody and said I was trying to find him a white knight. I told him it wouldn't be outside the realm that we would try to be hired by Bendix."

First Boston seems most eager to come in during the middle of deals. Joseph Perella keeps on hand a list of "street brawls" —complicated tender battles in which First Boston entered in mid-fight and pulled off what Mr. Perella considers a victory. In the Bendix-Marietta situation, First Boston's notion of a defensive strategy seems to have been to sell the client at a high price.

Because Bruce Wasserstein was on vacation, Perella met with Agee to try to become Bendix's investment banker. "I said, 'You only made one mistake so far, Bill, you hired the wrong investment banker,'" Mr. Perella recalls. "I handed him the list of street brawls. I said, 'Your problem is bigger than street brawls. We're First Boston and we can help you.' I thought they had made some misjudgments about what they were going after." According to Perella, Bill Agee said he did not want to make any decisions that day because it might look as though Bendix were somehow in disarray.

On Friday, September 3, a First Boston client whom Joe

Perella declined to identify but which the author learned was Combustion Engineering, asked Perella to help decide whether it should be a white knight for Marietta if the opportunity arose. Combustion and Perella asked for and obtained confidential Marietta information from Kidder Peabody, which had prepared the material as part of Marietta's tender-defense package. The packet contained financial information not available to the general public, and anyone with access to it was subject to a confidentiality agreement that said, in effect, the material will be used only for a deal that Marietta considers friendly.

Over the Labor Day weekend, while Joe Perella was reading the confidential Marietta package for Combustion Engineering, a client thinking of bidding for Marietta, First Boston tried to approach Allied Corporation to persuade it to bid for Bendix. Asked whether this was a conflict with Combustion Engineering's interests, Bruce Wasserstein said, "We were providing a service [to Combustion Engineering]. They had not engaged us."

Still another of the calls Bill Agee made was to Felix Rohatyn of Lazard Frères. Rohatyn, through a secretary, told the author he was too busy to be interviewed for at least six months. Others have related what has become a rather famous conversation on Wall Street. Bill Agee opened by asking Mr. Rohatyn to represent Bendix to help prevent Martin Marietta from buying Bendix on the cheap. Rohatyn is said to have replied that Bendix could not hire him, that he had a client who was interested in buying Bendix. "I had a very frank conversation with Felix," Mr. Agee said. "He asked me would the company be for sale and I said, 'sure.' " Mr. Agee said Mr. Rohatyn asked him to name a price, but that he asked Rohatyn to name one first. Rohatyn said he thought Bendix was worth $60 to $65 a share, Mr. Agee said, and he told Rohatyn he thought the proper price was more like $100. To discuss that was almost the equivalent of putting out a For Sale sign. "Rohatyn came away from that meeting feeling that Agee was not averse to a deal for Bendix," says Martin Lipton, the takeover lawyer who represented Kidder Peabody.

Bill Agee would soon find out who Felix Rohatyn's client was.

When Bill Agee had begun searching for a new investment banker he apparently thought he was in trouble, though others were not sure that he really was. By the time he finished the search, he *was* in trouble.

Chapter 10

The Gray-Pownall Variation

MARIETTA, UNITED COMBINE FORCES

Almost from the time it decided to countertender for Bendix, Martin Marietta had been looking for a "white knight." A typical white knight rides to the rescue of the target company by buying it on terms more acceptable than those of the raider —paying a higher price, offering the target's top managers employment contracts, or both. But Marietta was looking for a different kind of knight, one to help it attack its attacker. Getting a knight to help on offense was a novel strategy suggested by Martin Siegel of Kidder Peabody. He was afraid— correctly, as it turned out—that a Marietta countertender without help would not draw enough Bendix shares to frighten Bendix into withdrawing its bid for Marietta.

On August 31, the day after the countertender for Bendix was announced, Marietta began negotiating with United Technologies Corporation, a giant industrial conglomerate, to launch a second tender for Bendix and divide up Bendix's assets if Bendix refused to drop its bid for Marietta. "If Bendix would go away, fine. If not, we'd carve the turkey up," says Marty Siegel. Negotiations opened with Doug Brown, one of Siegel's subordinates, calling Stillman Brown (no relation to Doug), United's executive vice-president for finance, and inquiring about making a combined attack on Bendix. Later that day, with United indicating interest, Marietta president Tom Pownall talked on the phone with his old friend, United Chairman Harry Gray. They agreed to meet on Thursday, September 2. Marty Lipton of Wachtel Lipton offered the use of his office. He was an ideal go-between: both Kidder Peabody and United Technologies are among his regular clients. (In this case, Mr. Lipton says, he obtained a waiver from Kidder and Marietta so that he could represent United as well.) Because the Marietta-United talks involved allocating Bendix assets, it made sense to have the top men, rather than intermediaries, negotiating. Harry Gray and Tom Pownall understood aerospace, the Bendix assets they were apportioning; the investment bankers did not. On the night of August 31, Felix Rohatyn called Marty Siegel at home, Siegel says, and the two men began discussing the outlines of the deal.

By the time William Agee talked with Rohatyn, Rohatyn's firm, Lazard Frères, was representing United Technologies. When Agee indicated to Rohatyn that Bendix was for sale if the price was right, what he accomplished was to increase United's interest in buying his company. According to Jay Higgins of Salomon Brothers, Agee had indicated a similar ambiguity about whether Bendix was buying or selling, during discussions before the Bendix bid for Marietta was launched. When members of the Salomon team and some of his other advisors told Bill Agee that a tender for Marietta might result in a tender for Bendix by a third company, according to Higgins, Agee remarked, "Maybe we should go and find them." Saying this to his own allies did not damage Agee's position. But to discuss price with Felix Rohatyn could only have whetted United Technologies' interest in pressing a bid for Bendix.

United did not need much encouragement. Company officials already considered the Bendix attack on Marietta a golden opportunity for United to pick off Bendix cheap. According to a high United Technologies official, Felix Rohatyn had come to Hartford for a previously scheduled lunch on

August 27, two days after Bendix attacked Marietta, and proposed that United buy Bendix and sell the antitrust problems to Marietta. United, the official said, had agreed it was an excellent suggestion.

By the time Agee had gone to see Rohatyn, he was under attack from two directions—Martin Marietta was trying to buy Bendix and sell part of the company to United Technologies, and United wanted to buy Bendix and sell part of it to Marietta. By accident, Bill Agee had come to the office of the man representing a most dangerous opponent, and had shown that he was worried about being taken over.

To show indecision or ambivalence to an opponent in the midst of a contested tender battle is like bleeding in the water near a shark—some people call Harry Gray of United Technologies the "Gray Shark" for his role in four bitterly contested takeover battles in the 1970s. "Harry Gray is a finisher," Tom Pownall says.

Mr. Gray, who is sixty-three years old, has often said that he wants United to have sales of $20 billion a year by 1985, the year he is scheduled to retire. Buying Bendix and its $4 billion of annual sales would close about two-thirds of the gap between United's 1982 revenues of $13.6 billion and Harry Gray's desired $20 billion. Buying *both* Bendix and Martin Marietta, which was a possibility if the two companies acquired positions in each other and needed to be rescued, would have put United at the $20 billion level in a single transaction.

When Tom Pownall talked to Harry Gray, he found that Gray and his takeover men at United had been following the Bendix-Marietta battle from the day Bendix announced its takeover bid. Marty Lipton says that Bendix had been on United's list of potential takeover targets for years, but United "always rejected it on the basis of insuperable antitrust obstacles." For the most part, these obstacles involved Bendix's aircraft engine controls business. United is in that business, too. But in Marietta, United had a willing buyer that would offset the antitrust problems. Tom Pownall's goal, suggested by

Marty Siegel, was to have United buy the parts of Bendix, primarily automotive and machine tools, that Marietta did not want. Harry Gray reversed the deal: he offered to buy Bendix and to sell Marietta the engine control business and other assets that United did not want.

If being pursued by Martin Marietta tended to make Bill Agee nervous, being pursued by United Technologies and Harry Gray was *guaranteed* to put him on edge. With United bidding for Bendix, Agee would be in a two-front war. Even if he devoured Marietta, there was a chance United would devour him.

Harry Gray has spent most of his life pushing his way to the top. Like many of the people involved in the Bendix-Marietta war—Tom Pownall, Jay Higgins, Ed Hennessy of Allied Corporation—Harry Gray comes from humble origins. His official biography states that he was born in 1920 in Milledgeville Crossroads, Georgia, near Augusta. Gray's father was an impoverished truck farmer. His mother died when he was six years old; shortly after, his father moved Harry and his sister Gussie to Chicago, and then disappeared. Still according to Mr. Gray's account, Gussie, fifteen years older than he, was about to place him in an orphanage but changed her mind on the way into the building, and Harry spent his grade school and high school years living in her apartment, sleeping on a folding cot.

Gray worked his way through the University of Illinois–Urbana, majoring in journalism, graduated in 1941 during World War II and became an infantryman in Europe, rising to the rank of captain by the war's end. He was awarded a Silver Star for the Battle of the Bulge and also has a Bronze Star with a *V* for valor. After the war he taught journalism at the University of Illinois while earning a master's degree. Leaving academia for the world of commerce, where he apparently felt more at home, Gray became advertising manager for a Chicago automobile dealership; he says he was the first adman to use the now familiar technique of having the dealer do his own radio commercials. He became the dealership's sales manager but left when the dealer refused to include him in on the profits. He then went into bus sales, but the Korean War reduced the steel supplies available to the bus industry. The Greyhound Corporation, however, impressed with his bus-selling skills, hired him to help solve problems at its Greyhound Movers subsidiary. He left Greyhound at least in part because the company did not have a stock option plan and did not plan to install one. In 1954, seeking a piece of the action, he became one of the first employees of Litton Industries, one of the earliest conglomerates. Litton's founder, Charles (Tex) Thornton, believed in stock options and bestowed them on successful employees.

At Litton Mr. Gray's first assignment was to organize an electrical components group by finding companies to acquire, buying them and forging a cohesive operation out of what he had bought. He did that well enough to be named a Litton vice-president in 1959. In 1963, a Litton vice-president and still running the components group, he was pinned under a guardrail when the motorcycle he was riding hit an icy patch and skidded. In twisting his body to reach the key to turn off the ignition, he broke his hip. While in the hospital recuperating from the accident, he had Litton rent the room next to his, install phone lines and put a secretary at his disposal. He worked out of the hospital for four months, then went home and worked out of his living room for four months more. By 1969 he was number three in the hierarchy, but seemed to stand little chance of becoming number one. Roy Ash, just two years older than he, was the heir apparent to Tex Thornton. Because few companies want their two top executives to be almost the same age—they both retire at about the same time —Gray could not even aspire to the number two job at Litton, so when United Aircraft offered him a job in 1971 that gave him a clear shot at becoming the top man within a few years, he left Bel Air, California, for Hartford, Connecticut. He became United Aircraft's top executive in 1972.

United's main business was its Pratt & Whitney division, which makes jet engines, and Mr. Gray was determined to expand the company to keep it from being overly reliant on the aircraft industry. He also wanted to make the company large enough so that no corporate raider would be able to attack it. But instead of making many small acquisitions, the way Litton Industries had done, he decided to make a relatively small number of big acquisitions; and remembering his early struggles, he installed a system that allowed successful United employees to acquire large bonuses.

In September of 1972 Harry Gray hired Edward Hennessy, Jr., then chief financial officer of Heublein Incorporated, to be United's chief financial officer, and the two became among the first corporate chieftains to realize the bargains that had been created in the mid-1970s by the combination of inflation and falling stock prices. United was involved in the first hostile tender offer of the contemporary wave—the Inco-ESB battle of 1974 in which Inco, a nickel company, took over ESB, a battery company, despite ESB's opposition. United entered the battle as a white knight for ESB but walked away when Harry Gray felt the price was becoming uncomfortably high. In 1976, having changed its name to United Technologies, the company bought Otis Elevator in a bitterly contested battle. It took over Carrier Corporation, an air-conditioner manufacturing company, in 1979 despite resistance from the company and the residents of Syracuse, New York, Carrier's headquarters. In 1977 United bid for Babcock & Wilcox, a maker of steam generators, but let the J. Ray McDermott Company buy B&W when the price got too high.

United has not made any hostile acquisitions since 1979 when Ed Hennessy left after the Carrier deal to run the Allied Corporation. Hennessy, who has privately claimed credit for some of United deals—Gray publicly claims credit for them—now says that Allied does not believe in making hostile acquisitions.

Harry Gray is famous for being able to cut to the heart of the matter and for having the self-control not to make high bids for contested acquisitions so as to be considered a "winner" by the news media. "Mr. Gray pays only what he thinks is appropriate," Marty Lipton says.

By September 2, the Thursday before Labor Day, it was becoming clear that the Marietta countertender for Bendix would not succeed unless Marietta got help. "The market didn't really accept our tender," Tom Pownall said. "That was worrisome. Siegel thought we needed someone to provide strength to this."

Late that afternoon Pownall met with Gray. Even though he had never been in a hostile tender battle and Gray had been in many, Tom Pownall said, he did not feel ill at ease. The two men had a long private meeting in Marty Lipton's office. "Harry Gray and I got locked in a room for a couple of hours," Pownall said. "He is someone I have known for a long time. He's shrewd, bright and capable. He's been through it many, many times and I've been through it never. [But] he doesn't stomp on someone he knows, respects and likes, and that's our relationship."

The two men made a tentative deal that was heavily in United's favor—but Marietta did not have much of a bargaining position. They agreed that United would tender for 11.9 million Bendix shares at $75 a share, about half the company, and would pay United stock worth about $50 a share for the second half of Bendix. For Bendix, of course, the United offer was even worse than the Marietta offer, which was valued at $75 in cash for the first half of Bendix and about $55 of Marietta securities for the second half.

The United-Marietta contract is on file with the Securities and Exchange Commission and is therefore a matter of public record. The contract says that Marietta agreed to pay $600 million for Bendix assets, among them the $44 million of Marietta stock that Bendix owned, plus $300 million for the Bendix engine controls business. The other assets were to be agreed on later. Marietta would pay United the $600 million as soon as United finished the cash portion of its tender for Bendix. United reserved the right to drop its tender—and to receive $2.5 million from Marietta to cover expenses—if Bendix purchased the Marietta shares tendered to it.

This was a deal virtually without risk to Harry Gray. If no deal was consummated, United stood to lose at most a few million dollars in expenses—almost a rounding error in a company so vast. If United formally withdrew its offer, the $2.5 million from Marietta would cover most or all of the costs. If United were successful it would receive a large infusion of cash: United's tender for 11.9 million Bendix shares for $75 in cash each would cost just under $900 million. But immediately afterward Marietta would pay United $600 million, reducing the company's net outlay to $300 million. When the second half of the Bendix acquisition went through, United would issue new shares of its stock, while acquiring Bendix's assets— which included cash, marketable securities and RCA stock worth about $500 million. United would thus end the deal with $200 million more in cash and easily marketable RCA stock than it started with. (The marketability of the RCA stock, that Bendix had owned, was proved on March 30, 1983, when Allied sold the stock to Salomon Brothers for about $129 million in the biggest dollar transaction in the history of the New York Stock Exchange. Within fifteen minutes, Salomon resold the shares to institutional investors, earning an estimated $2 million profit on the transaction.)

Although Harry Gray and Tom Pownall agreed on the skeleton of their deal in a few hours on Thursday, September 2, putting flesh on the bones took lawyers the entire Labor Day weekend. The major sticking point, Tom Pownall said, was that Harry Gray insisted the Bendix aircraft engine controls business was worth $300 million, but Marietta was not sure that was a fair price. "We didn't want to pay $300 million for something that was worth $150 million," Tom Pownall said.

The Marietta team, including Marty Siegel, worked all

weekend to get information to place a value on the controls
business. Now Marty Siegel's contacts from the 1980 deal in
which he had sold Warner & Swasey to Bendix came in handy.
Siegel said he was surprised at sources' eagerness to help. "My
Deep Throats reported in," he says. "One guy drove a hundred
miles to get another guy, who had just moved and didn't have
a phone in. Someone else called from a cottage in Michigan."
(Some of Siegel's sources have provided information to the
author on an off-the-record basis and have confirmed to him
that they talked to Siegel.) Without the information his sources
provided, Siegel says, Marietta might not have been able to
sign the United deal.

Although there seem to have been no leaks to the press
during the frantic Labor Day weekend, Arthur Fleischer, Jr.,
Bendix's lawyer, said his team picked up information that Marietta was talking to United Technologies. Fleischer ordered a
crash antitrust review so that Bendix would be ready to file an
antitrust suit to counter the United bid.

Ed Hennessy of Allied also found out something was going
on between United and Marietta when he interrupted a Labor
Day cruise on his boat to put in at Nantucket and play tennis.
Until that weekend, Mr. Hennessy has said, he had not had
time to catch up with newspaper stories about the Bendix-
Marietta war, but he read the papers while he was cruising. At
Nantucket, while waiting for a tennis court, he says: "I heard
someone with a voice that was very familiar running to the
phone. He was talking with somebody from New York that I
know very well, and he kept coming back to take the telephone calls. It was Harry Gray. I'm sitting there with several
other people waiting to play a game of doubles. The phone was
going off every once in a while."

Hennessy says he did not say hello to his former boss, and he
also says that when he returned to Allied after Labor Day, "I
made some calls," and started to get involved in what at that
point was a Bendix-Marietta-United Technologies struggle.

By the end of Labor Day, Monday, September 6, Marietta's

management and Kidder Peabody were convinced that Harry Gray's $300 million price tag on the Bendix controls business was not only fair but possibly low. At a special Marietta board meeting on Tuesday, September 7, the directors approved the deal with United.

Things were getting very complicated. United filed its offer with the Securities and Exchange Commission on Wednesday, September 8. It could not file on September 7, as originally planned, because the Marietta board meeting took longer than expected. There were now two tender offers outstanding for Bendix. (The United Technologies tender had the unintended effect of pushing back by a day the date that Marietta could buy the tendered Bendix shares. Before United's offer was filed, Marietta would have been free to buy Bendix shares after midnight on Tuesday, September 21, when the offer would have been open the fifteen business days required by the securities laws. But when a second company makes a tender offer for shares of a company for which there is already a tender offer outstanding, it may delay the date the first tender offerer can buy the shares. Under another provision of the securities laws, a second tender for at least five percent of a company's shares means that the first bidder cannot buy the shares tendered to him for at least ten days after the second offer was filed. If a tender offer is in its tenth day and a new offer is filed, the first offerer must wait ten days after the second offer, which has the effect of delaying the first offer by five days. If the second offer is made on the fifth day of an existing offer, it would have no delaying effect because the first offer had to be open at least fifteen days anyway. Because the United offer was filed on the sixth day that Marietta's offer was outstanding, Marietta had to wait an extra day—and so it could not buy Bendix shares until after midnight of Wednesday, September 22.)

On September 7, the day United announced it was joining the fight, Bendix announced that 58 percent of Marietta's shares had been tendered. Those shares, combined with the

4.5 percent of Marietta that Bendix already owned, gave Bendix the potential to control more than 60 percent of Marietta, except Bendix could not buy the stock until after midnight, September 16.

To make certain the tendered Marietta shares would not be withdrawn, Bendix on September 7 made a shrewd move. It increased the price it was offering from $43 a share to $48. That increase would make it very difficult for a Marietta white knight to lure shares out of the Bendix pool. Anyone withdrawing shares from Bendix would be giving up a reasonably sure $48 and would have to take a chance on another proration pool and another fifteen-day waiting period. To overcome these disadvantages a white knight would have to offer substantially more than $50 a share for Marietta—and Bendix did not think a knight could be found to pay such a price. In a sense one might say the $48 offer was also a peace gesture to Marietta.

But the entrance of United Technologies as Marietta's ally lent credibility to the Marietta tender. Instead of being involved in a $1.5 billion takeover of Bendix, which would strain Marietta's resources to the limit, Marietta was now talking about a $600 million purchase of assets. That seemed a reasonable bet, and Bendix shares began to be tendered as Wall Street concluded that there was now a good chance that Marietta would go through with the Bendix purchase. The Bendix board apparently thought so too; it gave Bill Agee and other Bendix executives golden parachutes on September 7, a step that had not been taken when only Marietta was tendering for Bendix.

The web was growing more tangled. Barring a reversal in the courts or a last-minute move by Marietta, Bendix would be in a position to own a majority of Marietta stock after midnight on September 16—the first time it could buy the tendered Marietta shares. But Bendix was also in danger of being eaten up by the Marietta–United Technologies combination. If Bendix bought the tendered Marietta shares, United was likely to exercise its right to end its tender for Bendix. But there was no guarantee that United would do so. In fact, United could continue its tender—and possibly even reduce the price it was offering on the grounds that Bendix plus Marietta was less valuable than Bendix alone.

What was worse from Bendix's point of view was that United did not need Marietta in order to solve the antitrust problems caused by buying Bendix. Having figured out what it thought was a good way to solve those problems, United could arrange to sell the antitrust problems to another company if Marietta was no longer available.

In their eagerness—indeed, desperation—to get an ally to help fight Bendix, Marietta and Kidder Peabody had set in motion a force they could not fully control: Harry Gray. Marietta could call off its own tender for Bendix if Bendix withdrew its tender for Marietta, Marietta could possibly get Harry Gray to drop United's tender for Bendix as part of a three-way settlement. But Marietta could not guarantee that no other company would *ever* attack Bendix again.

(Bill Agee says his fear of having Bendix taken over by Harry Gray in 1982, or later, contributed to some of his later actions in the Bendix-Marietta battle. Ending the matter with the three-way peace that Marietta and United offered would have left Bendix exposed to being taken over in the future. Buying Marietta, despite the formidable risks involved, might seem in a way to maintain Bendix's independence. A purchase of Marietta would use up Bendix's surplus cash and also incur substantial amounts of debt. The weaker Bendix balance sheet that would result would in turn make Bendix a less desirable takeover candidate. Indeed, getting rid of surplus cash is a standard ploy to discourage a takeover. By unleashing Harry Gray, Marietta made Bill Agee so concerned about having Bendix taken over that he chose to buy Marietta and assume the risks of that purchase rather than call off the Marietta bid and be vulnerable to United Technologies.)

With United's entrance into the battle on September 7 both Bendix and Marietta were in two-front wars. Bendix had to worry about being bought by Marietta acting by itself, or by Marietta and United acting as a team. Marietta had to worry about being bought by Bendix, or by United Technologies if Bendix and Marietta each owned majorities of each other and needed a rescuer to sort things out. The only company not in danger of being bought was United Technologies, which was and is too big to have to worry about a hostile takeover. But by having made a relatively cheap offer for Bendix—the United offer averaged out to about $62.50 per Bendix share— United was vulnerable to having a higher bidder snatch Bendix away.

Even though both United and Marietta were tendering for Bendix, Wall Street professionals tendered their Bendix shares to Marietta rather than United. Marietta would be in a position to buy Bendix stock at least ten days earlier than would United Technologies. There was also a possibility that a Bendix anti-trust suit would tie United up; there was no chance for either Bendix or Marietta to sue each other on antitrust grounds because each company was trying to buy the other.

Marietta had to keep its offer for Bendix open for both leverage and protection. If there were no Marietta tender outstanding for Bendix stock, Marietta would have no quid pro quo to offer to induce Bendix to drop its bid for Marietta. And if Marietta did not have a shot at buying Bendix, it would have to worry about the United offer for Bendix. United could allow Bendix to buy Marietta, then buy the combined Bendix-Marietta company.

As if things were not sufficiently messy, Ed Hennessy and his Allied Corporation were beginning to get into the act. Beginning the Tuesday after Labor Day, Ed Hennessy was trying for Bendix. And so was Joseph Perella, the co-director of First Boston Corporation's mergers and acquisitions department.

Joe Perella was still trying to persuade Bendix to hire First Boston. As previously mentioned, Perella spent the Labor Day weekend reading confidential Martin Marietta financial information on behalf of Combustion Engineering, a First Boston client that had been interested in becoming a white knight for Marietta. By Tuesday morning, September 7, Perella has said, he and the client had concluded that a white knight deal did not make sense. Combustion returned its copy of the confidential Marietta information to Kidder Peabody, according to Mr. Perella, and he destroyed his copy. Bruce Wasserstein, Joe Perella's fellow mergers and acquisitions co-manager, had been trying to get Allied interested in bidding for Bendix—but Allied, it seems, was attempting to work through Salomon Brothers, which had handled many Allied financing deals. Note that the two co-managers were circling around Bendix, though from different directions: Perella in search of a white knight for Marietta; Wasserstein in search of a takeover of Bendix by Allied. Bill Agee had let loose, it would seem, a pack of predators when he had launched his own move on Marietta —and now the principal target was himself and Bendix.

When news of United's involvement in the Bendix-Marietta affair moved on the Dow Jones newswire the afternoon of September 7, Mr. Perella says, he called Bill Agee's secretary and left a message that went essentially like this: "Whatever reasons you had for not bringing First Boston in are now irrelevant. If you want to use First Boston, call my partner, Bruce Wasserstein."

Joe Perella says he could not wait for Bill Agee to respond to the call because he had to catch a flight to Houston to attend a victory celebration being given by American General Corporation to mark its acquisition of the NLT Corporation. First Boston had replaced Salomon Brothers as American General's banker in the middle of the deal to acquire NLT, and Salomon retired to the sidelines. In the Bendix-Marietta war, First Boston was now asking Bill Agee to do unto Salomon Brothers what American General had done: to replace it with First Boston in the middle of a well-publicized tender war. Wars within wars, wheels within wheels . . .

On September 9 First Boston was formally hired by Bendix. But Salomon was not dismissed because Bendix did not want to anger the firm, which is a powerful force in the securities market.

Higgins says he told Agee that hiring a second firm "would be a disaster, because the bankers will be playing intramural games."

Not surprisingly, the First Boston-Salomon combination was not a felicitous one. Although neither man will say so publicly, Jay Higgins of Salomon and Bruce Wasserstein of First Boston do not especially like each other. Jay Higgins, as mentioned, comes from a poor background and climbed close to the top of Salomon Brothers, the second largest (in terms of capital) securities firm in the country. Bruce Wasserstein, who comes from a wealthy family, became a co-director of First Boston's mergers and acquisitions department shortly after joining it. Unlike Salomon, whose policy tends to restrict public statements, First Boston, a more recent entrant into the major leagues of mergers and acquisitions, has been highly public.

It is not unusual for investment bankers who work for competing clients by day to be colleagues and comrades outside the office. Not so Higgins and Wasserstein, it seems. In a variety of ways not directly traceable to them Higgins and Wasserstein have let it be known that each does not think highly of the other's credentials or competence. According to investment bankers from other firms, who specifically requested not to be identified because their firms frown on becoming associated with public disputes, First Boston suspects Salomon of spreading unfavorable stories about the firm, and Salomon suspects that First Boston has been the unnamed source of comments and stories in the *Wall Street Journal* and other publications that have published stories critical of Salomon.

Hiring First Boston and not dismissing Salomon gave Bill Agee two investment bankers who had problems with each other, including a lack of agreement on the strategy Bendix should follow. Salomon appears to have been leaning toward accepting a peace settlement from United and Marietta. Bruce Wasserstein told the author that by the time First Boston was hired, he felt the best strategy was to investigate the possibility of selling Bendix at a higher price than the $62.50 average that United Technologies was offering.

Meanwhile, both Higgins and Wasserstein say, Agee was talking to white knights without either of his bankers' knowledge, and appears to have told different stories to different advisors. Jay Higgins, for example, says that Bill Agee told him that the Fried Frank law firm had been working on a Marietta acquisition for a long time, while Fried Frank partner Arthur Fleischer, Jr. said the firm was hired by Bendix on August 18, just a week before the Marietta tender was launched. Looking back on the whole rather tangled matter, one not unreasonably might see it as an outgrowth of Bill Agee's apparent ambivalence about whether he was trying to buy Marietta or to sell Bendix.

Back to the fray, the Higgins-Wasserstein-Agee conflicts were exacerbated by the absence of Joseph Perella, Wasserstein's partner at First Boston, because Perella, having seen confidential information about Martin Marietta over the Labor Day weekend, was not allowed to become involved in representing Bendix. And thereby hangs a tale. Joe Perella says that First Boston's lawyers said that the firm could represent Bendix as long as he was not involved in any way. Now, there are no hard-and-fast rules about what is and is not a conflict of interest in such situations, but the traditional behavior for an investment banking firm in First Boston's circumstances would be simply to decline Bendix as a client altogether. It is unusual for an investment banker to take on a representation from which one of its two top men is excluded on potential conflict-of-interest grounds. Similarly in most law firms. (Bruce Wasserstein told the author that Bendix had been told Perella had been kept out of the case by conflict of interest problems. But both Bill Agee and Alonzo McDonald say they do not remember being told that. McDonald seemed a bit annoyed when the author told him about Joe Perella's conflict. "I would have been opposed to retaining them had I known that any member of their firm had had confidential access to the [Marietta] situation," Mr. McDonald said. " We had enough trouble with investment bankers. We didn't need that sort of trouble. If we had known that, I don't think we would have hired them." Wasserstein cited Arthur Fleischer, the lawyer, as someone who would confirm that Bendix had been told the nature of Perella's problem. Fleischer told the author that he could not recall.) Other investment bankers have said privately to the author and others that it was not appropriate for First Boston to accept Bendix as a client, given the circumstances. Because of the investment bankers' code (not unlike the doctors' and lawyers')—Thou shalt not run down the profession in public—no bankers made a public fuss about First Boston's participation. Joe Perella says: "There's nothing embarrassing about it," and asks if what First Boston did was somehow improper, why did not Martin Marietta or Kidder Peabody do something about it. There is, in fairness, more than a little jealousy in the criticism the competition makes of First Boston. First Boston has earned some of the largest investment-banking fees in history—$14 million for helping DuPont buy Conoco for $7.6 billion, $17 million for helping Marathon Oil sell out for $6.3 billion to U.S. Steel. It is not diffident about its success. First Boston periodically runs advertisements declaring itself number one in the mergers and acquisitions business. The firm has also benefited from favorable publicity— including full-length stories in Fortune, the *Wall Street Journal* and the New York *Times*—which tends to upset bankers who have not been so favored by print coverage. First Boston coverage stems from an interesting story capably promoted by First Boston's public relations staff, reinforced by Messrs. Wasserstein and Perella. Also, from examining First Boston's financial data, it would appear that its mergers and acquisitions operation is far more important to its profits than M&A operations are to other investment bankers. First Boston is a relatively small company, and its stock is publicly traded, hence financial data are available. With the exception of Salomon

Brothers, which is part of Phibro-Salomon, a multibillion-dollar corporation, the other major tender-offer bankers are privately owned and no precise data are available. However, the others appear to be larger than First Boston, and to have smaller M&A operations. Adding to the pressure on Wasserstein and Perella to produce ever-larger fee revenues is that First Boston's stock was exceptionally strong in 1981 and 1982 in part because of the large fees generated by mergers and acquisitions. A fall-off in those fees might well damage the stock. The M&A department appears to be First Boston's second largest money-maker after securities trading.

By contrast, mergers and acquisitions are relatively small potatoes at Salomon Brothers. Salomon is so large that on occasion it buys entire issues of well over $1 billion of Treasury securities directly from the United States government and puts them into its own inventory to be resold. For a firm like that, M&A fees are far less important than they are to First Boston, and far less stress is put on the M&A department. In the midst of the Bendix-Marietta war, Allied did a so-called debt-equity swap with Salomon, giving Salomon newly issued stock in return for existing Allied bonds Salomon had bought from institutional investors. The profit on that deal, plus the approximately $2 million Salomon cleared on the previously mentioned sale of Allied's RCA stock, probably equaled the $2.9 million fee that Bendix paid for Salomon's M&A services. With a firm like Salomon behind him, Jay Higgins could and can afford to be less aggressive than Bruce Wasserstein, whose department is a vital profit center for his company. It should also be noted that several other investment bankers were trying to get a piece of the Bendix-Marietta action. And there is no question that other investment banking firms are fee-hungry—fees, after all, are what investment bankers are in business for. But it would also appear that among them First Boston was special in its attitude of operating on offense, defense or in representing a white knight for either side.

On any case, the absence of Joe Perella meant that Bendix

was getting only the more publicized half of the First Boston team rather than the team. Perella and Wasserstein complement each other and are a formidable pair; they do not seem as effective when they operate separately and alone. Wasserstein is brilliant—when one talks to him, words, ideas and concepts spew forth, some of them showing great insight. He tends to see mergers as a great game and is always on the lookout for new gambits. His forte appears to be offense—he has perfected the front-loaded, two-tier bid, and also the "crown jewel" strategy of locking up a target's prime assets on behalf of a white knight—but his defense work does not seem as strong. He gets higher prices on behalf of his defense clients but rarely does the client end up not being sold. Wasserstein, an intense man, seems to love the battle for its own sake; the people involved tend to be obscured in the smoke of combat. Joe Perella seems a perfect partner for Bruce Wasserstein. He is calm, witty, explains things carefully and struck the author as being altogether forthcoming. He may lack some of Wasserstein's brilliance, but he also comes across as more reassuring, balanced in his views and presentation. Certain other investment bankers told the author that they prefer to deal with Perella, who is more a member of the club.

Combining Bruce Wasserstein and Bill Agee, in the absence of Joe Perella's moderating influence, put together two impatient men who seemed driven to succeed. At the same time, by hiring First Boston, William Agee was dealing with what is arguably the best investment banking house on Wall Street when it comes to playing war games and inventing new moves. What might, however, have better served Bendix, its shareholders and employees was a banker willing and able to restrain him.

Of course, as subsequent events showed, Bill Agee did not want to be restrained.

Chapter 11

Double Check

BENDIX, MARIETTA IMPERIL EACH OTHER

While William Agee was hiring Bruce Wasserstein of First Boston to serve as Bendix's primary investment banker, its target, Martin Marietta, was carying out a campaign to capture a key block of Bendix stock—the 4.5 million shares held in the Bendix Salaried Employees Savings and Stock Ownership Plan. The SESSOP was by far the largest collection of Bendix shares in one place. The SESSOP shares, owned by about 16,000 Bendix employees, represented about 23 percent of Bendix's 19.3 million shares of common stock and a bit less than 20 percent of the 23.7 million that would be outstanding on a "fully diluted" basis—that is, if holders of securities convertible into Bendix common stock converted them, and all the holders of stock options exercised them.

In its planning, Bendix assumed that the SESSOP stock was firmly under management's control and would therefore not be tendered if Marietta counterattacked against Bendix. "Everyone thought the twenty-three precent ownership by our own employees was an enormous shark repellant," Bendix president Alonzo McDonald, Jr., told the author. There was good reason to think that. Even if Bendix employees wanted to desert the company en masse and tender their shares, there was no way for them to do so. The SESSOP had many restrictions, and one of them made it impossible for SESSOP participants to withdraw their shares until September 30 at the earliest, unless Bendix waived the rules. Bendix, of course, would not do so.

Without the SESSOP shares, Marietta's tender for Bendix had almost insurmountable problems. It was vital to Marietta that its tender for Bendix draw at least 11.9 million shares—just over half of Bendix's stock on a fully diluted basis—by midnight on Thursday, September 9. That was when the proration pool for the Marietta offer for Bendix closed. Marietta, of course, was offering a two-stage deal—$75 in cash for the first half of Bendix, $55 (or less) of Marietta securities for the second half—with the goal of filling the proration pool. The $20 difference between the first and second stages was intended to stampede Bendix holders into tendering early to get into the proration pool—the shares eligible for the $75 part of the offer. If even the $20 difference could not attract enough shares to fill the proration pool, it would be an unmistakable sign to professional investors—and to Marietta's board of directors—that the offer was almost sure to fail. Not filling the pool could have led to professionals withdrawing their shares, and that would have meant that Marietta would have lost its leverage on Bendix. Marietta, after all, was not so much trying to buy Bendix as to scare it.

Despite the credibility of Marietta's offer gained when United Technologies appeared, simple arithmetic made it all but impossible to fill the proration pool without SESSOP shares. Marietta needed 11.9 million Bendix shares. Not counting the SESSOP stock, there were fewer than 15 million common shares left. Marietta could not expect to get any of the 800,000 Bendix shares that were under option to Bendix employees. And many holders of the Bendix securities convertible into about 3.6 million shares of Bendix common stock were not likely to tender either. Convertible securities trade at a premium above the value of the shares into which the securities can be converted. To tender Bendix convertibles, a holder had to convert the security, then tender the resulting common stock. If Marietta did not buy the tendered stock, a former convertible holder could not undo the conversion. He would be left with common stock that would always be worth less money than the convertible security. The risks of tendering were thus far greater for holders of convertible securities than for holders of common stock.

In any case, drawing 11.9 million shares required Marietta to attract almost eighty percent of the non-SESSOP common stock—an almost impossible task. And so the Marietta raid on the SESSOP. Although individuals owned the SESSOP stock, the shares were registered to Citibank of New York City, whose trust department administered the plan and held the stock as custodian for the SESSOP participants. When Martin Marietta began its countertender for Bendix, both Bendix and the Citibank trust department agreed that the bank did not have the authority to tender SESSOP shares to Marietta. The author has been told this by Agee, McDonald and numerous other people. If the bank did not tender the shares, there was no way for Marietta to attract the SESSOP stock, because the owners themselves could not withdraw SESSOP stock in time to tender it.

But on September 8, the day before the proration deadline of the Marietta offer for Bendix, Marietta attacked. L. Robert Fullem of Dewey, Ballentine, Bushby, Palmer & Wood, Marietta's New York City law firm, has said that he warned Citibank that Marietta's two-tier offer for Bendix exposed the bank to potential liability if it failed to tender the SESSOP shares on behalf of the shares' owners. If the Marietta bid for Bendix succeeded, Fullem said, Bendix employees who owned SESSOP shares that qualified only for the low part of Marietta's offer might be able to sue Citibank for the difference between the $75 first stage and $55 second stage. This represented a potential liability of some $90 million.

On Thursday September 9, Mr. Fullem has said, he threatened Citibank with a lawsuit by Marietta and a second one by a Bendix employee, unless the bank tendered the Bendix SES-SOP shares. He argued that Bendix employees would have until September 22 to withdraw their shares from the Marietta pool if they did not want to sell; but if Citibank did not tender the shares the employees would be denied a choice.

It is not clear that Citibank had the power to tender the shares; in a 1981 tender for four million of its own shares, Bendix said in a formal prospectus describing the offer: "The trustee of SESSOP does not have discretionary authority to tender shares pursuant to the offer." On September 9 Citibank was preparing a letter, never sent, to SESSOP participants explaining that the stock would not be tendered to Marietta.

But late that night Citibank did tender the stock. According to a Bendix press release, the company did not find out until 10:30 P.M. that Citibank planned to tender, and by then it was too late to do anything. At 10:30, Bendix said, a messenger delivered a letter to Harold Barron, Bendix's general counsel, notifying him of the decision to tender. Barron, the release said, "immediately responded to the messenger that the act was unauthorized by the provisions of the plan and demanded the immediate withdrawal of the offer. The messenger responded that there was no one available at that hour to whom he could address his demand or who could act for the bank."

On Friday, September 10 Marietta announced that 14.5 million shares of Bendix had been tendered and the proration pool was filled to overflowing. Without the 4.5 million SESSOP shares, there would have been only 10 million shares in the pool, well under the 11.9 million shares Marietta was seeking. The filling of the Marietta pool hurt Bendix badly by making it *look* like Marietta might be able to win. "Psychologically, it was unbelievable," Bill Agee told the author. "It was a serious, serious blow."

Agee attributes Citibank's decision to tender the Bendix SESSOP shares to "apparent conflicts of interest" on the bank's part. United chairman Harry Gray sits on the board of Citicorp, the bank's parent company, and a top Citicorp executive, Willard Spencer, sits on United's board. Agee offered no particular evidence to back up his charges; he merely implied that the bank had somehow been pressured by Gray.

"I think it's interesting," Agee said, "that Harry Gray is on the fiduciary committee of Citibank [which oversees the trust department], and he happens to be on the board, there happen to be some interlocks." The bank has said, in a statement, that its only purpose in tendering the SESSOP stock was to give Bendix SESSOP holders an opportunity to sell to Marietta if they so chose.

Even though more than 95 percent of the SESSOP shares were ultimately withdrawn by Bendix employees, Marietta had scored a considerable triumph. It announced that 75 percent of Bendix's stock had been tendered—a gross exaggeration but one that Bendix never rebutted. The 14.5 million tendered Bendix shares represented 75 percent of the Bendix common stock outstanding at the time, but only about 60 percent of the shares outstanding on a fully diluted basis. It is the custom in takeover situations to use fully diluted numbers because in a takeover, convertible securities are converted and stock options are exercised. Bendix could have responded by calling Marietta's math into question, and by pointing out that the Bendix offer for Marietta drew about 60 percent of Marietta's stock—the same proportion on a fully diluted basis that Marietta's offer for Bendix drew—without a $20 difference between the first and second stages of the offer.

The only explanation for that apparent public relations failure, as well as for the failure to safeguard the SESSOP stock, would seem to be that Marietta, in effect, caught Bendix napping. William Agee and Alonzo McDonald say they were keeping a close eye on the SESSOP stock—but clearly Marietta managed to keep an even closer eye on it. Bendix apparently did not know that Marietta was working so hard to pry loose the SESSOP block, which was considered untouchable.

Bendix's public relations strategy, like its SESSOP strategy, remains puzzling. Alonzo McDonald, who tends to a political view of things safeguarded Bendix's flanks in Washington. By sending one of his chief subordinates, Michael Rowney, to Washington and thereby putting Bendix's Washington connections into play, McDonald forestalled Marietta's attempts to hold up Bendix through congressional or Pentagon pressure.

But Bendix's news-media strategies were not so sophisticated. The company decided not to allow members of the Bendix team to comment beyond the company's press releases, which were often couched in legalistic terms. Robert Meyers, Bendix's director of communications, told the author the company withheld comment because it did not want to tip its hand to Marietta. "If we had won, everyone would say it was a brilliant strategy," he said.

Marietta, it would seem, had a better strategy—and managed to implement it without tipping its hand to Bendix. Marietta's story was skillfully told by Martin Siegel of Kidder Peabody, and by members of Kekst & Company, a New York City public relations firm, even though Marietta executives themselves only rarely commented. (Bendix hired one of the nation's best-regarded financial public relations men, Richard Cheney of Hill & Knowlton, but apparently disregarded much of his advice and restricted his freedom to tell Bendix's story.)

According to a Kekst executive, who asked to remain unnamed, Kekst wanted to make Bill Agee's personal life an issue, but Marietta forbade it. Marietta, however, did not need to make Bill Agee an issue. He already was one—and the Bendix PR strategy only tended to make matters worse. Because they had to produce a daily story and could get little new information or insights from Bendix either on or off the record, many journalists played and replayed the Bill Agee-Mary Cunningham record, or rehashed the March 1982 statement by RCA: "Mr. Agee has not demonstrated the ability to manage his own affairs, let alone someone else's." (Mr. Agee asserts that RCA chairman Thornton Bradshaw apologized to him for that statement; Mr. Bradshaw declined to be interviewed.)

Bendix's attempts to cope with the SESSOP debacle were not especially deft. It ordered Citibank to withdraw the tendered SESSOP shares unless individual Bendix employees said they wanted their shares tendered. But a federal judge in New York City ruled that the shares would remain tendered unless individuals ordered them withdrawn; a sort of negative-option situation. Marietta charged in a lawsuit that Bendix pressured employees in several ways, including keeping lists of those who failed to return tender-withdrawal cards to their superiors. There appears to be something to this charge: a Bendix employee fired after the author interviewed him said that his superior kept such a list, and that one reason he was dismissed was that he objected loudly and publicly to the pressure brought to bear on him. The former employee asked not to be named because he said he does not want a reputation as a troublemaker to follow him to a new job. He is one of the few who refused to withdraw shares; ultimately, fewer than 100,000 of the 4.5 million SESSOP shares remained tendered.

In addition to apparent pressure from superiors to withdraw tendered shares, William Agee told plan-participants by letter that those who did not withdraw their shares would be ineligible to participate in the SESSOP for six months. The SESSOP, to which Bendix and its employees both contributed, was one of the company's major fringe benefits.

Even though the bulk of the SESSOP shares were withdrawn, damage had been done: another example of how Marietta, supposedly on defense, was at least taking the play away from Bendix.

The SESSOP struggle was only one of the problems besetting Bill Agee following United Technologies' entrance into the battle.

For starters, according to interviews he gave in late September, he was not getting much sleep in the latter stages of the struggle. He seems to have had a problem making up his mind whether his primary goal was to buy Marietta or to sell Bendix for a rich price. He also considered other alternatives. "I met

with lots of people," he told the author, "talking about everything from selling a division, [selling] the whole company, taking the company private, everything you can imagine."

Adding to such confusion was that Mr. Agee appeared to
have gotten conflicting advice—both because of whom he
hired to represent Bendix and because of the way he ran the
show. After United's appearance, Mr. Agee and Jay Higgins of
Salomon Brothers spoke to each other very little. When Agee
hired First Boston Corporation and Bruce Wasserstein, he did
not, as mentioned, dismiss Salomon: "You've got a choice," Mr.
Agee said to the author. "Do you kick them in the face two
ways or just one way . . . We didn't need any more enemies."
But Bendix's two investment bankers, Higgins and Wasserstein, disliked each other and had different ideas about how to
proceed. Jay Higgins, by his own account, counseled concilia-
tion with Marietta; Bruce Wasserstein wanted a more aggressive course.

Arthur Fleischer, Jr., Bendix's lead lawyer, was urging a
legalistic strategy that depended heavily on lawsuits and was
based on the assumption that no court would allow Marietta
and Bendix to buy majorities of each other. Because Bendix
could buy first, this implied that Marietta would somehow be
blocked from buying Bendix. ("This was a situation where people carried a concept to its logical conclusion, expecting that
at some point an institution would say, 'Okay, you've gone far
enough,' " Mr. Fleischer has said, "but it never happened.")

It seems understandable that investment bankers Jay Higgins and Bruce Wasserstein see the battle in differing tactical
terms, while attorney Arthur Fleischer sees things in legal
terms. Each according to his training. It is, though, up to the
leader, in this case William Agee, to lay down overall strategy.
Differences among team members are usually resolved in
meetings and the team adopts a unified approach. Agee sent
out conflicting signals, and seems to have had only one full
meeting—and that a few days after the Bendix bid for Marietta
was launched. Large meetings can be contentious and un-

wieldy, but they have their uses in situations such as Bill Agee found himself, with strong-willed advisors pulling in different directions. A full-scale meeting allows everyone to hear what the other team members have to say, and to critique each others' ideas. But, says Bendix public relations director Bob Meyers, William Agee tends to be uncomfortable in big meetings: "That's not Bill's style." So there were small meetings, in which only Bill Agee heard all of what various participants in various meetings had to say; other members of the team were pretty much left in the dark.

Agee, who did not fully confide in his investment bankers and lawyers, also did not confide fully in Alonzo McDonald, his second in command. "There were many, many scenarios," Agee told the author. "You know some of them . . . Al McDonald knows of all of them except one. There are some that only I know."

It would appear that the person in whom Agee did confide was Mary Cunningham Agee, who has said that she was his primary advisor during the takeover battle. "It was almost decision-tree analysis I was giving him," Ms. Cunningham was quoted as saying in Savvy magazine ("Unlimited Partnership," November 1982). "[I said,] 'The following is unfolding and here are the options, here is how your decisions are changing, here are the consequences.' "

Consider the difference in the ways Thomas Pownall of Martin Marietta and William Agee of Bendix conducted themselves during the biggest crisis of their business lives. Pownall confided in Martin Siegel of Kidder Peabody, in some of the Dewey Ballantine lawyers and at almost all times had at least one other Marietta executive available to talk to. He also talked to longtime friends such as John Byrne of the Geico Corporation (who lent him the "Don't Give Up the Ship" lucky tie), and Harry Gray. Agee, on the other hand, appears primarily to have had Mary Cunningham, who had no experience as an aggressor in a hostile tender offer. By Ms. Cunningham's own account, as printed in Monthly Detroit magazine's March 1983 issue, she gave her husband gifts and dinner invitations to ease the tension. He seems to have spent much time only with her talking about the deal.

The problems Agee was confronting in September of 1982 were far more serious than those Ms. Cunningham had faced two years earlier when publicity led the Bendix board of directors to force her out of the company. At the time Ms. Cunningham was twenty-nine years old and had only a job to lose. In September of 1982, Mr. Agee was forty-five years old and faced the loss of not only a job but of the reputation for financial wizardry he had spent twenty years building. When Ms. Cunningham had her problems in 1980, she first vacillated on the question of resigning, until the directors requested her resignation. Then, by her own account, she took losing her position so seriously that she considered suicide . . . "When people consider suicide," Savvy magazine quoted her as saying, "it's generally when everything is taken out of their control. That's what happened to me." Such is not exactly the coolness under fire that one might hope for in an advisor during a crisis.

With the pressure mounting on Bendix and Agee, the company tried a long-shot, high-risk strategy to extricate itself from its trouble—a strategy that Agee in early 1983 told the author was "a terrible mistake." That strategy was to fend off Marietta and United Technologies by adopting "shark repellant" amendments to Bendix's corporate charter. These amendments, which required approval from owners of a majority of Bendix's shares, would have made it impossible for a company making a two-tier offer such as Marietta's or United's to take Bendix over.

The question of adopting shark repellants had been raised more than a year earlier by the Bendix legal staff, which sent Alonzo McDonald a long memo describing charter amendments the company might adopt to make it virtually invulnerable to a hostile tender. Bendix had done nothing about those recommendations. McDonald told the author that neither he nor Agee had acted on the memo because it was a laundry list of the things Bendix could do, but was not a short, concise list of what Bendix *should* do. "We glanced at it," Mr. McDonald said. "From my point of view, it was an excellent compilation of boilerplate. It involved most of the items repugnant for a public corporation to consider if its primary interest happens to be shareholder value." Had the lawyers presented a list of amendments tailored to Bendix's circumstances, McDonald said, he would have acted on the memo.

One of the responsibilities of a company's top managers is to anticipate problems. When the lawyers raised the question of Bendix's vulnerability, one might suggest that it was arguably the job of both Mr. McDonald and Mr. Agee to do something about the problem rather than not to act because they did not like the form in which the lawyers' ideas for dealing with it was submitted. Had the shark-repellant amendments been in place it would have been near-impossible for Marietta to counter-attack against Bendix. As it was, the company persisted in trying to pass the amendments in the middle of a contested tender—the worst possible time.

Many Bendix shareholders had tendered their stock and wanted the takeover to go through. Bendix did not need just a majority of the shares voting at the special shark-repellant meeting . . . it needed a majority of all Bendix shares outstanding. Even voting all the SESSOP shares in favor of shark repellants would have left the company well short of a majority.

The shark-repellant amendments were initially proposed by Bendix on August 30 but were not seriously pushed until after United Technologies entered the battle, by which time it was very difficult to round up a majority. The special meeting was scheduled for September 21, just one day before Marietta would be free to buy tendered Bendix shares. Making a major effort to round up votes to pass the shark repellants made it appear that Bendix was seriously worried about being taken over—the exact opposite of what the company wanted to convey.

Had the repellants somehow been adopted, the battle would have been over. Without a chance to gain control of Bendix, the Marietta board would surely not have allowed the company to borrow $900 million to buy Bendix shares. In fact, one of the conditions in Marietta's tender offer was that the shark repellants not be adopted; if they were, Marietta was free to drop the offer.

Meanwhile, Bendix was delaying United Technologies with antitrust obstacles, but they were far from a sure thing. It was possible that United would figure out a way around the obstacles and then gobble Bendix up. And stopping United did not necessarily mean stopping Marietta. It was still possible that Marietta would buy a majority of Bendix, take control, end the antitrust actions Bendix had brought, then divide the company with United Technologies.

Threatened though it might be, Bendix was in less immediate danger from Marietta than Marietta was from Bendix. Despite any number of maneuvers, Marietta had the same problem it had started with: it could not overcome Bendix's six-day lead, and Bendix showed no sign of being so frightened as to call off its tender. Even though a majority of Bendix shares had been tendered to Marietta, Bendix showed it was not buying Marietta's terms: Marietta would buy Bendix's Marietta stock at a price to be negotiated; the tender offers and lawsuits by Bendix, Marietta and United would all end; and the three companies would go about their respective businesses.

And delaying tactics on Marietta's part—such as getting a "partial white knight" to tender for just enough Marietta stock, 5 percent, to force Bendix to wait ten more days before buying tendered Marietta shares—would play into Bendix's hands. Bendix could find a partial knight, too, and stall Marietta for ten days. And the more time Bendix had, Marietta felt, the greater Bendix's chance of rounding up sufficient votes to adopt the shark repellants.

Point counter-point . . .

On the weekend of September 11 and 12, Marty Siegel of Kidder Peabody, and the Marietta lawyers came up with yet another novel strategem that represented smart tactics, but questionable strategy. Indeed, the strategem was unprecedented, and so outlandish that almost no one on the Bendix side believed that Marietta was serious.

In yet another display of its dry corporate humor, missile-maker Marietta called the new move "assured second-strike capability." But "doomsday machine" or "deadman's trigger" was perhaps a more apt description. A doomsday machine as found in science fiction movies; all life on earth is destroyed because the machine, once started, cannot be turned off. The point of a doomsday machine is to show the other side that even if it wins, it loses. But this maneuver, like the decision to involve Harry Gray and United Technologies in the battle, created a force that Marietta could not control.

Tender offers are usually filled with escape clauses to allow an offer to be called off in case of "materially adverse" developments in lawsuits, or a deterioration in the target company's business or financial condition, or the issuance by the target of new shares, or the declaration of an unusually large dividend. On Monday, September 13, in full public view, the Marietta board disconnected all the fail-safe buttons except two. Marietta was now legally obligated to buy the Bendix shares that remained tendered after midnight on September 22 *regardless of whether Bendix by then owned a majority of Marietta,* unless Bendix withdrew its bid for Marietta or passed amendments to the Bendix charter. To make certain that Bendix did not miss the point, Marietta president Thomas Pownall issued a statement saying that Marietta wanted it "explicitly understood" that it would buy the tendered Bendix shares "even if Bendix may have earlier purchased Martin Marietta shares under the terms of its tender."

Unfortunately, what Marietta was doing was not "explicitly understood" by Bendix—or even taken seriously. It was another communications failure, caused by the fact that neither Bendix nor Marietta understood the motives or the people on the other side. Bendix did not realize the depth of Marietta's distaste for Bill Agee's kind of management, and Marietta's tendency to identify itself with the national defense effort and to be willing to die in a good cause. Marietta did not understand that to Bendix, the entrance of Harry Gray signaled that Bendix had to eat Marietta or be eaten itself. Bendix viewed the doomsday machine in Bendix's own terms: a semantic obstacle that could be easily overcome with the right kind of semantic maneuver.

The leaders of the Marietta effort, Tom Pownall and Marty Siegel, were straightforward men not given to semantics. They thought the message they sent was so clear that no sensible corporate executive would risk both companies by buying Marietta shares.

But the leaders of the Bendix effort—Bill Agee, Mary Cunningham, Arthur Fleischer, Al McDonald and Bruce Wasserstein—were different kinds of people. They were into word games, niceties of meanings. Because no one on the Bendix side could imagine blowing up one's own company to save it from capture, they did not understand that Marietta was prepared to go down in flames if its bluff was called.

(An example of this difference came on September 16 when Bendix thought it gave Marietta an escape by adopting two minor changes to the Bendix bylaws. The Marietta condition did not specifically list the Bendix shark repellants; it simply gave Marietta the right to withdraw its tender if the Bendix corporate charter were amended. One of the new Bendix bylaws set the number of directors at fourteen. The other, according to Bendix, provided "that no person may serve as a director of Bendix who has violated any substantive duty owing to Bendix or to any corporation a majority of whose outstanding shares are owned by Bendix." To Bendix, these changes gave Marietta enough leeway to disconnect the machine. To Marietta, the changes were irrelevant, because even though its tender did not specify which charter amendments would nullify the offer, everyone knew that Marietta had the shark repellants in mind.)

"The doomsday machine was absolutely nothing to us . . . We didn't believe any responsible management would decapital-ize their company," Alonzo McDonald told the author. "Did we think they were irretrievably committed to it?" Bill Agee said to the author. "No." But Marietta directors *were* irretriev-ably committed. Despite the ingenious escapes Bill Agee and Arthur Fleischer later offered Marietta, the company's direc-tors felt they were compelled to buy the tendered Bendix stock because they had given their word to do so, and their lawyers produced an opinion to that effect. Not until almost the last minute did Bendix understand that Marietta was de-termined to let the doomsday machine detonate. By then, the machine could not be stopped.

Marietta's Tom Pownall told the author that even though he and the other Marietta directors felt the company had made its resolve crystal clear, he should have had a man-to-man talk with Bill Agee to make him understand that Marietta was deadly serious. "The one thing I should have done and didn't do," Tom Pownall said regretfully, "was talk to him. I should have found him, wherever he was, and I should have directed some very strong talk to him." And Bill Agee says, "I should have been insistent to see Pownall sooner."

The two men did not fully realize the great gulf between them until the week of September 20, after Agee had bet $1,200,000,000 of Bendix's money that Marietta would not go through with its tender, and Marietta was about to spend $900 million on Bendix stock. By then it was too late.

And by the time Agee and Pownall finally did get together, the game's fourth player had taken a seat at the table. Allied Corporation, whose chairman, Edward Hennessy, Jr., had been pressing to join the fray since Labor Day, was about to add a fourth ring to the Bendix-Marietta-United Technologies circus.

Chapter 12

The Agee-Hennessy Variation
BENDIX, ALLIED COMBINE FORCES

By September 13, the day Martin Marietta unveiled its doomsday machine, the Allied Corporation was already beginning to affect the Bendix-Marietta battle. The entrance of Allied was almost inevitable, given Allied's need for profitable operations in the United States, Edward Hennessy, Jr.'s rivalry with United Technologies' Harry Gray as a dealmaker and the cheap price Gray was offering for Bendix.

From May of 1979, when Ed Hennessy took it over, through September of 1982, Allied had bought four sizable U.S. companies, spending almost $2 billion in the process. Allied was heavily dependent on oil and natural gas for its profits, but most of its oil and gas operations were outside the U.S. Allied's U.S. operations—including chemicals, fibers, plastics, electronic products and health products—were not very profitable.

So in the fall of 1982 Allied had more than $100 million in unused United States federal income tax credits, with little prospect of earning enough money on its U.S. operations to make use of them. In 1981, to realize some value from the credits, Allied sold some at a discount to other corporations. That same year Bendix was making so much money in the U.S. that it bought credits from other companies to reduce its tax bill. Combining Allied and Bendix would produce what analysts call "tax synergy." Allied credits could be used to offset some of the Bendix profits. In effect, Allied could use tax credits to reduce the cost of buying Bendix.

For financial reasons, then, Allied was a logical candidate to rescue Bendix from Marietta's white knight, United Technologies, which had no such unused tax credits. Ed Hennessy was trying to supplement Allied's chemicals, fibers and plastics businesses—which for the most part required large capital expenditures but did not earn much money, with new businesses that could generate profits and required low investment. Bendix's businesses were much more attractive than many of Allied's own businesses. Since companies the size of Bendix do not often come on the market, Ed Hennessy was eager to land the company if he possibly could.

On a personal level, too, Bendix was undoubtedly attractive to Hennessy. Before taking over at Allied, Mr. Hennessy had been the number two man at United Technologies. Both Ed Hennessy and United's Harry Gray are financial men by training and consider themselves takeover experts. The two, as mentioned, collaborated on most if not all of United's major acquisitions during the 1970s. But understandably the spotlight at United was focused on one man—and that man was not Edward L. Hennessy, Jr.

Harry Gray's arrangement with Marietta to buy Bendix was so favorable that Allied could pay more and still have a good deal. United was going to pay $75 a share—just under $900 million—for 11.9 million Bendix shares, and United securities worth about $50 per share for the other nearly 11.8 million Bendix shares—some $600 million in all. This made a purchase price of $1.5 billion (not counting the Bendix debts that United would assume). Marietta would pay United $600 million for the Marietta stock Bendix owned and for parts of Bendix's aerospace business and other assets, thereby reducing United's cost to $300 million in cash and $600 million in securities. Further, if United succeeded it would get some $500 million of Bendix cash, securities and RCA stock, producing a net cash inflow of $200 million on the deal and reducing the overall cost to United for Bendix's remaining businesses to $400 million. For that United would own a substantial auto parts business, the second largest machine tool operation in the country, plus odds and ends that could be sold to generate more cash. In effect, Harry Gray's United would be buying Bendix with Bendix's own assets.

On Wall Street Ed Hennessy of Allied is generally regarded as a somewhat impatient and excitable man whereas Harry Gray is regarded as something of a human computer. Taking the Bendix deal away from Gray and United would represent a substantial business as well as psychological victory for Hennessy, given the background relationship of Hennessy and Gray.

Ed Hennessy, fifty-five years old, loves to win. A highly competitive man, he grew up in West Roxbury, Massachusetts, the son of a lumber salesman. He boxed until he was defeated in a Golden Gloves bout, and spent three years in seminary at Notre Dame, leaving when he decided he had no calling for the priesthood. When asked a few years ago to name his two favorite authors, he selected Saint Thomas Aquinas and Saint Jerome. He is also fond of Gregorian chants.

"When I got out of the seminary," he said in an interview with Forbes magazine in 1981, "my mother said to me, 'You can't make a living translating Latin and Greek, so you ought to find something else to do.' So here I am."

He was an assistant controller at Textron from 1950 through 1955, attending Fairleigh Dickinson University at night and graduating with a bachelor of science degree. After Textron came group controller with Lear Siegler (1956–60), controller at International Telephone & Telegraph (1960–64), director of finance for Europe, the Middle East and Africa for Colgate-Palmolive (1964–65), vice-president and senior vice-president at Heublein Incorporated (1965–72), United Technologies (1972–79) and finally, Allied.

The biggest influence on him, Mr. Hennessy says, is Harold Geneen, the former ITT chairman, whom he calls "my mentor." (On Christmas Eve of 1982, he says, Geneen called to say he had just finished reading the 277-page prospectus describing the Allied-Bendix-Marietta deal, and that it was a good one for Allied. "I said to him, 'For Christ's sake, don't you have anything better to do on Christmas Eve?' But that's Harold Geneen.")

Geneen was famous for running ITT strictly by the numbers. He demanded detailed accounts from all his executives, and met with them frequently and at length, meetings that terrified almost everyone involved except, of course, Geneen. Hennessy traces his rise in Geneen's affections to a night when he told the big man off in front of other executives. As Hennessy recalls it, it was about 1:00 A.M., eight hours after he had been scheduled to present a report, when Geneen began criticizing it and its author. Hennessy told Geneen it was obvious he had not read the report because the questions he was asking were all answered in it. Hennessy then stalked out, not knowing if he would have a job to return to in the morning.

The reason he did leave ITT, Hennessy says, was that he was working in Europe and "Geneen was going to transfer me to another country. My wife said, 'No way. We're going home. You can go to another country, but I'm going home.' Geneen had made a commitment we'd only stay there a number of years, and my time was served. But then he was going to change his mind and send me somewhere else."

In his early days at Allied, which was in worse financial shape than it appeared to be, he sold or closed money-losing or marginally profitable businesses and caused seven hundred employees at Allied's headquarters in Morristown, New Jersey to be fired, thereby cutting overhead by $30 million a year.

His office is dominated by a large picture of a Philippine eagle, presented to him by Armco Steel. Allied was being sued by Armco for $80 million when Hennessy arrived, and he settled the suit—which involved a contract under which Allied was to provide coking coal for an Armco plant—by paying $20 million cash and a coal mine valued on Allied's books at $14 million. In return he got the picture. When he took it home, Mr. Hennessy says, his wife suggested, firmly, that it belonged in his office. Hennessy later gave Armco's chairman a Steuben glass eagle.

Hennessy says nothing bad about Harry Gray—the two men agreed publicly in 1979 that Hennessy's major reason for leaving was that Gray did not plan to retire until 1985 at the earliest and that Ed Hennessy did not want to wait that long for a chance at United's top job.

Hennessy can make his point obliquely but also clearly. During an interview with the author he pointedly said, "I do not worship at the altar of the Fortune Five Hundred"—an obvious reference to Harry Gray's oft-expressed desire to make United a $20-billion-a-year company by 1985. And in the previously mentioned 1981 interview with Forbes Hennessy took credit for some of the United acquisitions—Essex International, Otis Elevator and Carrier Corporation—of which Harry Gray is also rather proud. In the case of Essex, United's first major acquisition, "I couldn't get anybody even interested in it at United" for several months, Hennessy said.

When over the Labor Day weekend Ed Hennessy saw Harry Gray in Nantucket discussing Bendix, the Hennessy competitive juices must have once again begun flowing. Tuesday after Labor Day he called Salomon Brothers to try to get an interview with Agee but was unable to obtain one. Meanwhile, before Bendix had hired his firm, Bruce Wasserstein of First Boston had been trying to reach Hennessy to see if Allied could be interested in buying Bendix. By September 14, the day after Marietta unveiled its doomsday machine, Hennessy and Wasserstein were talking, according to documents on file at the Securities and Exchange Commission.

Hennessy wanted to buy all of Bendix. Bendix was interested in lining up Allied as a partial white knight. Under the securities laws, if a tender offer for 5 percent or more of a company's stock is begun while another tender offer is under way, the first buyer cannot purchase any tendered shares until ten days after the second offer has been made. If Marietta was close to taking over Bendix, Bendix wanted to be able to use Allied to gain a ten-day delay. During that time the tendered Bendix shares would be withdrawn from Marietta and tendered to Allied, if the price was high enough.

Bruce Wasserstein said he was talking with Allied about a possible purchase of part or all of Bendix because, "When we were hired, we were hired to defend [Bendix] against United Technologies." Mr. Wasserstein told the author that he had concluded that the "doomsday scenario" in which Bendix and Marietta would buy control of each other was far more likely than William Agee and some other advisors thought, and First Boston was taking prudent steps to cope with the problem.

On September 15 United Technologies made a last offer to Bendix. It said that if Bendix dropped its opposition, United would pay $85 a share for the first half of the company, up from $75. This appears to be the point at which United and Marietta changed their deal. Instead of buying $600 million of assets, Marietta agreed to buy $700 million. That $100 million increase covered most of the $119 million—11.9 million shares at $10 each—by which United raised its offer for Bendix.

But even an $85 first-stage offer did not solve Bill Agee's problem because United left the second stage at $50. If Bendix accepted that offer, the Bendix Salaried Employees Savings and Stock Ownership Plan (SESSOP) holders, as well as Bendix executives with stock under option, would still get less than the prevailing market price of Bendix shares.

September 16 was the crucial day—the day Bendix had to decide whether to buy the tendered Marietta shares, the doomsday machine notwithstanding, or to accept a peace offering. There were frantic efforts made that day to head off a confrontation—all in vain. William Agee and Alonzo McDonald had decided to buy the Marietta stock—they were not impressed with the doomsday machine and they feared Bendix itself would be bought cheap in the near future unless Bendix bought Marietta. In an interview with the author, Mr. McDonald said: "When Agee and I started this, we had the will to buy. And that's exactly what we started out to do, and there was never any doubt that if we were permitted to, we were going to buy."

At this point, of course, Agee and McDonald did not have what they considered a reasonable offer for the sale of Bendix, so they had to press ahead with buying Marietta. In their determination to buy, Agee and McDonald overlooked the significance of the Marietta doomsday defense, which was designed to, as it were, blow up both companies if Bendix bought the tendered Marietta shares. If Bendix bought Marietta, things would be out of Marietta's hands, and it would have no choice but to spend $900 million to buy a majority of Bendix's stock. Financial fallout from the machine would devastate both companies, which would have spent all their cash and consumed most of their borrowing power to buy each other's shares. The resulting Bendix-Marietta company would have about $2.7 billion of debts and just $1.1 billion of net worth, and would have to sell assets wholesale to raise enough cash to survive.

Except for Salomon Brothers' Jay Higgins, whom Bendix tended to ignore, Bendix's advisors were upbeat about buying Marietta. And the Bendix board of directors, which one might have thought would hesitate before betting more than a billion dollars by buying Marietta stock without having a clear idea of the outcome, was not going to stop William Agee from doing just about anything he wanted. Any opportunity for the Bendix board to reign in Mr. Agee had ended in 1981, when he had maneuvered Harry Cunningham, Alan Schwartz and Paul Mirabito off the board, and when Robert Purcell had resigned.

Meanwhile Martin Marietta was putting together a few last-minute contingency plans (though it was relying primarily on the doomsday machine). For a few hours it appeared Marietta had succeeded in getting U.S. District Judge Joseph Young of Baltimore to halt the Bendix-Marietta struggle before it got altogether out of control. Judge Young was hearing a Marietta suit against Bendix. Fearing that there was an increasing chance of the companies actually buying each other and creating a financial and legal nightmare, Judge Young ordered a ten-day freeze for both companies to allow time for reflection. Bendix wanted to buy Marietta and was not interested in a cooling-off period. Late Thursday night, after the Bendix board had given Agee authority to buy Marietta, Bendix succeeded in obtaining a court of appeals decision reversing Judge Young's order. For Marietta, the judicial route had failed.

Marietta was also considering a partial white knight deal with the LTV Corporation. LTV chairman Paul Thayer was a friend of Marietta's Thomas Pownall (as well as being a director of Allied Corporation). The goal was to have LTV tender for enough Marietta shares to hold off Bendix for ten days, and to trade the Marietta shares for certain Marietta assets.

But Marietta and LTV could not agree on a price. And even if they could have made a deal, the transaction would have given Marietta a substantial income tax liability without generating cash with which to pay the bill. Once upon a time a company could trade some of its assets for some of its shares, and obtain a valid legal opinion that there was no income tax due on the transaction even if the value of the stock was greater than the value at which the traded assets were carried on the company's books. The government closed that loophole —or possible loophole—some two weeks earlier, on September 1, 1982, as part of that year's tax-increase bill. The loophole was closed largely because of reaction to a 1980 deal in which Esmark Incorporated made a $745 million transaction with the Mobil Corporation. Mobil made a friendly tender for about forty percent of Esmark's stock, then traded the stock for Esmark's Trans-Ocean Oil subsidiary. Esmark paid no income tax on the transaction.

But even if Marietta were willing to accept a low LTV price and a tax liability, a partial white knight would not solve its

fundamental problem. In ten days Bendix would still be waiting, and in the meantime Bendix, too, could obtain a partial
white knight. The delay was working in Bendix's favor by
giving it more time for its effort to push through its shark-
repellant charter amendments.

On the morning of September 16 Jay Higgins of Salomon
Brothers and Bruce Wasserstein of First Boston made separate
calls to Martin Siegel of Kidder Peabody, Marietta's investment banker, to make certain they stayed in touch to see if
peace could be negotiated. Even though Salomon had not
been actively involved since September 9, when First Boston
had been hired, Mr. Higgins participated in some of the formal
meetings because Bendix was still, at least officially, a Salomon
client. It was rather typical of the lack of coordination on the
Bendix team that Jay Higgins and Bruce Wasserstein were
both trying to negotiate peace between Bendix and Marietta
though unable to negotiate peace between themselves.

An illustration of the Higgins-Wasserstein relationship is an
anecdote that Mr. Higgins relates about Mr. Wasserstein. On
September 15 Higgins and other Salomon people met Mr.
Wasserstein outside William Agee's office. "Wasserstein said,
'When the question comes up tomorrow whether we should
buy the shares, there is no way First Boston will tell the directors to buy shares. But if you want to be a hero, tell Agee to
buy the shares. That's what he wants to hear.' " Wasserstein
says he may have said something like that, but that he was
obviously joking when he said it. He also says Higgins is intentionally misinterpreting what he said.

The Bendix board meeting was a rubber-stamp gathering to
give William Agee authority to do what he wanted. With the
exception of Higgins, who was wary of the risks involved in
buying Marietta, the other advisors were optimistic. Marietta
might buy Bendix shares, the advice went, but Bendix would
almost certainly prevail in a court battle over control, and
could still cope with the problem, although with some pain.

Agee told the board it was possible that the companies

would buy each other, but that he would do everything possible to forestall such an event. The mutual buying, he said, would produce a company "constipated" with debt, as well as skewed financial ratios that would violate conditions of some Bendix bank loans and bond issues, but it would not result in bankruptcy or dismemberment of the companies.

Remarkably, the Bendix board voted to delegate authority to five directors—Bill Agee; Al McDonald; William Tavoulareas, president of Mobil Corporation; and Thomas Stafford and Jonathan Scott, businessmen who were friends of Mr. Agee. The five directors were given the power to buy Marietta stock, settle with Marietta or raise the price to give Marietta a friendly deal. The other board members went home. In similar circumstances, the Martin Marietta board stayed in session past 10:00 P.M. before deciding to buy the tendered Bendix shares.

According to Mr. Agee, the five-person committee met once, but the final decision authorizing him to buy Marietta shares was made by telephone. He said he and Mr. McDonald called the other three directors individually and obtained their approval. In effect, the Bendix board was leaving Bill Agee on his own.

On the tactical front, Harry Gray of United Technologies and his aides helicoptered in from Hartford, Connecticut to the Manhattan offices of Martin Lipton of Wachtell, Lipton, Rosen & Katz, the law firm representing both Kidder Peabody and United. After Marietta asked that United agree to withdraw if a Bendix-Marietta settlement could be arranged, United agreed to do so, provided it was paid five million dollars of "breakup" money. The request to United was made as part of Marty Siegel's negotiations with Bruce Wasserstein.

It would appear, however, that Mr. Wasserstein was, so to speak, stringing Mr. Siegel along. By talking about a three-way peace with Marty Siegel, Bruce Wasserstein kept the power to save Bendix from Harry Gray, if necessary. But if the freeze were lifted—as it was between 9:00 and 10:00 P.M.—Bendix could buy Marietta and not need a three-way peace.

In early interviews, Mr. Wasserstein suggested to the author that peace had been at hand the night of September 16, and that the only problem was that Marietta did not want to pay enough money. Both Mr. Agee and Mr. McDonald vehemently denied that they ever authorized Mr. Wasserstein to settle— although Mr. Agee says he authorized "exploratory" talks to keep Bendix's options open.

While Judge Young's freeze was on, Wasserstein and Siegel were talking about how much Bendix would accept for the 1,632,500 Marietta shares it owned as part of an overall peace settlement. The men started the day well over $30 million apart. Wasserstein was talking about a purchase price of $48 a share (what Bendix was offering for Marietta) and Siegel was talking about $27 a share (just below what Bendix had paid for Marietta). By 9:00 P.M., with the judicial freeze still in force, the two men had agreed to speak every hour on the hour. Wasserstein had an advantage—he was calling Siegel because Siegel did not know where he was and could not call him. Wasserstein and Arthur Fleischer, the lawyer for Bendix, were in a Chinese restaurant near the Palace Hotel in New York, where the Bendix suite was located. Wasserstein would call Siegel from a phone booth, and he and Fleischer reported to Agee, McDonald and Mary Cunningham.

During the 9:00 P.M. call, the gap between what Wasserstein said he would take on behalf of Bendix and what Siegel was offering had narrowed considerably. Siegel was up to $35 a share, about $57.1 million. Wasserstein was down to $37.50, about $61.2 million, and says there was a question of about $2.5 million more for expenses.

While waiting for Wasserstein's 10:00 P.M. call, Siegel obtained permission from Marietta to meet the $37.50 price. (Marietta president Tom Pownall told the author that he had given Siegel authority to settle at $37.50 and that he thought peace was at hand.)

But peace was not at hand, or even close. Messrs. Agee and

McDonald were still determined to buy Marietta, and said they had no idea what Wasserstein had been discussing with Siegel. In an interview with the author in April of 1983, Mr. Wasserstein—who on several occasions told the author peace had been close the evening of September 16—said that he had never told Siegel that Bendix would accept a $37.50 settlement if Marietta agreed to pay it. Wasserstein said this after the author told him what Agee had said. All he had been doing, Wasserstein said, was testing the waters.

When the author told Marty Siegel what Wasserstein said, he was furious. "That's not the case at all," he said, "I thought I was negotiating in good faith with an authorized representative of Bendix." Mr. Siegel said he discussed cost figures with United Technologies, and that Mr. Wasserstein told him he had discussed cost figures with Bendix, and had led Mr. Siegel to believe they were negotiating a peace settlement.

Peace became a moot question about 9:30 P.M. when the court of appeals overturned Judge Young's freeze order, freeing up Bendix to buy Marietta. Marty Siegel, who was waiting for Bruce Wasserstein's 10:00 P.M. call to offer $37.50 to end the battle—or so he thought—never received the 10:00 call, nor the scheduled 11:00 call nor the midnight call. Siegel then began searching for Wasserstein, not knowing he was incommunicado in the Bendix suite at the Palace Hotel.

Alonzo McDonald, who was afraid Marietta would try a last-minute maneuver—he says he heard Marietta lawyers were trying to get Warren Burger, chief justice of the United States Supreme Court, to overturn the court of appeals' reversal of Judge Young's ten-day freeze order—saw no purpose in having Bruce Wasserstein talk to Marty Siegel. "In the last six minutes of the game," McDonald said, "there is nothing to talk about. We were going to buy."

Mr. Wasserstein told the author he wanted to make a last call to Marty Siegel to get Marietta's last, highest bid to purchase the Marietta stock Bendix owned, and to see if there was a price at which Marietta would do a friendly deal. "You'd find their absolute last dollar that way," he says.

Shortly after midnight, Agee ordered the billion dollars spent and the shares bought. The black hole, into which both companies would pour their capital, was opening.

When midnight went and there was no word from Bendix, Marty Siegel sent the United Technologies contingent home. Mr. Siegel and Marty Lipton felt Bendix would use its power to buy as a lever to force Marietta's Tom Pownall to the bargaining table—but it apparently never occurred to them that Bendix would buy first and talk later. "We were astonished that they bought," Mr. Lipton says.

When Marty Siegel's phone rang early Friday morning, September 17, and he heard Bruce Wasserstein's voice, he expected to be told that Bill Agee was offering a meet-with-me-or-we'll-buy ultimatum. Instead, Wasserstein told him that Bendix had bought the stock. Siegel was shocked: "I said, 'He's a fool.' "

Bendix had bought control of Marietta—it thought—but the battle was far from over. In the next week, the struggle would turn from a corporate takeover contest into a spectacle.

Chapter 13

Endgame

BENDIX MOVES TO TRAP MARIETTA

Throughout his business career William Agee had managed to get out of troublesome situations unscathed—he is a very smart, quick, innovative and charming man, exceptionally able in many ways and has the ruthlessness necessary to dispatch adversaries that he has at his mercy. But in the final weeks of the Bendix-Martin Marietta conflict, he came up against two men he could not outwit, charm or overpower: Thomas Pownall of Martin Marietta, and Edward Hennessy, Jr. of the Allied Corporation.

Despite Agee's threats and importunings, Tom Pownall clung stubbornly to his position: Marietta had no choice but to go through with its tender offer for Bendix; the doomsday machine could not be disconnected. A stubborn, straightforward man with a military mindset running a company filled with former military men, Pownall felt that Marietta had no honorable alternative but to buy the tendered Bendix shares. Neither Pownall nor the Marietta board of directors were afraid to die at their posts: after all, that is what soldiers are paid to do.

Bill Agee could not budge Tom Pownall, who meant what he said. He also seriously underestimated Ed Hennessy, a considerable gamesman. Hennessy made it clear he badly wanted

to buy Bendix, so Bill Agee behaved as though he were negotiating from strength—which he was not. Hennessy, however,
allowed him to think that he was—and took his company away,
albeit at a rich price.

Agee's goal in his negotiations with Hennessy was to get
Allied to tender for enough Bendix stock to delay Marietta's
tender, but not for enough stock to allow Allied to control
Bendix. Hennessy, of course, wanted to buy all of Bendix or—
failing that—to buy choice Bendix assets at a low price.

Under the deal Agee thought he had made with Hennessy,
Allied would have ended up with about 20 percent of Bendix
for a total cost of $383 million, and was pledged not to try to
take Bendix over until 1986. The deal was structured so that
Bendix could buy Marietta. In terms of annual revenues Bendix-Marietta would have been about as large as Allied and
substantially more profitable. It was far more likely that Bendix-Marietta, which was not pledged not to buy Allied, would
in the long run take over Allied rather than the other way
around.

Ed Hennessy was too smart to go for such a setup. He
wanted either part of Bendix, or all of it—and had no intention
of putting almost $400 million into a company that one day
could take over his own. Hennessy won out by backing Agee
into a corner, cutting off his alternatives, then telling him he
had to sell to Allied or risk financial disaster.

In the denouement Agee tried to sell both Bendix and Marietta to Allied, and probably realized that he was sacrificing
himself in so doing. A kind of classic Samson pulling down the
temple on the Philistines—I am sacrificing myself, but I will
take my enemies with me. But Marietta escaped through a
one-minute loophole in the securities laws, and so when the
roof caved in, it fell on Bendix alone.

The Bendix-Marietta-Allied-United Technologies endgame
was a series of intricate moves, involving esoteric aspects of the
securities laws. Before getting into the ending, one needs to
recall some pertinent facts:

• Bendix now owned 70 percent of Martin Marietta, but did not control the company because it did not control the board of directors.

• Marietta would be free to buy the tendered Bendix shares after midnight on Thursday, September 22, unless another force intervened.

• Under the securities laws, Marietta could be temporarily blocked if Bendix could find a bidder willing to tender for 5 percent or more of its stock. If such a bidder emerged, Marietta would not be able to buy any tendered Bendix shares until at least ten business days after the new offer began. By then, Bendix would almost certainly have been able to call a special Marietta shareholder meeting, replace the board of directors and call off the Marietta tender for Bendix.

• United Technologies was still in the game. After Bendix had bought the tendered shares of Marietta on September 17, United had the right to drop its tender offer for Bendix, but was not obliged to do so. United kept its tender for Bendix open; as a result, Bendix had to worry about being taken over by United even if it succeeded in taking over Marietta.

Bendix's first move in the endgame was to try to overpower Marietta. Instead of stopping when it had just a majority, Bendix kept buying Marietta shares until it owned 70 percent of the company. The idea was to give Bendix such an overwhelming majority of Marietta stock that the Marietta board of directors—or, if necessary, the courts—would bow to Bendix's will.

Meanwhile Bendix was still trying to round up votes to pass the shark-repellant amendments to its corporate charter—repellants that would have blocked Marietta from controlling Bendix. If the repellants passed, Marietta could turn off its doomsday machine. (Marietta had reserved the right to end its tender for Bendix if the shark repellants passed.) The repellants would also give Bendix protection against United Technologies by making it impossible for a company to take over

Bendix with a two-tier bid not approved by the Bendix board of directors.

On September 17, at Bill Agee's request, Ed Hennessy stopped by in New York to talk. Hennessy, who is based in Allied headquarters in Morristown, New Jersey, was in Manhattan to attend a fund-raising event for Senator Strom Thurmond of South Carolina. (Allied has a major facility in the state.) Earlier that day Hennessy had decided there really might be a deal for Allied in the Bendix-Marietta-United triangle, and hired lawyer Joseph Flom and the investment banking firm of Lehman Brothers Kuhn Loeb to represent Allied. Mr. Hennessy told the author that he had not hired a lawyer or investment banker up to that point because he did not want to run up bills needlessly.

There was at least a touch of revenge in Lehman Brothers' accepting the Allied assignment. Lehman had been embarrassed in March 1982 when Bendix, then a client, took a major position in the stock of Lehman client RCA Corporation without telling Lehman about the investment. Now, Lehman was about to earn a $5 million fee from Allied for helping it to buy Bendix.

At this point, based on information they provided the author during interviews, it seems clear that Bill Agee and Bendix president Alonzo McDonald, Jr. were putting off the hard decision—what to do—by concentrating their attentions on keeping all their options open. In hindsight it also seems clear that the two men would have done better to have picked one strategy, at most two, and plunged ahead. Instead, with time running out, they were still considering some half-dozen options, with variations.

The preferred strategy was to negotiate a friendly deal with Tom Pownall of Marietta, buy the 30 percent of Marietta that Bendix did not already own and call off the Marietta tender for Bendix. There were various ways of trying to accomplish this, not the least of which was to continue pushing the shark repellants.

If Marietta could not be taken over peacefully and the shark repellants could not be passed, there was the "partial white knight" strategy, which Agee nicknamed "The Great Extender." This would allow Bendix to delay Marietta's bid long enough to take the company over and end the tender for Bendix. But that strategy ran the risk of having Marietta's management threaten to destroy the company—a "scorched earth strategy," as investment bankers call it—by selling valuable assets at cheap prices in the interregnum before Bendix could take control.

If the Extender did not work, there were the options of trying to sell all of Bendix, or trying to cope with a Bendix-Marietta devastated by the doomsday machine. Allowing United Technologies and its Harry Gray to take Bendix over appears to have been at the bottom of the list.

But as they juggled their options, Agee and McDonald seemingly failed to realize that few companies were interested in being a cat's paw for Bendix. A minimum of $75 million was required to tender for 5 percent of Bendix, and $100 million or more was preferable. Any company or investor-group putting up that much money wanted a genuine bargain or it would not play the game. Agee and McDonald seem to have been misled by the fact that many potential investors were interested in doing a partial tender. But the presence of several interested investors did not mean Bendix was negotiating from strength; it needed the deal, the potential investors did not and were not interested in having Bill Agee play them off against each other, as he attempted to do.

On Monday, September 20, Agee tried to pursue all his options simultaneously. He was stalling his Extender candidates, trying to make peace with Pownall, and also trying to pass the shark-repellant charter amendments. By attempting all of these moves simultaneously rather than concentrating on one, he ended up assuring that all of them would fail.

Agee spent several hours of September 20 talking face-to-face with Tom Pownall in the New York City offices of Dewey, Ballantine, Bushby, Palmer & Wood, Marietta's law firm. Agee had been pressing for weeks to meet Pownall, who until that point had had no interest in meeting him.

The two men spoke at length but did not communicate— they saw the problem in differing terms. From the point of view of Agee and his lawyers it was a simple matter for Marietta to turn off the doomsday machine. All it had to do was to call off its tender offer on some pretext, and take a chance on whether any Bendix shareholder deprived of a chance to sell to Marietta for $75 a share would decide to sue. Agee offered Pownall indemnification to protect him in such a case.

Agee told the author he kept waiting for Tom Pownall to tell him that if Pownall became chief executive of the combined companies "the legal problem would go away"—he himself, Agee added, was willing to make that sacrifice.

This was the way Agee saw the problem—who would control the combined company. It does not appear to be the way Pownall saw it. For Pownall it was a matter of honor, not amenable to tactical compromises. Marietta and Tom Pownall had promised to buy Bendix stock if Bendix bought Marietta stock and did not pass its shark repellants; Marietta and Pownall would keep their word, regardless of consequences.

Pownall's actions demonstrate that he sets considerable store by personal integrity. He negotiated a $700 million deal with United Technologies that was basically a handshake arrangement with Harry Gray, whom he trusted to work things out if there was a problem in splitting up Bendix's assets. Later, Pownall negotiated a similar if $900 million deal with Ed Hennessy at Allied.

Pownall apparently did not feel similarly about Agee. And Agee was not making himself more attractive in Pownall's eyes by posing a series of maneuvers to allow Marietta to escape from its vow. Among them: a proposal to have Bendix indemnify Marietta directors, and suggestions that Marietta ask a court to issue an injunction to block its own tender offer.

From Pownall's point of view Agee was a man who had attacked Martin Marietta without an attempt at negotiations.

And each time Agee wrote a "Dear Tom" letter he filed it with the Securities and Exchange Commission and released it to the Dow Jones news service, which publicized it. Pownall did not want to negotiate in the press.

Bendix's actions on Thursday night, September 16, were surely disturbing to Pownall. This was the night Marietta had believed it was close to a negotiated settlement with Bendix. But Bendix's investment banker had not kept his promise to call Marietta's investment banker every hour to negotiate terms, and had not resumed talks until after Bendix had bought Marietta stock.

Pownall was keenly aware that Agee was still pushing shark repellants. Marietta, which had bought a token 100 shares of Bendix stock in the open market, was soliciting negative notes to try to block approval. Pownall, having been fooled on the night of September 16, could be forgiven if he thought that Agee was playing him along while waiting to see if the amendments would pass.

Not surprisingly, the Agee-Pownall talks were unproductive, though the men tentatively agreed to continue the discussions in Bethesda on Tuesday, September 21.

September 20 was also Bendix "Unity Day." Bendix, which had started the battle, now wanted to demonstrate how badly its employees wanted their company to remain independent. According to Al McDonald, the day was designed to round up employee support, boost morale, gather votes in favor of the shark-repellant amendments and to make certain that employees who had not yet withdrawn their SESSOP (Salaried Employees Savings and Stock Ownership Plan) stock from the Marietta tender pool remembered to take their shares back.

Unity Day featured "I Love Bendix" balloons, hats, bumper stickers and pins. At Bendix headquarters in Southfield, a plane flew overhead with a banner. Cheerleaders, complete with pompons and short skirts, exhorted the troops.

Not only did Unity Day prove to be a waste of time, there was also more than a touch of irony in it: Bill Agee and Al

McDonald were seriously considering selling the whole company even as the balloons were being filled with helium and the cheerleaders were shaking their pompons. Also, Unity Day was a distraction, diverting McDonald, in particular, from more pressing tasks. Time was running out on Bendix, which had kept its options open, but still had not exercised any of them.

Bendix knew by then that it did not have the votes to pass the shark-repellant amendments. Other parties, however, did not know. As September 20 wore on, Agee's list of partial white knights was shrinking fast. One of them had been the ubiquitous LTV Corporation, the same company that had considered white knighting for Marietta. A second potential knight, a British company, wanted to tender for Bendix stock and to exchange the stock for Bendix's truck parts business. But the British firm did not offer a high enough price to suit Agee and the deal fell through. There was also an aborted deal with Donald Trump, a New York City real estate developer who coveted Bendix's RCA stock. The plan was for Trump to tender for something more than $100 million of Bendix shares, then trade them for Bendix's RCA shares. Mr. Trump, who contacted Bill Agee himself—"He was," Trump says, "an honorable man, and I hope you quote me as saying that"—says the plan fell through because it was too complicated and risky; a high-placed Bendix source told the author that Trump could not come up with the money.

So it came down to Allied and Ed Hennessy. Agee finished his talks with Hennessy convinced he had a deal—but Hennessy told the author that Agee did not have one.

According to documents on file at the Securities and Exchange Commission, the proposed Allied-Bendix deal was in two parts. One called for Allied to tender for 2.6 million Bendix shares at $80 each. This was about 10 percent of Bendix's stock, sufficient to trigger a ten-day extension. The $5 increase above the Marietta $75 offer would deflect criticism that Agee was trying to deprive Bendix shareholders of the right to receive $75 a share for their stock. The other half of the deal was far better for Allied. It would buy $175 million of newly issued Bendix preferred stock that carried a quite high 13 percent annual dividend, and was convertible into common stock at $67.50 a share. The dividend would more than offset the cost to Allied of borrowing money to buy the preferred stock, and Allied would own about 20 percent of Bendix-Marietta. Allied agreed not to try to take over Bendix-Marietta until 1986 without Bendix's consent—but there was no mention of a clause to stop Bendix-Marietta from taking over Allied.

The Bendix board, acceding to Agee's wishes as usual, approved the deal.

But the Allied board did not approve it.

A chronology of the Bendix-Marietta battle filed at the Securities and Exchange Commission by Allied and Bendix implies that the Allied board turned down the deal: ". . . The board of directors of Allied concluded it did not favor making an investment, as opposed to purchasing a controlling interest, in Bendix."

In an interview with Ed Hennessy and Allied's general counsel, Brian Forrow, the author asked why the Allied board had turned the deal down. Mr. Forrow corrected the author. The filing at the SEC did not say the board turned the deal down, Forrow said; it said only that the board "did not favor making an investment . . . in Bendix."

The reason the board did not approve the proposed deal with Bendix, Ed Hennessy said, is that "I never proposed it." And the reason for that, he said, is that every time he tried to pin Agee down in a discussion of what Bendix assets Allied would get in return for the almost $400 million of Bendix stock it was asked to buy, Agee changed the subject. "We never nailed anything down," Hennessy told the author. "That was the problem . . . During those negotiations we said, 'We have to swap these [shares] for assets, I'm not going to sit here as an investor in this company.' I was trying to tie down the assets we could get. It became so complex and so cloudy, there was really nothing to propose to our board once they met—but we did discuss it."

In addition, Hennessy said, Agee kept talking about who would sit on whose board of directors, and Hennessy felt he had no reason to play such games: "We were going to have directors that served on their board, and they were coming back and saying they'd have an equal number on our board, and I said, 'That's crap.' "

(When the author interviewed Messrs. Agee and McDonald in April 1983, both men seemed surprised when they were told Mr. Hennessy had said the proposed deal had never been submitted to the Allied board of directors. The two men said they thought the Allied board had turned the deal down. Hennessy said, "I called Bill Agee and told him it wouldn't fly" —but he obviously did not tell Agee the real reason.)

Ed Hennessy, in effect, had led Agee out on a limb and then sawed it off. Agee was in serious trouble. It was almost September 21. He was virtually out of Great Extender candidates, and the shark-repellant meeting, held in Southfield on September 21, was a fiasco. Unknown to Bendix, Marietta attorney James Simpson and support troops bearing cardboard boxes of shareholder proxies voting against the amendments had infiltrated the hall in which the meeting was held. Bendix, knowing it did not have the votes, tried to have the meeting adjourned. Simpson attempted to take the meeting over and have the amendments voted down. Amid chaos, Bendix forces declared the meeting adjourned and turned off the lights and microphones. Simpson and his supporters moved their show to a Southfield hotel, where they gleefully held a mock meeting and declared the shark repellants rejected. Score one for Marietta.

Mousetrapped by Ed Hennessy and Allied, Bill Agee made another tactical error on Tuesday, September 21. He allowed himself to be drawn into spending most of the day and part of the early morning of the following day in fruitless talks with Tom Pownall in Bethesda. By being in Bethesda it was impossible for him to negotiate in person with Ed Hennessy or other potential buyers of the entire company.

There was a touch of the surreal about the negotiations. Agee and his entourage were to fly to Bethesda on a Bendix jet stationed at the Butler Aviation terminal at Newark Airport. The Marietta lawyers and investment bankers were also flying down from Newark. The planes were parked in adjacent slots, and the Bendix and Marietta teams watched each other board the planes in Newark, and debark from them in Washington.

The Marietta team then proceeded to Marietta headquarters while the Bendix team went to a motel to await a call from Tom Pownall that the Marietta board was ready to hear Bill Agee.

Agee was putting great faith in his persuasive powers. He seemingly felt that if he could address the Marietta board, rather than Pownall, the board would accept one of his scenarios, call off its tender, and Bendix would prevail.

But the Marietta board had no interest in hearing Bill Agee, and left him to cool his heels in the motel for several hours.

Meanwhile Allied's Ed Hennessy was pressing Agee to make up his mind. "I knew he was shopping," Hennessy said of Agee's actions on September 21. He says he told him, "We'll tender for the shares, we're willing to have a board meeting tonight, but I have to know very quickly. He did not let me know that whole day."

Agee had come down to Bethesda without a firm commitment from Pownall to let him address the Marietta board at a specific time. He compounded that apparent error by not realizing the personal impact of his actions. The Bendix team included Agee; Bruce Wasserstein and others from First Boston; Arthur Fleischer and others from Fried Frank. It also included Mary Cunningham Agee, who had obtained emergency vacation days from her job at Joseph Seagram & Sons. *Agee had not brought with him a single other person from Bendix.* He had come to Maryland to encourage Tom Pownall to join the Bendix team, but his own actions made it clear that Bendix was a

one-man show. His error was not in bringing Mary Cunningham, though it perhaps did seem rather strange to be bringing
a vice-president from a different company. The error was in
not bringing anyone else from Bendix.

(Later Agee became angry at stories criticizing Ms. Cunningham's presence that were carried in the *Wall Street Journal* and other publications. In its characteristic dry fashion,
Marietta issued a statement that appeared on the surface to be
conciliatory but viewed on another level was something of a
put-down of Agee and Cunningham. "It was apparent that Mr.
Agee took some comfort from his wife's presence," the statement read in part, "but not then or later did any of us find that
to be either irritating or curious." The Marietta statement took
the form of a letter to the Washington *Post,* and probably
would have received only limited attention, except for Bendix,
which surprisingly distributed the letter nationwide by sending it out as a Bendix news release.)

Agee and Pownall talked for hours at Marietta headquarters,
but Agee's position was seriously eroding. Pownall was less
inclined to deal than before. Agee's shark repellants had failed,
and Marietta undoubtedly knew that the deal for Allied to buy
20 percent of Bendix had also failed. Bill Agee was running out
of his options.

Agee and Pownall went over the same old ground. Agee
proposed escape routes. Pownall and his attorneys were not
interested, not least because they did not pass what Marietta
called "the red face test." . . . "I was really, honest-to-God
searching my soul to see if there were any possible alternative
[to buying the tendered Bendix stock]," Pownall said. "I was
sympathetic that he had gotten himself stuck in a mess, and we
had gotten sucked in right behind him."

About 6:00 P.M. the Agee entourage, traveling to the airport
in two chauffeured cars provided by Marietta, decided to give
the talks one more chance. Fearing that Marietta might have
bugged the cars, the Bendix forces talked on a knoll near a
bank of phone booths, according to the Marietta account, con-

sulted with each other, then moved up the knoll and made their calls. One was from Agee to Pownall, asking for a chance to come back.

He did not want to see Agee again, Pownall says, but "how can you not make yourself available in the circumstances? You've got two companies that are just about to pull the plug on each other, and here's a guy pleading with you to think about these things."

Agee and his entourage returned. This time Marietta led him on. Frank Menaker, Jr., Marietta's general counsel, told the author that if Agee insisted on coming back again, he wanted to keep the Bendix chairman pinned down in Bethesda to prevent him from making a deal with another company.

The talks, altogether fruitless, went on for five more hours. "Mary came in here and interrupted a few times, and he'd go out and talk to her for a while," Pownall said. But, he added, he was not in any way offended by her actions; throughout the late evening and early morning, he said, people were wandering in and out of offices. Marietta people remember talking to Ms. Cunningham about the weather, and about how similar in style the Bendix and Marietta headquarters buildings were.

Agee's own description of the meetings: "Endless, endless."

Pownall agreed: "It was interminable. We were almost cross-eyed here. It was a zero discussion, it was a waste of time. The most depressing moment was when he came back here. It was so useless and pointless. It's almost as though he was afraid to leave here because when he left it would be all over."

And, in fact, it was.

Chapter 14

Checkmate

AGEE LOSES BENDIX

William Agee left Marietta headquarters in Bethesda in the early hours of Wednesday, September 22. The Marietta contingent also left then. The Bendix and Marietta teams watched each other board their respective planes at Washington National Airport, and watched each other deplane in Newark. One member of the Marietta team recalls that the Bendix people were whisked away in waiting limousines, while the Marietta people took taxicabs. Likely a case of less than meets the eye . . .

At midnight Wednesday, barring a court order or the appearance of a Bill Agee Great Extender, Marietta would be able to buy the Bendix shares that had been tendered to it, and the black hole would consume the net worth of both companies. Whichever team of corporate managers emerged on top of the combined company—after what would doubtless be a prolonged court battle—would be presiding over a company not only top-heavy with debt but with financial ratios so skewed that it would be in violation of covenants in some of its loans and bonds. Which in turn would make the loans and bonds immediately due and payable. The only way out of the mess would be to sell assets at a fire sale, and fire sales do not normally generate good prices.

Bendix tried to persuade U.S. District Judge Joseph Young of Baltimore to ban Marietta from buying Bendix stock on the grounds that the purchase was against the will of Marietta's majority shareholders, Bendix. Judge Young declined to do so. He had tried to impose a ten-day freeze on September 16 to allow both companies to devise a way to resolve the conflict; but Bendix had succeeded in getting his freeze order overturned. Now he would not freeze Marietta.

Bendix did manage a victory on September 22 by getting the Delaware Court of Chancery to issue an injunction barring Marietta from voting any Bendix stock it might purchase. If Marietta bought Bendix shares, it might well be purchasing what Bendix president Alonzo McDonald, Jr. called "eunuch stock." Note that the Delaware court did not bar Marietta from buying Bendix stock, only from voting it. Bendix lawyers were pleased with the decision, though the court order made no practical difference: Marietta still considered itself legally and morally bound to buy Bendix.

On September 22, Marietta's Thomas Pownall said, Bill Agee kept telephoning and offering new ideas to break the deadlock. "I told him we couldn't have a board meeting every fifteen minutes [to discuss the proposals]."

Shortly after noon Agee finally made up his mind, talked to Ed Hennessy of Allied and concluded a deal to sell him both Allied and Marietta. "[Agee] said, 'It's out of my hands, I sold your company,' or words to that effect," Tom Pownall reported. "He called me back and said it was Allied, and he was going to be president, no hard feelings. Maybe we could work together."

The deal called for Allied to begin a tender for 13.1 million Bendix shares at $85 of cash each, and to offer Allied securities worth $75 a share for the remaining 10.6 million Bendix shares. This was a front-end-loaded, two-tier offer, the very thing Bendix had attacked bitterly when Marietta and United Technology made their bids. But in the Allied-Bendix arrangement there was a relatively small difference between the two parts of the offer. By negotiating a $75 price for the second-stage sellers, Agee deflected any criticism for depriving shareholders of the right to sell their stock to Marietta or United for $75.

The Allied-Bendix deal, announced at 4:45 P.M., was described as a $2.3 billion deal, even though the price Allied was paying for Bendix totaled less than $1.9 billion. The assumption was that Allied's tender for Bendix would delay the Marietta tender and that Allied would buy the remaining 30 percent of Marietta for about $400 million.

Things did not work out that way. By the time Agee had made up his mind there was not enough time that day to draw up the tender offer documents. "The lawyers threw up their hands" when he told them he had made a deal with Agee, Ed Hennessy said, and told him the forms could not be completed and filed by 5:30 P.M., when the Securities and Exchange Commission's offices in Washington close. Even if the boards of directors of both companies speedily approved the deal, it could not begin on September 22 as originally intended.

Bill Agee could not sell Bendix to Allied on his own authority. He needed approval from the Bendix board of directors, which, true enough, had routinely rubber-stamped his decisions. But now, as the abyss neared, some directors expressed misgivings. When the board had given its approval for the purchase of Marietta shares on September 16, Agee and his advisors had said they could live with a situation in which Bendix and Marietta bought each other's stock. The Delaware court decision seemed to mean that Bendix would emerge on top. Why sell out to Allied, some directors wondered, if Bendix was going to prevail?

Agee's answer was obvious. Bendix would win, but it would be a Pyrrhic victory. It made more sense to sell to Allied, and it had to be done quickly. Four Bendix directors—Mobil Corporation president William Tavoulareas, G. D. Searle chairman Donald Rumsfeld, Harvard Business School professor

Hugo Uyterhoven and University of Texas dean Wilbur Cohen —huddled together. The first three men voted no on the sale to Allied; Cohen abstained. The four then resigned from the board and left the meeting. Their action, though dramatic, made no difference to the outcome. Later in the afternoon the Bendix and Allied boards approved the Allied-Bendix deal—but it never came to pass because of Martin Marietta's magic minute.

The minute was a gap in the securities laws. Marietta would be free to buy the tendered shares of Bendix at midnight, September 22, the last chance for holders of tendered stock to withdraw it. If Allied filed the necessary forms at the Securities and Exchange Commission on Thursday, September 23, its tender offer would have been deemed to have legally begun at 12:01 A.M. on Thursday. If Marietta could buy the Bendix stock in the sixty seconds between midnight and 12:01 A.M., the Allied tender offer would be too late to block the purchase.

Anticipating that possibility, Marietta ordered Citibank, which was holding the tendered Bendix shares, to prepare to buy them between midnight and 12:01 A.M. The bank made sure its clocks were precisely accurate, and prepared to close the deal in the allotted time.

The only way left for Allied and Bendix to block Marietta was to convince the owners of tendered Bendix shares to withdraw them from the Marietta tender pool. The $10 difference between the $85 Allied offer and the $75 Marietta offer was designed to draw shares from Marietta.

Convincing arbitragers that a deal will succeed or fail often becomes a self-fulfilling prophecy. If they have confidence that a tender will be consummated, the arbitragers buy and tender large quantities of stock. If they have no faith, they do nothing, and the tendering company has trouble attracting the shares it needs. The Marietta strategy had been to convince the arbitragers that it would actually buy Bendix, which many arbs doubted. The idea also was to convince large institutions either to tender their shares or to sell them in the stock market, where the arbs would buy them. (By selling shares rather than tendering them, a holder accepts a lower price than the tender offer promises, but eliminates the risk of being stuck with his stock if the tender offer fails.)

Investment banking firms and arbs talk to each other frequently during contested tender battles. The arbs want to pick up hints of possible new moves by the companies; the investment bankers want to test ideas on the arbs before proposing them to the client. When the Allied-Bendix forces began trying to see if the Marietta tender pool could be broken, Kidder Peabody and Marietta found out about it quickly.

Marty Siegel of Kidder Peabody mobilized his troops. Dozens of Kidder employees called the holders of tendered Bendix shares, urging them not to withdraw the stock. Kidder told the arbs and the institutional stockholders that Marietta intended to buy at $75, the Dow Jones announcement of the Allied-Bendix deal notwithstanding. About 6:00 P.M., Marietta issued a statement to that effect.

At this point the fact that less than a majority of Bendix had been tendered worked in Marietta's favor—though it had worked to Marietta's disadvantage in the early days. All of the stock in the Marietta pool was eligible for the $75 part of the offer. The $75 was for 11.9 million Bendix shares, but only 10 million were in the tender pool. Kidder could assure tendering stockholders that all their stock would qualify for the higher-priced part of the transaction.

Such was not true of the Allied offer. Because it was a friendly deal, virtually all the 23.7 million shares of Bendix would be tendered, but only 13.1 million—55 percent—would quality for the $85 part of the offer. The rest would receive $75 of securities. Faced with the prospect of having only part of their tendered shares qualify for the high end of the deal, the arbs could calculate that the Allied deal was worth only $80 a share. To get five dollars above the Marietta offer, the arbs would have to wait almost another month and run the risk of having the deal broken up by events. They decided $75 in hand was worth $80 in the bush, and almost all the tendered Bendix stock stayed in the Marietta pool.

Unable to block Marietta's purchase, Allied decided to make a separate peace. In the middle of yet another board meeting, Tom Pownall of Marietta received an urgent call from his friend Paul Thayer, chairman of LTV Corporation, who was a member of Allied's board. Thayer put Hennessy on the phone, introduced the two men, and Hennessy and his entourage of Allied executives, investment bankers and lawyers flew to Washington on an LTV jet to meet Pownall. (Marietta thought the Allied party would land at Dulles Airport and sent cars there. Instead, Allied landed at National Airport and took taxis to Bethesda.)

When Hennessy realized that Tom Pownall did not want to be bought by Allied and that Marietta held the balance of power, he and Pownall made a quick deal. They agreed that Marietta would buy 11.9 million shares of Bendix at $75, as per its tender offer, then trade the shares to Allied for some of the Marietta shares that Allied would acquire when it bought Bendix. The two companies agreed to value the shares at their average cost: $75 per Bendix share, $46.66 per Marietta share. (The cost per Marietta share was lower than the $48 tender price because Bendix had earlier bought 4.5 percent of the company at an average price of $27.05).

Because Bendix had spent almost $1.2 billion to buy Marietta stock while Marietta would spend a bit under $900 million to buy Bendix stock, Allied would retain $300 million of Marietta shares. Those shares would be 39 percent of the Marietta stock outstanding, after the Bendix and Marietta shares were swapped and Marietta retired the shares it received in the exchange. (At the time of this writing Allied holdings have been diluted to less than 39 percent of Marietta, thanks to Marietta having reissued some of the shares it obtained for its Bendix stock.) Pownall and Hennessy agreed that Allied would have seats on the Marietta board of directors, and concluded a ten-year "standstill agreement" that barred Allied from using its stock to control Marietta or to sell it to a third company until 1992. Marietta also obtained an option to purchase its shares from Allied at a price—$53 in 1983—that rises about 14 percent a year. (Should Marietta's stock price rise above $53 in 1983, the likely move for Marietta would be to buy the shares from Allied, then reoffer them to the public, thereby freeing up some $340 million for Allied—which would make Hennessy happy and would remove the threat that the Allied bloc of Marietta could lead to a takeover in the 1990s.)

In several ways the deal Ed Hennessy made with Tom Pownall was better for Allied than the deal he had negotiated with Bill Agee. In the original deal, Allied would have had to pay $1.11 billion in cash for 13.1 million Bendix shares at $85 each. With the Marietta deal, the cash outlay was only about $900 million—11.9 million shares at $75 each. (To be technical, Allied actually did not have to lay out any cash, because Bendix had already borrowed the money to buy the Marietta shares that Allied was exchanging for the 11.9 million Bendix shares. Since Bendix and Allied were to become a combined company, it made no difference which of them had actually spent the cash.) Hennessy avoided having to pay some $400 million for the rest of Marietta, and did not have to show any part of Marietta's debt on Allied's balance sheet.

In a festive spirit, the Allied-Marietta negotiations were quickly concluded. A few moments after midnight, Marietta bought the tendered Bendix stock, about 10 million shares, and ordered that the buying continue until 11.9 million shares had been bought. (The arbs rounded up those shares within a few days and sold them to Marietta.) "By one A.M. we were drinking champagne," Hennessy said. He returned home to New Jersey about four A.M., changed, shaved and made his way to New York City to tell Bill Agee that the deal had been changed. Agee, it would appear, had gone to bed thinking that he had sold both Bendix and Marietta to Allied, and awakened to discover that only Bendix had been sold.

Hennessy pressed Agee to finish the deal by accepting the

agreed-upon price of $75 of Allied securities for the balance of Bendix, but Agee was adamant. If Allied would not come to terms, he said, he would continue the battle with Marietta. Because Hennessy had agreed to pay $80 on average for Bendix and had gotten the first half for $75, Agee said, Allied should pay $85 in securities for the second half. The second half included Agee's personal stock, the Bendix Salaried Employees Savings and Stock Ownership Plan stock, and the shares that Bendix executives had under option.

Hennessy yielded. The $75/$85 offer was still better than the original deal he had made with Agee because Allied would pay more in securities and less in cash than originally contemplated. The original deal required $1.11 billion of cash and $800 million of securities; the revised deal required $900 million of cash and $1 billion of securities.

By concluding the deal, Hennessy kept Bill Agee from shopping for another buyer. And the deal worked out rather well for Allied's balance sheet since most of the securities it was issuing in return for Bendix shares were common stock and preferred stock with no redemption date. The common and preferred counted as equity on the debt-to-equity ratio. Had Allied borrowed more money and issued less equity, its debt-to-equity ratio would have been significantly less favorable.

Part of the Allied deal with Bendix called for Agee to become president of Allied. Ed Hennessy, however, had made certain not to make him chief operating officer of the company and not to give him authority over any Allied operations other than Bendix. Hennessy made it publicly clear that Bill Agee would have no real power at Allied. When Hennessy was asked at a news conference why a man with so little authority had the title of Allied president, Hennessy replied that the title was part of the deal.

When Allied, Bendix and Marietta disentangled, Uncle Sam picked up part of the bill. Financial people call it "tax planning." What had begun as a simple exchange of $892.5 million of Bendix stock for $892.5 million of Marietta stock turned into a series of sales that ran up artificial tax losses of almost $50 million. In December of 1982, when the exchange of stock took place, Marietta owned 11,900,100 shares of Bendix. Bendix, controlled by Allied, owned 25,852,500 shares of Marietta. Marietta had bought all but 100 of its Bendix shares at $75 each. Bendix had bought 23,950,000 shares of Marietta at $48 each, and the balance for $27.05. Because the unraveling did not take place until December, both Bendix and Marietta had already paid a regular quarterly dividend—83 cents per Bendix share, 48 cents per Marietta share. A corporation is allowed to exclude from federal income taxation 85 percent of all dividends it receives. The effective rate is 6.9 percent—15 percent times the 46 percent corporate tax rate. It can deduct short-term capital losses at a 28 percent rate. Marietta had received $9.9 million of dividends on its Bendix stock, (83 cents times 11,900,100) and Bendix had received $12.4 million of dividends on its Marietta stock (48 cents times 25,852,500). Both companies paid an effective rate of 6.9 percent on that income.

Bendix sold its Marietta stock to Allied for its costs, less dividends received, taking a loss of $12.4 million on the transaction. Marietta sold its Bendix stock to Allied for $74.17 a share—its $75 cost, less the 83-cent dividend—taking a $9.9 million loss. In both cases, the "loss" was equal to dividends received. But the effective federal income tax rate on the dividends was just 6.9 percent, while the "losses" could be deducted at 28 percent.

Allied sold Marietta 19,128,000 Marietta shares at $46.18 a share—the $46.66 Bendix had paid for them on average, less the 48-cent dividend. Allied could decide whether it was selling Marietta $48 shares or $27.05 shares, and decided it was selling the expensive shares. Allied had paid Bendix $47.52— the $48 cost, less the 48-cent dividend—for the shares that had cost Bendix $48 each in the tender offer. Allied sold $47.52 shares to Marietta for $46.18, taking a loss of $1.34 a share, or $25.6 million in all.

Which adds up to $47 million of artificial tax losses. And

that's not all. When Allied agreed to pay $85 in Allied securities for some Bendix shares, it used special securities designed to allow holders to pay low taxes. Of the $85, some $46.50 was in Allied common stock. The other $38.50 consisted of $25 of preferred stock, and $13.50 of "original issue discount" promissory notes. The preferred stock carries a rate that is adjustable, but is somewhat below the rate the U.S. Treasury pays for money. Allied is not a better credit risk than the U.S. government. The rate is low because payments on the preferred stock are considered dividends, and as mentioned a corporation can exclude 85 percent of them from federal income taxation. The preferred is aimed at corporate owners. Their 85 percent tax exclusion amounts to a tax subsidy from all other taxpayers.

The original issue discount notes are even more complicated than the preferred. To simplify matters, Allied pays only 6 percent cash interest a year on them, but pays an effective interest rate of 11.6 percent because it will redeem the notes in the future for a price greater than the value at which the notes were issued. Even though only 6 percent of interest is in cash, Allied can deduct all 11.6 percent on its tax returns.

On January 31, 1983, stockholder meetings were held in Morristown, New Jersey and Southfield, Michigan, to approve the Bendix-Allied deal. The Allied meeting was as festive affair. Allied ferried journalists from New York to Morristown, and held news conferences and provided breakfast and lunch.

The Bendix meeting was funereal. Bill Agee, appearing disconsolate, presided over a brief, sad meeting. Bendix's days as an independent company were over.

On February 2, 1983, Allied's Ed Hennessy fired Bendix president Alonzo McDonald, Jr.

On February 8, bowing to the inevitable, Bill Agee resigned, effective June 1, because Ed Hennessy refused to make him Allied's chief operating officer. Both McDonald and Agee had their golden parachute employment contracts to ease their pain.

Since September, Bill Agee has tried to present the outcome of the Bendix-Marietta battle as a triumph for "shareholder value" and a victory for himself. "I consider myself a hero," he has said.

In the longer view, Bill Agee, it seems reasonable to say, will be remembered as the man who started the Bendix–Martin Marietta war—and lost it.

Chapter 15

The Bigger Picture

SOME CONCLUSIONS

A giant company can cease to exist for a variety of reasons. The products it makes may become obsolete; competitors may be able to make the products better or cheaper; the company may fail to anticipate changes in the marketplace or in society as a whole; it may spend too much on expansion and not be able to repay its debts; it may spend too little on expansion and become freighted with out-of-date facilities. Or it may become the target of another giant company and be taken over.

The demise of the Bendix Corporation as an independent company is perhaps the most public example of what happens when the teachings of the Harvard Business School are carried to their ultimate conclusion. The notion that it makes no difference whether you are buying another company or selling your own, provided the price is right, is no mere abstraction to the people and communities who will suffer from the fall-out.

The *déchute* of Bendix, which was based in the Detroit suburb of Southfield, Michigan, is more than just an abstraction or case-history so far as the economy of the Detroit area is concerned. Except for the so-called Big Three auto makers—General Motors, Ford and Chrysler—Detroit had no other Fortune 100 company other than Bendix (though the Burroughs Corporation will probably make the 1983 list).

"It's a terrible thing to see Bendix disappear," says Leon J. Level, once one of Bill Agee's favored subordinates in the company. "It's sad not only for the hundreds of people who are going to lose their jobs but for the [Detroit] area as a whole. Losing the headquarters of a Fortune 100 company means more than losing high-paying jobs. It means a loss of people who are interested and concerned and contribute to the well-being of the community. Some of those people will move to New Jersey [where Allied is based] and most of the others will drift out of the area and find jobs with other companies. And there's a multiplier effect that will be lost. The United Fund contribution Bendix used to make—that's gone . . . There were supplier functions, and much of that will be gone. People flew in here from all over the world to do business at Bendix, and they stayed in hotels here, rented cars, ate meals in restaurants. And there is an incredible amount of intellectual activity in a company like the one Bendix used to be. All that is gone, and we will never get it back."

Level was not personally affected by the sale of Bendix. But despite having been favored by Agee—in 1978 Agee gave him the distinguished achievement award for a member of the headquarters staff—Level left the company in October of 1981 to become vice-president of financial planning at Burroughs. (Level, 42, was vice-president and treasurer of Burroughs at the time of this writing.)

Bill Agee, by contrast, considers the sale of Bendix a triumph. Because Bendix fetched a high price—the Allied Corporation paid an average of $80 per share for stock that had never sold above $67.50 before September of 1982—Agee believes he won, and has so stated.

In late September, a few days after Bendix had agreed to be taken over by Allied, Bill and Mary Agee sat in their Bendix-paid New York City hotel suite sipping champagne and declaring themselves the victors in the so-called Bendix-Martin Marietta war. In an interview with Robert Sam Anson for Savvy magazine, Bill Agee is quoted as saying: "In the eyes of everything that is important to me—my God, my company, my family—I think I'm a hero . . . Maximizing return for investors, that's what they always preach in Business 101, even if not everyone always practices it. Well, that's what we did. I'm proud of it."

Starting out to buy a company and ending up selling your own company under duress would not strike most people as a triumph. But Agee, by his standards, sincerely held, can claim to have won. Agee's standards are those taught at the Harvard Business School—although, in fairness to Harvard, it should be noted that Agee has carried the standards to an extreme.

The doctrine preached by Harvard and some other perhaps less illustrious business schools is that a properly trained "professional manager" can run just about any kind of business. Managers and businesses are essentially interchangeable. Books, ingots are all the same when managed rationally. If one does not like the businesses one's company owns, sell them or close them and buy other businesses with the proceeds. The people . . . ?

The case-study is the favored method of instruction. Students analyze a hypothetical company—sometimes even a real one—and suggest strategies for varying problems. It is a bloodless, intellectual game, in which the lives of people, the well-being of communities and indeed the stability of our social and economic structure, are surely secondary.

The overriding goal is to make an "adequate" profit. If a business will not be sufficiently profitable within a certain time, say three to five years, a professional manager should rid himself of it and move on to better things.

Some of this thinking is not unreasonable. May even be necessary. But carried to a logical extreme, the return-on-assets, professional-manager way of thinking produces serious problems.

The United States is not alone in the world. There are companies in other countries—Japan comes to mind—that operate in a non-Harvard Business School manner. These companies are willing to endure short-term pain for the prospect of long-term, substantive gain. They will suffer meager profits, perhaps outright losses, to build up their businesses in anticipation of the day when they will become sufficiently profitable.

It would also appear that many Japanese and European companies, our country's companies' major competitors, have a differing notion of what "sufficiently profitable" means. It is difficult to compare profitability among companies in different countries because the definition of "profit" varies, as do accounting standards for items such as, say, depreciation. But it would seem that U.S. companies' profit criteria are substantially higher in terms of the bottom line than those of competitors in other countries.

Under the Harvard doctrine, as epitomized by disciple Bill Agee's attitude and behavior, U.S. companies should yield business to competitors because there is not enough profit in it, and then "redeploy" assets into more profitable areas, providing they can be found. The result has been that U.S. companies, intent on keeping profit margins up, have gradually lost business to foreign competitors. And, of course, the more business lost, the greater is the corporate overhead—headquarters staff, computers, etc.—per unit of diminished production. The more overhead per unit climbs, the less profitable the remaining business becomes. A vicious cycle is created. The shedding of insufficiently profitable businesses in turn means exporting jobs and profits to other countries—which is what has happened to the domestic automobile market, the camera market and most of the U.S. motorcycle market, to name a few.

The flaw in the Harvard doctrine—and especially as practiced by the Bill Agees of the world—is that shareholders are a corporation's only constituency, and a stock price is the only significant criterion by which to judge a manager's success.

Corporations—especially giant corporations such as Bendix once was—also may reasonably be said to have a stake in the nation's social stability and economy-at-large. If all companies shut down businesses considered only marginally profitable, what happens to all the unemployed workers? Two of the great forces for social stability in the United States is that the vast majority of people be employed, and own their own homes. If people lose their jobs and homes, what next?

In his final years at Bendix, Bill Agee surrounded himself with many Harvard Business School graduates who shared his concept of managing an industrial company by the numbers rather than concentrating on fully understanding Bendix's businesses and directing them in an increasingly efficient and productive fashion.

It would appear that Bendix had begun to underinvest in some of its facilities—just as the U.S. automobile and steel industries did for so many years—because the potential profit did not appear sufficient to justify the investment. The problem, as the steel and auto industries belatedly discovered, is that underinvestment tends to catch up to a company all at once; one day a plant becomes obsolete and the company faces the choice of pouring in large amounts of modernization money, or closing down and walking away.

Perhaps the most "successful" portion of Bill Agee's tenure as Bendix chairman was the timely purchase and sale of a 21 percent interest in Asarco, the mining company, and the timely sale of three Bendix businesses in 1981. But even though these transactions benefited Bendix by producing cash to ride out the period of highest interest rates in U.S. history, three of the four transactions were zero-sum games for the economy as a whole.

In the Asarco case, Bendix bought its shares for $118 million in 1978 and sold them to Asarco for $336 million in 1981. Asarco, which paid Bendix a premium to keep the stock from falling into the hands of a corporate raider, was drained by the transaction and was obliged to sell parts of itself, including a portion of its most valuable holding, to raise the money. Falling metals prices put Asarco into a hole and as of this writing it has not yet climbed out.

Bendix sold its forest products business to a partnership that paid too much for the properties; the partnership could not pay its debts. And Bendix sold its geophysical business to Seiscom Delta, which—according to a *Wall Street Journal* story in April of 1983—is having trouble generating sufficient income to pay the debts incurred to buy the business from Bendix.

The only one of the four sales that appears to have been of mutual benefit for both parties involved was Bendix's sale of its offshore drilling manufacturing business to LTV. Bendix realized a good price, and LTV acquired a business that complemented businesses it already owned—though it bought the Bendix business near the height of the oil drilling boom and may have overpaid for it.

Bendix's gain was someone else's loss in three of the four instances. Bill Agee is to be commended for his astute market timing, but had Bendix made the same profits by making better and cheaper products rather than by trading, our economy and society as a whole would doubtless be far better off. And, in the end, no company is worth much if the nation's economy is sick and its society in turmoil. The unemployed and homeless are poor consumers.

But Harvard does not teach how to build and operate a better mouse trap. It teaches how to outsmart, to beat out the other guy. There is, to be sure, some merit in some of what Harvard teaches. Profit *is* important, return on assets *is* important, planning *is* important. Businesses are not public charities; neither are they employment agencies. If companies do not make a profit, they will go out of business and rightly so. Still, many people, Bill Agee and Mary Cunningham seemingly among them, appear to have departed the Harvard "Busy" School with the idea that the school's way of doing business is the only way, and that its graduates are therefore somehow wiser, even more worthy, than other mere mortals.

The Harvard B-School method is demonstrably not the only way to run a business. It may well not be the best way— certainly not for the health of society at large. Shareholders are not the only people who count. Real life is not a scenario;

people are not automatons. If short-term results become a company's primary criteria, as they appear to have been in the case of Bill Agee and Bendix, the company will almost surely self-destruct sooner or later.

Which leads to mergers and acquisitions as practiced on Wall Street—capitalistic doctrines gone out of control in practice.

There are perfectly good reasons why companies should be bought and sold. Some businesses are far better off under new managements. Shareholders who have had money invested for years have a right to benefit from the rising value of a company's assets, which is often not realized until a company is sold. And the risk of having one's company taken away in a hostile raid can be one of the few sources of external discipline on a company management that might otherwise feather its own nest or become self-satisfied, to the detriment of employees and shareholders alike.

The pluses, though, have been largely offset by some nine years of increasingly ferocious tender battles. Mergers-and-acquisition business began as an adjunct to other areas of investment banking, such as raising capital by selling bonds or stock, but the M&A function has very much taken on a life of its own. Wall Street is fee-hungry; M&A work can generate seven- and eight-figure fees. Since 1974, when the recent merger boom began, mergers-and-acquisitions business has become so profitable that it has become an end in itself for many investment banking houses—the tail, so to speak, wagging the dog.

Not only are merger deals lucrative, they can be great fun, so long as one does not happen to work for a company that gets sold out or makes a bad acquisition. To the takeover knights of Wall Street, corporate battles are an exhilarating game, offering opportunities to make big money, gain a national reputation, influence economic history and gain vicarious power by dealing on a first-name basis with some of the most powerful men in America while one is still, say, in one's thirties or early forties.

But the merger battles have become so high-stakes and fast-moving that people are forced to make fateful decisions—such as whether to enter a battle as a "white knight" or whether to sell a company out or unload some of its vital businesses—without having time to *think*. When, for example, a Bill Agee can come to Wall Street acting essentially as a free agent—it would appear that no one other than Mary Cunningham Agee really knew all of what he was doing—and lose a $4 billion company at the Great Casino, it is perhaps time to begin thinking about what has gone wrong.

In many instances—too many—investment bankers have turned into or fancied themselves warriors rather than performed as prudent counselors. When M&A work was an outgrowth of an overall relationship between an investment banking firm and a client company, bankers handling an M&A assignment were obliged to ask themselves whether the deal made overall good economic sense for the client. The banker was supposed to provide wisdom as well as carry out the client's wishes, or impulses of the moment. Now many bankers seem to consider themselves hired guns—not unlike lawyers who are obliged, or think they are, to do what the client wants, forgetting along the way the maxim, "control your client."

Perhaps most illustrative is the First Boston Corporation, arguably the best *mano à mano* combatant in the M&A field. First Boston makes few if any bones about being in the M&A business to make money, unrelated to its other operations. First Boston has shed much of the genteel restraint of some other M&A practitioners—it talks to the press, even seeks favorable publicity, criticizes other bankers. It surely deserves high marks for being openly, honestly, aggressively in pursuit of fees. First Boston tends to treat M&A work as a chess game, and Bruce Wasserstein is possibly the most inventive tactician in the business, though the fact that *people* are also involved perhaps gets lost among all the moves on the big board. Even Martin Siegel of Kidder Peabody, who views client companies' executives and employees as people, not merely customers, also tends to envelop what he does in abstractions. He talks, and convincingly, of how he shares his clients' joys and fears. But if you are not a client, that is another matter. He indicated no second thoughts about toppling Bendix—the employees of which are also people. (He would doubtless argue that it was his job to save Marietta, and besides, Bendix started the fight.) And consider Felix Rohatyn of Lazard Frères. Rohatyn is something of a businessman-statesman; he unquestionably helped rescue New York City from bankruptcy, and he speaks frequently about the need to sustain our aging cities; one of his clients is the City of Detroit and another is Wayne County, Michigan, where Detroit is located. The same Mr. Rohatyn, for a business fee, also set Harry Gray and United Technologies on a course that contributed to the takeover of one of the Detroit area's major employers—the headquarters operation of Bendix—and the loss of hundreds of jobs in Michigan. Investment bankers are insulated from the consequences of what they do, just as most lawyers are. They are, they would suggest, paid to represent clients, not to worry about the soundness of the client's business judgment or about the economic health of the country as a whole. And yet, one is entitled to expect or at least hope that men and women in positions of such influence and power would be more aware of the consequences of what they do.

The Bill Agees are also insulated from the results of their actions. Agee, for example, can justify selling Bendix on the basis of "shareholder value." But before selling the company, it is of interest to note, he made certain that he had a $4.1 million golden parachute, which will guarantee him a salary of $825,000 a year through 1987. He would not have gotten the parachute had he resigned from Bendix without the company being sold. And the Allied deal was lucrative for him in other ways: his personal shares of Bendix became worth $4 million, and Allied paid him some $1.4 million for his Bendix stock options, which became immediately exercisable as the result of the sale rather than being phased in over a period of years.

He also negotiated a title for himself—president of Allied Corporation—as part of the deal, and assured himself a seat on the Allied board of directors.

Mr. Agee's response, in effect, was that other Bendix shareholders were handsomely paid for their stock, especially the employee-shareholders who received $85 a share for the stock held in the Bendix Salaried Employees Savings and Stock Ownership Plan. He, however, did rather better than most. His total proceeds from selling Bendix were something over $9 million (before income taxes); $4.1 million for the parachute, $4 million for the stock, $1.4 million for the options—totaling more than eleven years of salary. How many Bendix employees did comparably well? For many employee-shareholders, Bendix stock selling in the $60-a-share range and a secure job is arguably a better deal than uncertainty and $85 per share.

A reaction of the Securities and Exchange Commission to the excesses of the Bendix-Martin Marietta affair has been to form a commission, itself including some of the foremost practitioners of the takeover, to suggest corrective medicine. It is difficult, though, to see the commission suggesting modifications that are more than cosmetic. The commission's most prominent members have prospered under the existing rules; they have little incentive to change them.

In a more perfect world they never made, the commission members would suggest changing the fee structure in takeover ventures. As things now stand, an investment banker's fee depends on whether his client "wins" or "loses," not on whether the deal makes economic sense for the client—never mind the country. A different sort of incentive would produce more salutary deals. Instead of payment based on whether the client wins, the fee might be based on whether the results achieved proved out to be good ones. Such "contingent payouts" are not uncommon in the business world when a business is sold; the sale price being based in part on how successful the business is under its new owners. In such fashion both buyer and seller have a financial incentive to make the deal genuinely workable. Since, however, we are dealing with the real world, and people whose watchword is "profits now," it is unlikely that the fee structure of investment bankers will be changed to any significant degree.

But there are some relatively simple and doable fixes for such underlying problems as self-defeating haste and the insulation of top corporate people from the impact of takeover battles.

Much of the strange behavior in the Bendix-Marietta affair was caused by *time* pressure. Decisions of great importance had to be made in a very short time, otherwise they would have been too late. Haste, tension and lack of sleep contributed to the outcome.

Under the rules in force at the time this is being written, a tender offer can remain open as little as twenty business days, about a month. But the target company has much less than a month in which to react. Unless it does something within a few days, large numbers of its shares will pass into the hands of arbitragers, and the battle is then usually all but lost. The "arbs," who will sell their shares to anyone, pose a danger to any target company.

Also, because there is so little time, the managers of the attacking and defending companies spend virtually all their waking hours dealing with the crisis. They get precious little sleep, their perspective narrows, their anxieties escalate. They too, after all, are human.

The pressure is made especially acute by front-loaded, two-tier offers, such as the Marietta offer of $75 for the first half of Bendix and $55 of securities that it offered for the second half. Such offers are designed to cause shareholders to tender early, and thereby to increase the time pressure on the target.

A possible solution might be to expand some existing tender offer regulations. Tenders should perhaps be held open for, say, sixty days instead of only twenty; at least this would give everyone more time to calm down and act reasonably. To help the over-burdened thinking process, transfers of shares in the target company could be banned for, say, at least ten business days so that executives would have time to react without having to worry about whether the "arbs" have already decided the outcome of the battle. And tender-offer rules could be amended to eliminate two-tier offers in which there is anything more than a minimal difference—say 10 percent—between the first and second stages of the offer.

Target companies could be forced to deal with the attack fairly, to give their shareholders an opportunity to sell their shares if they so chose. Shark-repellant provision designed to make takeovers virtually impossible without approval of the target's board of directors might well be banned as being contrary to public policy. And similarly with golden parachute contracts offered to top managers. One reason managers are paid such enormous salaries—many earn half a million dollars a year and up—is to take the rap if something goes wrong. The high salaries are compensation for the perceived riskiness of their jobs. If a top manager asks his or her company's shareholders to take a risk by not tendering their shares, the manager should be willing to take a risk too. (It is interesting to note that Edward Hennessy, Jr., chairman of Allied Corporation, announced in late April of 1983 that he and twenty other Allied executives were giving up their parachutes because of "adverse public reaction." Yielding those parachutes is not much of a sacrifice; Allied is now so large it is most unlikely to be taken over. Allied, of course, is still obligated for the $2.2 million parachute of former Bendix President Alonzo McDonald, Jr., as well as Bill Agee's $4.1 million parachute. Even if Allied should refuse to pay them, the parachutes are insured by a Lloyd's of London policy.)

It would also even things out a bit if the commercial banks that finance takeovers were made to be subject to some risk for their actions. In most cases, takeovers do not create new wealth, except for speculators; existing wealth is merely put into different pockets. The banks earn fees for making credit available to finance takeovers, and presumably earn a profit on the takeover loan itself by pricing the money above their own cost of funds. If things go well for the banks, the target will be captured and its banking business will be switched to the banks that backed the winner. If the target is not captured, the banks often get a fee—typically one quarter of one percent of the amount they committed to lend—that leaves them a profit.

Bankers should certainly be allowed to continue making such loans, but at least at their own peril. If a bank wishes to help Bendix buy Martin Marietta or Martin Marietta buy Bendix—deals that made no economic sense to society as a whole —they should be obliged to bear risk. The Federal Reserve Board chairman might explain to those banks that so long as they make such loans they cannot avail themselves of certain Federal Reserve services, such as the Fed's discount window. Using the window means borrowing money directly from the Federal Reserve, which generally charges a somewhat lower rate than do other lenders. A discreet denial of the use of the Fed window is one way regulators keep banks in line when they have no legal authority to impose their will on them.

The Bendix-Marietta affair illustrates not only the problems with the takeover mania on Wall Street, but with the way corporations are governed.

It is surely one of the strengths of American business that bright young men with no inherited wealth or family connections can aspire to—and indeed achieve—positions of wealth and power. The heads of all four corporations involved in Bendix-Martin Marietta are self-made millionaires from modest backgrounds. Bill Agee and Thomas Pownall of Martin Marietta grew up on small family farms; Harry Gray of United Technologies, an orphan for all practical purposes, grew up in poverty; Edward Hennessy, Jr., of the Allied Corporation was the son of a lumber salesman, and his early attempts at self-betterment included a brief stint as a boxer and three years studying to be a priest. Only in America, as they say and with good reason, could four people of such origins rise to head companies that rank among the country's two hundred largest industrial concerns.

But a weakness of the system, which admittedly can often infuse corporate America with vitality, is that someone who gets to the top too rapidly may not know how to behave when he or she gets there. The difference between, say, Bill Agee and the three other self-made men involved is that he rose very quickly indeed, with the aid of a winning personality, ability, luck and a Harvard Business School degree; they, on the other hand, rose slowly, became seasoned by failure and frustration along the way. They made early mistakes, suffered for them, apparently learned from them. Bill Agee, who led something of a charmed life until he became chairman of Bendix, did not suffer the personal buffeting and failures that most leaders are subject to before they attain the pinnacle.

In the end it was not the Bendix board of directors—which had the immediate responsibility for Bill Agee's behavior— that determined the outcome. It was the System as exemplified by Tom Pownall, Ed Hennessy and Harry Gray. Each an individual yet each having far more in common with each other than with Bill Agee, they in their fashions did what Agee's board did not, or was not able to, or did not wish to do. They deflected him from his original purpose, and they cast him out.

Whether Bill Agee will ever again achieve comparable power and position is, of course, unknown. But it is safe to say that, without so intending, he has made a lasting contribution if the example and lessons of the Bendix-Marietta war are studied with care and eventually bring about corrections badly needed by corporate America for its benefit as well as that of the man in the street.

Chapter 16

Where Are They Now?

William M. Agee, former chairman of Bendix and president of Allied, was to give up both jobs on June 1.

Mary Cunningham Agee is still a vice-president at Joseph E. Seagram & Sons, Inc.

Alonzo McDonald, Jr., former president of Bendix, is looking for a job.

Bruce Wasserstein, a managing director at First Boston Corporation, is still co-director of the mergers and acquisitions department.

Martin Siegel, a director at Kidder, Peabody & Company, is still head of its mergers and acquisitions operation.

W. Michael Blumenthal is still chairman of the Burroughs Corporation.

Harry Gray is still chairman of United Technologies Corporation, which in April of 1983 added shark-repellant provisions to its corporate charter.

Jay Higgins, head of Salomon Brothers' mergers and acquisitions department, gained revenge of a sort for his Bendix humilations. In late April, the Allied Corporation selected him to handle its planned $410 million purchase of the chemicals division of the GAF Corporation. The deal was presented to the Allied board of directors, with Bill Agee present, in what had been Bendix's New York City board room. Salomon stands to earn $1 million for its role in the transaction.

Thomas Pownall, president of Martin Marietta Corporation during its struggle with Bendix, is now chairman. He feels bad about having to sell parts of Marietta to raise cash to reduce the debt incurred in remaining independent. He no longer has the framed picture of Bill Agee and Mary Cunningham Agee in their bedroom that was in People magazine. In early 1983 he presented the picture to Allied chairman Ed Hennessy "because I had all the fun out of it I wanted" and Hennessy had told him he wanted to give the picture to Agee.

Edward Hennessy, Jr. is still chairman of
Allied Corporation, a director of Martin
Marietta, and may have the last laugh. In
April of 1983, Allied announced that its
profits for the first quarter of the year were
sixteen cents per share higher than they
would have been had Allied not bought
Bendix and part of Marietta. Despite what
he told Tom Pownall, Hennessy did not
give the blowup of the People magazine
picture to Bill Agee. He kept it.